# Domestic Violence

# The House of Prisca and Aquila

Our mission at the House of Prisca and Aquila is to produce quality books that expound accurately the word of God to empower women and men to minister together in a multicultural church. Our writers have a positive view of the Bible as God's revelation that affects both thoughts and words, so it is plenary, historically accurate, and consistent in itself, fully reliable, and authoritative as God's revelation. Because God is true, God's revelation is true, inclusive to men and women, and speaking to a multicultural church, wherein all the diversity of the church is represented within the parameters of egalitarianism and inerrancy.

The word of God is what we are expounding, thereby empowering women and men to minister together in all levels of the church and home. The reason we say women and men together is because that is the model of Prisca and Aquila, ministering together to another member of the church—Apollos: "Having heard Apollos, Priscilla and Aquila took him aside and more accurately expounded to him the Way of God" (Acts 18:26). True exposition, like true religion, is by no means boring—it is fascinating. Books that reveal and expound God's true nature "burn within us" as they elucidate the Scripture and apply it to our lives.

This was the experience of the disciples who heard Jesus on the road to Emmaus: "Were not our hearts burning while Jesus was talking to us on the road, while he was opening the scriptures to us?" (Luke 24:32). We are hoping to create the classics of tomorrow, significant and accessible trade and academic books that "burn within us."

Our "house" is like the home to which Prisca and Aquila no doubt brought Apollos as they took him aside. It is like the home in Emmaus where Jesus stopped to break bread and reveal his presence. It is like the house built on the rock of obedience to Jesus (Matt 7:24). Our "house," as a euphemism for our publishing team, is a home where truth is shared and Jesus' Spirit breaks bread with us, nourishing all of us with his bounty of truth.

We are delighted to work together with Wipf and Stock in this series and welcome submissions on a wide variety of topics from an egalitarian, inerrantist global perspective.

For more information, see our Web site:

https://sites.google.com/site/houseofpriscaandaquila/.

# Domestic Violence

*Identification and Restoration*

JEAN A. DIMOCK

FOREWORD BY
MELISSA LUZZI

WIPF & STOCK · Eugene, Oregon

DOMESTIC VIOLENCE
Identification and Restoration

The House of Prisca and Aquila

Wipf & Stock
An Imprint of Wipf and Stock Publishers
199 W. 8th Ave., Suite 3
Eugene, OR 97401

www.wipfandstock.com

PAPERBACK ISBN: 978-1-6667-8604-0
HARDCOVER ISBN: 978-1-6667-8605-7
EBOOK ISBN: 978-1-6667-8606-4

04/04/24

# Contents

# Foreword

WHEN I WAS ASKED to write the foreword for *Domestic Violence: Identification and Restoration*, even its title intrigued me. Because of my training, doctorate in Marriage and Family Therapy, and work in the field as a licensed therapist, program developer, and trainer, I find it imperative to view violence between partners as a family issue, especially when there are children involved.

A family engulfed in domestic violence (DV) is a complex system intertwined with various other complex systems. How the individuals in those various systems interact with the different family members will deeply affect how a protective mother and her children cope and heal from DV, as well as how and if the batterer chooses to change. The decisions made by lawyers, the court, and social services can either promote harm or healing as can the responses of the church, schools, extended family, and community.

With this book, Dr. Jean Dimock provides a one-volume source of information for general readers, professionals, and victims caught in the web of DV, including the parents of the victimized mother, a population that has been overlooked, even in the research. Considering the prevalence of DV, *Domestic Violence: Identification and Restoration* is a tremendous resource and reference for multiple audiences, including religious leaders and professionals who work with victims of DV in the court, legal, human services, and school systems. As Jean stated, her desire is to make the world safer and healthier through her work acting as a catalyst for just and loving action for the victims of domestic violence.

Through her doctoral research and thesis devoted to DV, Dr. Dimock gained the expertise to write this book. Additionally, she served as a New Hampshire guardian ad litem and has spent nearly twenty years as a domestic violence expert working with women across the country.

She learned about and experienced their world. Like the book, Jean applies her knowledge and application of experience and research to life situations.

Jean's writing is thought provoking and encourages discussion. I found myself wanting to call her and applaud some changes in the field since the mid-90s. At that time, when I began working for a non-profit as a therapist, offering counseling services for women and children who were victims of domestic violence and sexual abuse, the assumptions were different. At that time, the common phrases "it takes two to fight," "children are resilient," and "children need a father, in spite of his violent and abusive behavior" did not consider the context of domestic violence dynamics. However, such beliefs are not only untrue but harmful. In regards to the system of domestic violence, there is a victim of crime and a perpetrator. If children are involved, there are additional victims. It takes only one person in a relationship to abuse power and control. In addition, current research is supporting the negative effect of domestic violence on a child's development, even before they are born! And with the increased focus on the importance of the development of secure attachment and neuroscience, the imperative of supporting the protective parent is clearly in the best interest of the child.

Sadly, "Children need a father, in spite of his violent and abusive behavior," remains a common assumption. I ask, "What are we teaching children about emotionally healthy relationships if they are fearful of spending time with a person of whom they are justifiably afraid?" Would you want to spend extended time with someone who hurt someone you loved? Domestic violence is a complex topic. Experts do not even agree how to address the complexities. How, then, is a child to understand what is happening without an opportunity to heal and absorb through the lens of what is developmentally appropriate? When the mother is abused, the children are negatively affected emotionally, psychologically, physically, and sometimes spiritually. Their sense of how they see themselves, others, and the world is negatively skewed. Children are being abused even if they are not direct recipients of the abuse.

Domestic violence is relational abuse engulfed with deception and betrayal. Through continued research and biblical scholarship, appropriate and rational action can take place and application of knowledge in various disciplines and venues can also take place. As the result, the blight of domestic violence can and should be addressed with compassion, justice, and responsibility. Real healing happens in community and requires community.

Dr. Melissa Luzzi, LPC, NCC, EMDR-C
MA, Doctorate of Marriage and Family Therapy
Licensed counselor (for nearly 30 years)
Professorial duties have included Denver Seminary, Argosy and National Universities
Contributing author to *Healing the Hurting: Giving Hope & Help to Abused Women*

# Acknowledgments

F IRST, I AM ESPECIALLY grateful to my husband, Fred. Creating a life with you has been the best thing we have done outside of our commitment to the Lord in 1975. We have been married for fifty-five years. Those years have been filled with joys, frustrations, challenges, and successes, but we dealt with each of the difficulties together and became stronger together as a result. I fully recognize the grace God gave you as we both worked to see this book come to fruition. You may not have typed any of the words, but you filled in my task gaps and supported me with understanding and encouragement every moment along the way. *Domestic Violence: Identification and Restoration* is our book and our achievement.

Thank you to our son, Jonathan, who confirmed the value, beauty, and excellence that comes from connecting people. Many of these extraordinary people became helpful toward the execution of this book, and I want them to know how much they are appreciated. I am grateful for our daughter, Stephanie, who demonstrates how hard work and perseverance makes it possible to move toward a goal, even one that seems impossible to reach. Our granddaughters, Paloma and Peregrine, periodically provided expressions of energizing love along the way, for which I have been, and continue to be, thankful.

Dale Potter, my cousin and a very sound and organized thinker, overwhelmed me in the most positive and helpful way when I needed his input, which makes me unabashedly grateful. Humility prevents Dale and his beautiful wife, Patti, from revealing that they prayed for us during the formation of this book, but I know they did. I am also grateful for Patti, who planted a seed that sprouted and grew, and brought me back to the roots of my Christian upbringing and faith. Thank you, Dale and Patti.

My mind-blowing friends Jann McMurry, Lou Bacon, and Sarah Hale Folger have contributed what no one else could, in a way no one else could, because of the type of sisterhood I have with each of these exceptional women. Jann, you are more than trustworthy as a double-check on my theology. You amazed me as you helped me move through some required theological brain stretching. Our conversations and explorations led us to some great scriptural places. Lou, our conversations about all things psychology have increased my knowledge, increased my research, and provided a greater understanding of more psych subjects than one can imagine. Our heads are so good together. Brainstorming with you is more fun than a person should have, but this book is better for it. And I could always count on you to make me laugh. Sarah, after being in each other's lives for thirty-six years, we know each other very well. You knew what I needed and did not wait to be asked, but offered to be my second editor. In this capacity, you have outdone yourself, making valuable suggestions and getting your task done swiftly and thoroughly. Your prose at the end of Chapter 3 touched my heart. I am beyond grateful for each of you, Jann, Lou, and Sarah.

Grace May not only served as the first editor for this book, but also gave me great encouragement with her kind words. Sandra Whitley's words of affirmation concerning the need for such a book kept ringing in my ears and gave me increased motivation: "Our daughters need this book." This writer is so appreciative of Deb Beatty Mel and Maud Sandbo and their expertise that readied this volume for print. Thank you, Grace, Sandra, Deb, and Maud.

Drs. Aída Besançon Spencer and William David Spencer have an insatiable and infectious love of learning that has produced unsurpassed scholarship, for which their students—I having been one of them—can be eternally grateful. Their brainchild, the House of Prisca & Aquila, has blessed writers and readers alike. I am sure countless people are thankful for their work and encouragement. Closing without thanking the entire community of HPA members would be remiss. As we talk together, think together, and share ideas together, our collective intelligence increases. As we help each other, potential burdens in working through the writing and publishing process disappear. You all amaze me. Also, working with Wipf and Stock's wonderful people made the process much easier than anticipated. Thank you, all.

Many, many thanks to Dr. Mark Windt, my allergist, who kept me healthier and breathing better; to Teigue Young, my exercise physiologist, who taught me that if doing a little makes a good difference, doing more becomes noteworthy; and to Dr. Jeffrey Myers, my chiropractor, whose humor, patience, and expertise kept my body and this project cranking without pain.

Mom, I cannot thank you enough for the loving, wise, and single-handed upbringing you gave your three children and "our" foster twins in the first two years of their lives. Your faith undergirded everything you did and said, which impacted all our lives. You patiently and prayerfully awaited my faith commitment and, now that you no longer travel this sod, you wait for me again. As this work progressed, you were here with me. I saw your beautiful smile in my heart's eye and heard your words that reminded me of the many truths you taught your children. You encourage me still.

All the adult and child victims of domestic violence, including the parents of the victims, who contributed to the multi-part case study that begins each chapter, have a special place in my heart. I am indebted to each and every one of you. You have proven yourselves to be courageous and generous not only in your daily lives, but also in allowing some part of your story to be told.

I thank the Lord for everyone mentioned here and for all those who brushed by my life, even those I may not remember, but perhaps provided encouragement, ideas, or who may have jump-started a thought process.

My deepest gratitude extends to the Lord who stayed with me throughout the seemingly never-ending process of completing each chapter. He never left me. He never will.

# Introduction

D OMESTIC VIOLENCE. INTIMATE PARTNER violence. Family abuse. What do those terms bring to mind? Do we think of the daily struggles of women and children in domestic-violence homes? Or do we understand domestic violence as an action undertaken by an angry person, maybe more than once? Do we understand the unpredictability of the abuser? Do we wonder why a woman so treated simply does not leave and take the children with her? Do we question how an abuser can treat his family in such treacherous ways? Do we fully appreciate the danger a woman and her children are in? For those who work in the domestic violence field or who have made it their business to know because of a family member's or friend's experience, and those who are victims and survivors of domestic violence, answers to these questions come very easily.

But, too often, well-meaning people think of domestic violence as something that happens between adults and concerns only the adults involved. They assert that if the parents are simply separated, the problem will take care of itself. Neither idea is accurate; both are false. Alas, these ideas often guide parenting plans devised by guardians ad litem and the court system, which do not have the best interests of the children in mind. The philosophy that domestic violence is an issue between adults predominates when it comes to decisions and assertions made by most judges, guardians ad litem, and lawyers opposing the victim . . . and sometimes the victim's own lawyer.

These decision makers too often operate within the narrow context of family law considerations. This does not work for domestic violence cases, and leads to injustice and harm for both women and children. Children's best interests are often not considered through the lenses of clear, bold evidence from current research into domestic violence and the truth of what happens within the family, including from the perspective of the child. Rather, these bad decisions are often the result of ignorance, myths, and an incorrect sense that "the experts" know all they need to know and do not need any more information to make good decisions.

The systemic nature of domestic violence means that it damages families from every socioeconomic level, every faith (or lack of faith), every educational level, and every culture. Studies have shown, however, that "rates of partner abuse appear to be lower in societies where women have more power and authority outside of the family as well as inside."[1] Although domestic violence looks essentially the same around the world and has similar features throughout different cultures, the laws that exist within the United States and their observation (or lack thereof) by the legal profession are mainly in view in this volume's discussion of legal issues or court experiences.

This volume does not address the experiences of same-sex couples. Research has shown that the "behavior profile of lesbian and gay male batterers appears to correspond closely to that of heterosexual abusers."[2] In fact, the "life-time prevalence of IPV [intimate partner violence] in LGB [lesbian, gay, bisexual] couples appear [sic] to be similar to or higher than in heterosexual ones."[3] Thus it is hoped that our discussion will also be helpful inasmuch as it is applicable to those in same-sex relationships as well.

This book addresses men-on-women violence, since it is more prevalent. Women-on-men violence generally looks different and is subject matter for a different book. The use of coercive control by men in domestic violence situations provides the foundation of their behaviors as they make efforts to assert their power. For the sake of simplicity, female pronouns will be used to refer to the abused partner and male pronouns will be used to denote the abuser.

There is an unmistakable importance in helping mothers, children, and perpetrators in domestic violence situations, but considering the fact that the violence constitutes an emergency for the physical, emotional, and mental health and welfare of women and children, this volume addresses them as the primary concern. At the same time, a sound and grateful expression of thanks extends to those who work with batterers to help change their lives and find new ways of relating to others.

1. Bancroft and Silverman, *The Batterer as Parent*, 4, n. Heise et al.
2. Bancroft and Silverman, *The Batterer as Parent*, 4, n. Leventhal and Lunday, Renzetti.
3. Rollè et al., "When Intimate Partner Violence Meets Same Sex Couples," para. 4.

When family violence is invisible, partners and children are at risk of continuing abuse. Both women and children are affected physically, neurologically, emotionally, mentally, and in many other ways. Without intervention, risks abound for all the victims involved. Anyone involved in the court system—law enforcement, medical professionals, therapy and counseling professionals, faith communities, educators, and even the next-door neighbor to a family experiencing domestic violence—needs in-depth knowledge concerning the subject. Failing to identify and correctly address domestic violence allows harm to persist in every community across the nation and the world.

In the U.S., different terminology is sometimes used among professionals who do the same kind of work in different states. Sometimes terminology that is used for specific areas of operation within the court system may have a different name in another state. There are institutions in each of the states that perform the same task, but each state refers to these institutions by different names and are guided by different statutes. Please consider the following:

- The terms *visitation* and *parenting time* refer to time the noncustodial parent spends with the children. Sometimes quoted material refers to this time spent with the noncustodial parent as *visitation*, but outside of these quotes, the term *parenting time* will be used. In general, professionals within the court system prefer the term *parenting time*, since we visit neighbors, friends, those in the hospital, or elsewhere. Parenting time refers to actual parenting, not visiting.

- The terms *law guardian, guardian ad litem,* and *custody evaluator* are used interchangeably to describe someone who is appointed by a judge (or marital master) to investigate and make recommendations to the court concerning the best interests of children when there are parenting disputes over issues such as custody and parenting time.

- The term *family court* is used to denote the part of the court system that deals with divorce and separation, and also assesses parenting plan issues in dispute (e.g., custody, parenting time, child support, etc.).

- The terms *child protective services, social services,* and *Department of Social Services* are used interchangeably for government health and human service agencies that investigate reports of child abuse or neglect.

- *Survivor* and *victim* are used interchangeably throughout; both terms refer to those who are victimized by intimate partner violence or domestic violence.

- *Father*, *dad*, and the like refer to the partner, stepfather, or ex-partner of the protective mother.

- In a domestic violence context, the term *batterer* does not necessarily refer only to that person who has elevated his behaviors to the point of using physical harm. The term also refers to one who exhibits behaviors that can easily lead to physical abuse: these may include threats of harm, throwing objects, displaying fist(s), driving dangerously, killing the family pet, etc. In this discussion, the term *batterer* refers to both one who has caused physical harm as well as one who has exhibited intimidating behaviors that threaten physical violence.

The case study in the beginning of chapters 1 through 8 is an amalgamation of several different stories with identifying details removed and the names of the adults and children changed to protect them and their privacy. Any similarities to a person's situation exist either by coincidence or because domestic violence carries many similarities from case to case. Some fictional details were added to complete a picture of what intimate partner violence looks like and what victims, including children, often experience.

The last chapter provides a look at what happens to well-connected parents of the victim and her children, who are also victims. The case study for that chapter is, again, a combination of different parents' stories, from different families, with the names changed.

This book is offered with the hope that it will do three things: help women and children caught in domestic violence families, educate professionals as well as general readers who will help women and children, and ignite further research which, again, will help victimized women and children.

A goal in writing this volume was to put as much fundamental and indispensable information as possible in one place so that the reader will have not only a compact, easy reference, but also a deep understanding of domestic violence. Scriptural encouragement is included toward the end of each chapter to support and comfort those wounded by domestic violence, to help motivate others to engage in the necessary process of putting an end to domestic violence, and to encourage others to participate in the healing process for those harmed.

# 1

# Batterer Identified

## Case Study

WHILE LORI AND DAMON were dating, there did not seem to be any indicators of what would become a domestic violence situation after marriage. Lori's parents, Deborah and Bob, were suspicious after Lori's miscarriage early in the marriage, when Lori told them that Damon had chosen not to go to the hospital with her when she suffered the loss of their baby. She felt his absence during this time of emotional and physical distress.

A few years after marriage, when their first child, Poppy, was eighteen months old, Lori and Damon were preparing for their second baby. During her pregnancy, Lori was doing coursework to become an obstetrics nurse practitioner. Lori and her parents would often be included in social groups that included Lori's classmates. At a summer gathering, one of them, Nancy, who had become good friends with Lori, took Deborah and Bob aside, with Lori's permission, to explain her concerns about their daughter. Nancy shared that she had spoken to Lori about the bruising she happened to spot on her legs, and Lori confirmed suspicions that they had come as a result of Damon's abuse.

Among some of the situations Lori recounted to Nancy was an incident that occurred just before a visit from her parents. Although Damon knew well ahead of time about their visit, he became angry just before they arrived, and said that Lori should not have invited them. He completed his vicious tirade by raping her just minutes before they arrived.

Lori also told Nancy that Damon threatened her regularly and devised plans that would keep her at home. For example, Damon said that if she left him, he would take both the children and she would never see them again. Damon also impeded her ability to leave the house by taking away her cash and credit cards, except for the one he had acquired by forging her name and which had only her name associated with it. He would never be responsible for that card, and insisted that all the professional landscaping and plants be charged to it.

On a day when Lori had internship appointments with clients, Damon left for work early as usual. Before he left, he emptied the house of Lori's clothes, put them in his truck, and then drove away. When Lori got up, she fed and dressed Poppy and proceeded to get ready to leave the house for the day. She quickly realized that there were no clothes to wear. Her closets and drawers were empty. Fortunately, she had dressed in attractive, satiny red and black pajamas the night before when she went to bed. Remembering that she had left a pair of black shoes and a black blazer in the hallway coat closet, she put them on over her pajamas, picked up Poppy and her medical bag, and drove to her appointments after taking Poppy for a play date at a friend's house. The next time, Damon took her keys.

Before Lori had decided to become a nurse, Damon continually thwarted her attempts to return to school and work by accusing her of having affairs with professors and coworkers. He also worked hard to turn her and her parents against each other, even though Lori had a loving and caring relationship with her parents. Later on, he told Lori that her parents said she was crazy, when nothing of the sort had taken place. Damon also complained to Lori's parents often about Lori not valuing their marriage. He claimed Lori was not working on the marriage at all, and tried to convince Lori that her parents sided with him, not her.

## Definition of Batterer

### FOUNDATION OF CONTROL

Understanding the foundation of a batterer's actions is helpful in order to define what a batterer is. The need for control provides an underpinning of his[1] actions, and this need for control leads to abusive words and actions toward his partner as well as any children and stepchildren. Signs of this need for control may not be recognized by a partner before the couple begins

---

1. For the sake of simplicity, female pronouns will be used to refer to the abused partner and male pronouns will be used to denote the abuser. This book addresses men-on-women violence, since it is more prevalent.

to live together or gets married, or may not be identified until pregnancy, or when the first child is born. A woman's efforts to counter her partner's controlling tactics lead to escalation by the abuser, along with justifications for his actions and words.

The abusive partner will increase his tactics to gain or keep control when a woman makes an effort to maintain or gain her independence.[2] In the above case study, Damon made increasing attempts to control Lori when she showed her independence by furthering her education. The batterer also makes efforts to control the children in the relationship, which will often look similar to the methods used on the mother. The means of control can take many different forms. For example, professionals working with domestic-violence families need to be keenly and continually aware that there will be repercussions exacted on the mother and children if the abuser believes there have been honest disclosures about what is going on in their family life. These reactions represent attempts to gain or keep control. To control his partner and children, a batterer becomes violent and manipulative. Those controlling behaviors are displayed within primary family relationships. People outside the family most often perceive the abusive partner as agreeable, unless someone directly challenges his behavior or if he views others as interfering with his control over his partner or children.[3]

Outside the family, people do not necessarily see the sense of entitlement the abuser has, but those in the family see and experience this entitlement, and also hear the abuser's justification for it. Entitlement is the belief that one deserves special privileges or treatment. In the above case study, Lori's desire to have her parents visit was important to her, but Damon viewed his needs as having greater weight. To him, Lori's decision to invite her parents was selfish and uncaring toward him, even though he knew about the visit ahead of time. "The belief that violence toward a partner can be justified is a strong predictor of which men will batter" and helps to determine "which boys exposed to domestic violence will grow up to abuse their own partners."[4]

Drug and alcohol abuse are not the cause of a batterer's abusive behaviors, but can be a factor in heightening its volatility.[5] At the same time,

2. Bancroft and Silverman, *The Batterer as Parent*, 6.
3. Bancroft and Silverman, *The Batterer as Parent*, 24.
4. Bancroft and Silverman, *The Batterer as Parent*, 7.
5. Bancroft and Silverman, *The Batterer as Parent*, 7.

"substance abuse does appear at higher rates in batterers."[6] If a batterer who abuses drugs and alcohol recovers from addiction, he is simply a sober batterer. In this case, he has dealt with his sobriety, not his controlling, abusive behaviors.

## Exerting Control

Now, we can define *batterer*. When we think of a batterer, we generally think of one who batters, which would include hitting, kicking, shoving, or any other aggressive or violent physical occurrence using one's body or object on another person. However, in terms of domestic violence, a person can be a batterer even if physical violence has not yet become a factor. Perhaps he has not yet hit, spit, kicked, shoved, or done anything physically aggressive to his partner, but he has threatened to do so either verbally or in menacing actions. In other words, he has thrown objects across the room when agitated, or perhaps displayed his fists, or driven dangerously in a threatening way. When the threat of eventual physical violence is significant, it is likely to eventually occur, so he is called a batterer because these actions threaten physical abuse.

Bancroft and Silverman remind us that there is a difference between violence termed as domestic violence and "violence that is primarily annoying (as opposed to intimidating) and that is not accompanied by a pattern of coercion."[7] So, here we address violence that stems from intimidation, forceful attitudes, and the desire to control.

Those directly involved within domestic-violence families are the batterer, the partner, and any children in the family. Frequently, it is said that batterers *often* involve children in these families, but in truth, children are *always* involved. Even when the batterer uses tactics to exert control over the partner and does not directly exert those tactics on children, the children are indeed involved, as they can see what is happening. Witnessing violence used against a parent has negative effects on those children. The difficulties children experience as a result of viewing or hearing abuse will be described in later chapters.

The basic strategies that are used to control with domestic violence are common across cultures: "The tactics and attitudes of abusers can vary from country to country, from ethnic group to ethnic group, from rich

6. Bancroft and Silverman, *The Batterer as Parent*, 166.
7. Bancroft and Silverman, *The Batterer as Parent*, 73.

man to poor man. Abusers from each culture have their special areas of control or cruelty."[8] Bancroft explains, for example, that a man from Latin America would be more retaliatory if his partner paid attention to another male, while a middle-class white abuser is more retaliatory if his partner talks back or yells.[9] For this reason, as well as others, one must never tell an abused person that her experiences are perfectly understood. We may understand in general terms, but we can never know the specifics of someone's struggles. In any case, the abuse consists of "assaults on the woman's self-esteem, controlling behavior, undermining her independence, [and] disrespect" regardless of cultural background.[10]

Here are some of the most common behaviors used by the batterer:

- Exhibits jealous behaviors
- Blames, projects, rationalizes, and even denies bad behavior
- Infantilizes the mother
- Imposes repercussions for disclosure and issues threats related to disclosure
- Misuses Scripture or other spiritual writings
- Threatens to take children away
- Uses children against the mother
- Rapes partner
- States that it is the partner who needs help (e.g., therapy), not him
- Deliberately endangers children in mother's presence
- Uses guilt to get his way
- Restricts the victim's associations with friends and family
- Withdraws finances
- Kills pets/animals to threaten
- Threatens to commit suicide (the point at which he is the most dangerous)
- Threatens to harm children

8. Bancroft, *Why Does He Do That?*, 76.
9. Bancroft, *Why Does He Do That?*, 77.
10. Bancroft, *Why Does He Do That?*, 76.

These common behaviors and actions can be categorized as physical abuse, sexual abuse, or threats of abuse; psychological and emotional abuse; financial abuse (e.g., withdrawing funds from the victim or hiding financial information); spiritual abuse (misuse of Scripture to control the victim); and social abuse (attempts to harm or eliminate relationships with family, friends, and coworkers). This chapter's case study shows examples of how Damon used many of these tactics to control Lori. Remember that a batterer is termed as such even when there has been no physical abuse, because when there are actions or behaviors that threaten violent physical contact, physical abuse will occur.

## Cycle of Abuse . . . Or Not

The consideration of a cycle of abuse came to the fore in 1979 when Lenore Walker, a clinical forensic psychologist, wrote *The Battered Woman*. According to Walker, there are three recognizable stages within the cycle: tension-building; explosion and battering; and honeymoon phase.[11] During the tension-building phase the abuser becomes increasingly agitated, and shows this agitation through words and perhaps violent actions that do not make physical contact with his victim. He may show jealousy or displeasure over any one of numerous things his partner does (overcooking the chicken, failing to clean the bathroom, etc.). This stage can last for various lengths of time and its duration is not always predictable. Eventually, in the explosion and battering stage, the tension-building will lead to violence or abuse directed physically at the victim. Too often, the mistreated partner believes the abuse to be her fault, but the responsibility for the abuse belongs only to the batterer, even when the victim does irritating things to annoy him in order to get the battering stage over with. Finally, in the honeymoon phase, the batterer apologizes, may promise to change, and may explain why the battering took place. Here is where he puts the responsibility for his abuse onto the partner. For example, rationalizations such as "If only you wouldn't . . ." or, "You have a way of pushing my buttons," erase his responsibility. Too often, the damage victims experience prevents them from seeing the truth, and they accept the batterer's excuses. Then tensions build again, restarting the "tension-building" stage and continuing the cycle. In some cases, the behaviors become increasingly brutal over time.

11. Degges-White, "Intimate Partner Abuse," para. 3.

Many who work with victims and survivors of domestic violence view the "honeymoon" phase as misnamed. This is not a honeymoon period for the abused, because she knows the abuse and violent behaviors will escalate again. Also noteworthy is the understanding that some victims do not experience a cycle. In Lori's case, Damon's irritations and physical abuse were constant, and physical violence could take place at any time. There is no cycle; there is no tension-building stage; and the honeymoon stage does not exist.

## Batterers' Influences

### OVERALL ENVIRONMENT

Bancroft tells us that a boy's values and beliefs come from all that he experiences in his culture.[12] As adults, we sometimes reflect on our past. We might consider how our parents raised us and think about other experiences that happened within our family. We also reflect on those things that influenced us in our overall environment and with our friends, teachers, pastors, books, movies, jokes, etc. The totality of our experiences inside and outside the family contributes to the shaping of our values and beliefs as we grow and develop. Within Western culture, we have heard that boys "must sow their wild oats." At the same time, particularly within faith communities, girls are taught to remain virtuous. When girls are given the message that a boy's aggressiveness means that they like the girl, it blurs the lines between love and abuse.

Not until after the mid-twentieth century did general Western culture view the beating of women to be problematic. Before this, a man would usually not be faulted for physically abusing his wife, because the greater community held the belief that sometimes a woman needed to be kept in line. Legislation prohibiting extreme beatings of women in the late 1800s was not "enforced consistently at all until the 1990s."[13] Hundreds of years, if not thousands (if one considers the misogynistic and pagan influences of Plato and Aristotle on St. Augustine and St. Thomas of Aquinas respectively) have to be corrected with respect to how men and Western culture view women and their treatment and what we believe concerning women's ability to think equally as well as men. Men are not superior to women; nor

12. Bancroft, *Why Does He Do That?*, 319.
13. Bancroft, *Why Does He Do That?*, 321.

are women superior to men. Yet erroneous teachings throughout the ages concerning a woman's abilities and place in the home and community have dominated and still affect how women are treated today.

Easily accessible pornography on the internet and portrayals of women and girls on television and in movies has strongly influenced growing males concerning how women should be viewed and treated. The media often present rape and sexual abuse as acceptable, and even stimulating or sensual.

## *Religion.*

Doctrines in most prominent religions either teach that women are subservient to men, or influential writings and interpretations that endeavor to explain the scriptures for these religions describe men as having superiority over women. Where men of faith have a sense of entitlement, it often comes from teachings rooted in religion. For example, within Christianity, erroneous teachings commonly promote the idea that the status of men is higher than that of women, as opposed to teaching that men and women have equal status and equal ability to engage in leadership positions or whatever calling God has given them. Teachings within any religion that leave women in a lesser position than men will open the gate to men treating women as inferior beings, which too often encourages an already controlling man to engage in demeaning verbal and violent physical behaviors.

## *Entertainment.*

Women are often demeaned in movies, video games, television programming, lyrics to songs, and other forms of entertainment. Too often, media support a misogynistic culture. Young males, who are forming attitudes about life and acceptable behaviors, too often become saturated with music lyrics that call women by humiliating names, objectify them, and describe violence against women as normal and acceptable.

For example, a tune entitled, "Blurred Lines," performed by Robin Thicke and featuring Pharrell Williams, says: "I hate these blurred lines / I know you want it / But you're a good girl."[14] The music video included a

---

14. Thicke et al., "Blurred Lines."

topless woman.[15] Eminem's "So Much Better" is awash in disrespect, bad language, and descriptions of violent acts against a woman; for example: "Keep playing with me you're gonna end up with a huge goose egg / you fake, lying slut . . ." and "you want to lose two legs . . ."[16] Teens in particular listen to music that not only denigrates women, but also describes acts of violence. There are innumerable other examples. Sometimes these tunes are defended by those who state the lyrics are iconic or provide humor, or they are dismissed as "just songs" and therefore inconsequential. The truth is that these songs validate inclinations toward abuse of women. They do not provide humor to a sound and moral mind, and they are not just songs, but are indeed some of the tools used within a culture wittingly or unwittingly to distort the worth of women and girls.

The movie industry has provided the public with numerous examples of generally acceptable movies with a misogynistic theme. Again, only a few will be mentioned. In *Grease*, Sandy changes from a virtuous young woman to one that is more sexually pleasing to Danny. James Bond movies provide the viewer with "Bond girls," who are soundly objectified. In *50 Shades of Grey*, Anastasia Steele is "dominated" by Christian Grey every step of the way.[17] While many movies have content that should not be witnessed by children and teens, young viewers often find a way to watch and subsequently witness destructive examples of how women can or should be treated. *Grease* had many young followers whose parents deemed the story line "cute" and were distracted by the memorable tunes rather than assessing the messages being conveyed.

### *Children's Literature.*

Belle, in *Beauty and the Beast*, found herself quarantined from the world by the beast, who was very harsh with her. Ultimately, her love converts him into a kind man. Many women are ensnared in their abusive relationships because of the idea that their abuser or batterer will change if they love and serve them adequately. Of course, this is a myth—one that is perpetuated by this fairy tale.

*Hansel and Gretel*, by the Brothers Grimm, provides a look into a home with an abusive stepmother who influences Hansel and Gretel's very

15. Yasharoff, "Pharrell Williams on Realizing 'Blurred Lines' was Problematic," para. 4.

16. Resto et al. "So Much Better."

17. Olivares, "The 13 Most Misogynistic Movies," para. 6–8.

poor and reluctant father to treat them abusively. He agrees to lead the children into the woods to abandon them, so there would be two fewer mouths to feed back home. Eventually, Hansel and Gretel loaded their pockets and apron with jewels from a dead witch's house and somehow made their way back to their parents, hoping they will change their minds because now they would be rich and could afford to feed all four of them. Unthinkable abuses happen in real life even if we do not want to believe they do, and children want to maintain that connection to an abusive parent, even though we may not understand why.

Bancroft reminds us of one such children's book from the Berenstain Bears series, *Trouble with Homework*:

> . . . both the mother and children cower when Father becomes angry . . . At one point he knocks over a chair and clenches his fists above his head. At the end of the story, the children have pleased Dad by doing what he wanted, and Mom smiles happily to see them cuddled up with Dad on the couch.[18]

Dad Berenstain taught his family to do what makes him happy and he will be agreeable rather than display acts of aggression. There are many examples of children's books and stories that provide a skewed look at relationships and good behavior within a family.

## PARENTING

### *Relationship Training.*

While boys receive much teaching outside the home, the home remains a very influential place where morality, values, and male and female roles are learned. Without parental awareness, many erroneous messages about women can take root. Those parents who do not nurture and model for their developing children male/female equality and respect will teach either by omission or commission that men are superior to women. Furthermore, they learn that it is the responsibility of the female to provide sexual pleasure to males, simply by not teaching the importance of respect for a partner within a sexual relationship. In more extreme examples, a boy may witness his mother or stepmother being berated, threatened, or physically abused. When a child sees that his mother's partner is not held accountable

---

18. Bancroft, *Why Does He Do That?*, 326.

by law enforcement or the court system, the treatment his mother receives is validated.

## Abuse.

Every child should experience safety with and acceptance from his or her parents, but not all children live in an environment that provides these essentials. This leads to long-term difficulties that reach into adulthood.

When we refer to abuse, what words and actions qualify? Abusive acts can be categorized as "physical abuse, emotional maltreatment, neglect, sexual abuse and witnessing family violence."[19] The degree to which an adult is affected by an abusive upbringing depends on many factors, including the "frequency and duration of maltreatment and if more than one type of maltreatment has occurred."[20] Of course, the more frequently a child experiences abusive behavior, the more likely the outcomes will be worse as they reach adulthood. While there are many combinations of factors (e.g., the age of the child, type of abuse, the relationship to the abuser, etc.), frequency and duration provide an overall standard of predictability. When one hears the term "abuse," the automatic thought is often physical abuse, but abuse comes in many forms. The emotional abuse of humiliating a child can also have long-term effects. Continual shaming of a child produces an adult who feels "unloved, unwanted, and fearful."[21] As adults, they often replicate the parenting they received, thus creating the same fear in their children that they experienced as children. What is learned as children can emerge "in the form of self-destruction or cruelty to others."[22]

According to Bevan and Higgins, a learning-theory approach has been used to determine how physical abuse and witnessing family violence in childhood lead to "intergenerational transmission of violence."[23] The learning-theory approach posits that we gather information from our environment through our senses, and we then interpret or process the information that will, along with internal stimuli (what we feel, such as love, hunger, pain, etc.), potentially affect our thinking and behaviors. Their study of thirty-six men who engaged in domestic violence showed that, even more

19. Hunter, "Effects of Child Abuse and Neglect," para. 2.
20. Hunter, "Effects of Child Abuse and Neglect," para. 4.
21. McBride, "Shaming Children," para. 7.
22. McBride, "Shaming Children," para. 11.
23. Bevan and Higgins, "Is Domestic Violence Learned?," 223.

than physical abuse or witnessing family violence, neglect played a significant part in predicting the abuse of one's spouse physically. Witnessing family violence that did not include physical abuse associated itself more readily with "psychological spouse abuse and trauma symptomatology."[24]

Hunter's research shows that "violence and criminal behavior is another frequently identified long-term consequence of child abuse and neglect for adult survivors, particularly for those who have experienced physical abuse or witnessed domestic violence."[25] The occurrence of aggressive behaviors toward family members by those who were exposed to family violence growing up is increasingly likely among children who identify with the aggressor.[26] We will examine further how a child can be manipulated to develop a bond with the abusive parent even when they are mistreated.

A batterer will often learn how to behave toward women by observing their mother's partner. Boys absorb the idea that men should be in control and females need to submit. Whether stated by the mother's partner or whether the mere implication exists through experiences in the family, a child is taught gender roles and what "real men" are like. A boy growing up in this environment can be resentful of the batterer's violence, yet, at the same time, abuse their partners when they are adults because of what they learned as children.[27]

Approximately half of abusive men come from homes where the father, stepfather, or mother's partner has been abusive. Still, about half of abusive males do not come from abusive families; cultural surroundings or those elements outside the family can be enough to sanction violent behavior.[28] Remember that neglect is also a form of abuse. Of course, no excuse for abusing someone is valid, whether that abuse is the result of cultural or family influences.

### *Insecure Attachment.*

Before examining attachment styles, understanding the difference between bonding and attachment is important, as they are often mistaken for one

24. Bevan and Higgins, "Is Domestic Violence Learned?," 223.
25. Hunter, "Effects of Child Abuse and Neglect," para. 18.
26. Bevan and Higgins, "Is Domestic Violence Learned?," 225.
27. Bancroft and Silverman, *The Batterer as Parent*, 50.
28. Bancroft, *Why Does He Do That?*, 325, 329.

and the same. Bonding happens between a child and caretaker when the caretaker meets the child's needs, such as changing diapers, making lunch, playing, teaching, helping with batting practice, and the like. Attachment begins at birth with emotional interchanges that include nonverbal communication. Attachment pertains to the child's feelings about the parent. The quality of attachment between child and parent is a predictor of later social and emotional outcomes. The bonding process has not been demonstrated to be connected to child outcomes.[29]

There are a few main types of attachments infants and children can experience with their parents as they are developing. There are many different names given to the styles of attachment, depending on whether one examines a college psychology text, *Psychology Today*, responsible articles, internet sites, medical journals, or professors teaching an early childhood curriculum. And there may be anywhere from three to five different styles named within these sources. Bowlby's stages of attachment theory will be the basis for our discussion. John Bowlby, a psychoanalyst, theorized that there is a connection between children's ability to form relationships and their earliest experiences with their parents. He, along with Mary Ainsworth conducted much research in the 1950s and offered evidence for what is called the *attachment theory*.[30]

When infants are "placed in an unfamiliar situation and separated from their parents," they "will generally react in one of three ways upon reunion with the parents,"[31] according to Bowlby's research-based theory, described here:

> Secure attachment: These infants showed distress upon separation but sought comfort and were easily comforted when the parents returned;
> Anxious-resistant attachment: A smaller portion of infants experienced greater levels of distress and, upon reuniting with the parents, seemed both to seek comfort and to attempt to "punish" the parents for leaving;
> Avoidant attachment: Infants in the third category showed no stress or minimal stress upon separation from the parents and either ignored the parents upon reuniting or actively avoided the parents.[32]

29. Benoit, "Infant-Parent Attachment," para. 7.
30. Ackerman, "What is Attachment Theory?," para. 17.
31. Ackerman, "What is Attachment Theory?," para. 5.
32. Ackerman, "What is Attachment Theory?," para. 5.

While Bowlby focused on infant-caregiver relationships, he suspected a correlation between infant attachment and romantic relationships.[33] Subsequent research has expanded upon the connection between infant/child attachment with a caregiver and their eventual adult relationships, in part exploring the influence of early attachment upon romantic relationships.

Studies across cultures have determined that mothers universally desire the secure attachment pattern in infancy.[34] Adults who are seeking partner relationships also indicate they prefer those qualities in a partner that match those connecting qualities of secure attachment, but not all decide on secure partners.[35] Attachment styles experienced during infancy and childhood do guide behavior into adulthood, but the question remains as to whether an attachment style experienced in infancy can be overridden into adulthood.[36]

In later years, researchers advanced a fourth style of attachment known as disorganized attachment (or fearful-avoidant attachment), in which a child fails to find ways to cope with distress upon separation from a caregiver. They exhibit "aggression, disruptive behaviors, and social isolation."[37] When adults have a disorganized attachment style, they become overpowered by their feelings, experience mood swings, entertain fears of getting hurt and getting too close, and ultimately have difficulty developing healthy relationships.[38]

Kesner and McKenry's research indicates that "unmet attachment needs, originating from the internal working model, may precipitate violent behavior by the adult male."[39] In other words, when someone who has operated under an insecure attachment style perceives or experiences separation from a partner, fear and anger result and violence can erupt. Violent responses indicate a lack of security. At the same time, children who do not experience secure attachment with a caregiver, regardless of attachment style, will display fear and bouts of anger as a result.

In viewing the reasons why an adult engages in domestic violence, many things need to be considered in addition to childhood and adult

33. Fraley, *Adult Attachment Theory and Research*, para. 7.
34. Fraley, *Adult Attachment Theory and Research*, para. 19.
35. Fraley, *Adult Attachment Theory and Research*, para. 19.
36. Fraley, *Adult Attachment Theory and Research*, para. 28.
37. Ackerman, "What is Attachment Theory?," para. 36.
38. Ackerman, "What is Attachment Theory?," para. 39.
39. Kesner and McKenry, "Childhood Attachment Factors," 420.

attachment styles: "violence in the family of origin . . . attachment styles of partners, degree of dissimilarity in adult attachment style endorsement with their partners, and their reported levels of life events stress."[40] How can a child form secure attachment with a parent who is violent against the other parent? Additionally, there are many emotional challenges for the abused parent who may not always be available to their children in an attentive and expressive way as a non-abused parent might. The research is ongoing.

## Legal System

Up until nearly the twentieth century, it was legal for a man to beat his wife. In fact, a man could beat his wife with a stick as long as the stick was no wider than his thumb. Legal help for women abused by their husbands did not exist until the late 1800s, but even then, the laws were often not enforced until the 1970s.[41] After four years of formulation, the Violence Against Women Act became law in 1994. In 2000 and 2005, the VAWA met with expansion and improvements. Nonetheless, domestic violence continues to infect every community across the nation and continues to afflict and influence the children in these families.

## Gender Inequality

When men within any culture are viewed as having a higher status than women, gender inequality results. When this happens, men have the ability to control women in many aspects of life, from prenatal experience (e.g., sex selection), to infancy (e.g., infanticide), to childhood (e.g., genital mutilation), to adulthood (e.g., marital rape, other abuses toward his partner), to pregnancy (e.g., coerced pregnancy or coerced abortion), to old age (e.g., higher rates of elder abuse on women).[42]

Many factors contribute to domestic violence in addition to gender inequality. Nonetheless, domestic violence rates are "lower in societies that have lower rates of gender inequity," and lower gender

40. Kesner and McKenry, "Childhood Attachment Factors," 421.
41. Bancroft, *Why Does He Do That?*, 321.
42. ActionAid UK, "Gender Equality: The Key to Ending Violence Against Women," 2.

inequity proportionately influences the severity of violence toward women and children.[43]

## Personality Characteristics

Batterers will generally behave one way outside the home and another way at home. Outside the home, they will seem to be helpful, friendly, all-around good people, but behavior at home switches to a very different presentation. At home, they are feared, and create tension through manipulation, authoritarian edicts, and sometimes child abuse, violence, threats, and other controlling behaviors. Having a different persona outside the house is one of many ways to exert control. Those outside the home find it difficult to believe that the batterer is a batterer. The amenable behavior works well when professionals, such as guardians ad litem and social services, investigate the family to determine what the family, particularly the children, are experiencing.

Calvete's article primarily considers abusers receiving treatment or those who were in prison:

> The results of this research shows that domestic abusers tend to obtain high points for some types of personality disorders, especially narcissistic, antisocial and borderline disorders. They also present symptoms of depressive disorders and consumption of drugs and alcohol. Some studies also show that neurological problems are relatively frequent.[44]

Because there is no clean profile of a batterer related to geography, personality, and mental health pathologies, most recent research has been "directed towards identifying meaningful perpetrator subtypes (i.e., identifying commonalities that differentiate subgroups of perpetrators from one another and from non-perpetrators)."[45] Grana, et al. conducted research in Spain and categorize batterers into three different types based on violence level/frequency and psychopathology: Type I (low level of violence and frequency of violence and low level of psychopathology), Type II (moderate level of "violence and psychopathology"), and Type III (high level of "deviation in

43. Safe Steps, "Submission to the Senate Finance and Public Administration Inquiry," para. 25–26.

44. Calvete, "Mental Health Characteristics," 30.

45. Grana et al., "Subtypes of Batterers in Treatment," para. 2.

psychopathological characteristics . . . and higher severity and frequency of violence towards the partner").[46] They did their research with a sample of 266 men between 18 and 69 years who engaged in gender violence and who were referred by the court and placed in court-mandated programs.[47]

The New York Behavioral Health website also describes three main categories of abusers: predatory, affectively motivated, and instrumental.[48] Predatory abusers approach their victims without emotion, but with calculation, causing "severe physical and emotional trauma."[49] They have no sympathy for the victims and "often present with borderline personality disorder and sociopathic tendencies."[50] Affectively motivated abusers will generally have attachment disorders with no personality disorders, and, unlike predators, they will have empathy for the victims as the result of their angry outbursts, although they generally exhibit a lower level of physicality than predators.[51] Instrumental abusers are "at least somewhat aware of the impact of their actions on the victims," and are considered the midrange group.[52] They plan ahead, are methodical, and have a specific goal in mind in order to get something they want in return—a chosen outcome.[53]

## Myths

Myths about batterers are plentiful and often skew perceptions, leading to wrong assessments and mistakes in intervention.[54] The importance of understanding these myths cannot be overstated.

### Substance Abuse

Most men who abuse are not addicts; abusive men who are addicts will abuse their partner when they are not drinking or high. Becoming sober

46. Grana et al., "Subtypes of Batterers in Treatment," para. 1, 45.

47. Grana et al., "Subtypes of Batterers in Treatment," para. 14.

48. New York Behavioral Health, "Domestic Violence—Characteristics," para. 3–5.

49. New York Behavioral Health, "Domestic Violence—Characteristics," para. 3.

50. New York Behavioral Health, "Domestic Violence—Characteristics," para. 3.

51. New York Behavioral Health, "Domestic Violence—Characteristics," para. 4.

52. New York Behavioral Health, "Domestic Violence—Characteristics," para. 5.

53. Ennis et al., "Instrumental and Reactive Intimate Partner Violence," para 1.

54. Bancroft and Silverman, The Batterer as Parent, 19.

does not solve the problem of abuse. Drugs and alcohol do not automatically lead to abuse of one's partner. Furthermore, many substance abusers do not behave in either controlling or abusive ways, and not all batterers are addicts.[55] Addiction and abuse each need different resolutions. If a man does not deal with the problem of addiction, there cannot be any change in the abusive man's behavior toward his partner. Yet, even if the addiction problem is successfully dealt with, there are no guarantees that the partner abuse will stop. Still, the abuse cannot be successfully dealt with unless the addiction problem is also successfully dealt with.[56] Batterers often use their addiction to excuse violent behavior when their propensity toward partner control and violence exists apart from drug and alcohol use.

According to Soper, different studies show drugs or alcohol to be associated with 40–60 percent of intimate partner violence (IPV) situations, but conversely, "spousal abuse has been identified as a predictor of developing a substance abuse problem and/or addiction."[57] Compared with those who have no IPV experience, women who experience abuse by their partners are 70 percent more likely to abuse alcohol and/or drugs.[58]

## MENTAL HEALTH ISSUES

A person's mental health issues should not be viewed as the cause of battering, but may, in some instances, be an "important aggravating factor and . . . an obstacle to efforts at rehabilitation. . . ."[59] Battering rarely occurs outside the walls of the family, which indicates a certain amount of control, and often planning.

Antisocial personality disorders (sociopathy and psychopathy) are mental health complexities that can affect a batterer as well as any other person. Robinson provides a picture of sociopaths and psychopaths. Neither has empathy or the ability to identify with another's difficulty or loss. Both have a conscience that is lacking; a psychopath has no conscience and a sociopath has a flimsy one. Sociopaths make it clear that they are only

55. Bancroft, *Why Does He Do That?*, 202.

56. Bancroft, *Why Does He Do That?*, 208.

57. Soper, "Intimate Partner Violence and Co-Occurring Substance Abuse/Addiction," para. 3–4.

58. Soper, "Intimate Partner Violence and Co-Occurring Substance Abuse/Addiction," para. 4, 14.

59. Bancroft and Silverman, *The Batterer as Parent*, 22.

interested in themselves and can be hotheaded, acting before thinking. Psychopaths are "good at mimicking emotions and pretending interest" and are more "cold hearted and calculating" with no fear of consequences. Both "use manipulation and reckless behavior to get what they want."[60]

The description of a man with antisocial personality disorder gives better understanding of the difficulties he has with a partner. He tends toward dishonesty (including ongoing affairs) and abuse. "Antisocial personality disorder is dangerous and highly resistant to treatment, so a man who has both this diagnosis and a history of battering may be a serious risk to his partner, former partners, or children."[61] While there are similarities between batterers and those with antisocial personality disorders, Bancroft explains one of the differences: a batterer exhibits his behaviors with his partner, and a sociopath exhibits these difficult behaviors in and out of the home.[62]

## ANGER

The problem with batterers is not anger or a lack of impulse control. They behave agreeably in the community and when law enforcement appears at the family home. Many professionals decide to send an abusive client to anger management counseling or classes, but showing someone how to control anger does not help in domestic violence situations. Their anger is not the problem.[63] The foundational problem is the demand for control and the resulting abuse, manipulations, and selfishness.

## CHILDHOOD ABUSE

According to Bancroft, research does not show us a sound link between men who have been abused as children and men who ultimately engage in intimate partner abuse. Violent men who were abused as children generally exhibit their violence toward other adult men. At the same time, those men who engage in domestic violence and who have had abusive childhoods are

---

60. Robinson, "Sociopath vs. Psychopath," para. 4–19.

61. Bancroft and Silverman, *The Batterer as Parent*, 23.

62. Bancroft and Silverman, *The Batterer as Parent*, 23.

63. Bancroft, *Why Does He Do That?*, 38.

especially violent and dangerous.[64] A bad childhood has not been shown to be a direct cause of partner abuse. This excuse is often used to deflect from the batterer's own responsibilities for the abuse and gives his partner someone else to be mad at.

## ABUSIVE PAST PARTNERS

To take attention away from himself, an abusive man will often blame his controlling behaviors on a past partner. Doing so will possibly solicit sympathy on his own behalf. He will often blame his past partner for doing the very things he is doing to his present partner.[65] She was controlling. She had an affair. She was demanding. He essentially turns himself into the victim. He blames his bad behavior on a former partner, telling his current partner that he is jealous because she had an affair and therefore, he is mistrusting. Or he gets abusive when he is reminded that the trash needs to go to the curb because his former partner always told him what to do. And on it goes.

## TOO MUCH LOVE

Another common excuse used by the abusive partner is to claim to feel so deeply about his companion that he causes them deep pain, because feeling passionately about someone can lead to aggressive behaviors. This notion is substantiated in movies, romance novels, television shows, and sadly, sometimes at home. There is an expression in our home that has been applied to many reports and stories found on the news, in movies, and in many other areas of life: "Love doesn't behave that way." When we truly care about someone, we do not behave abusively. Love does not behave that way.

## THERAPY AND COUPLES COUNSELING

Psychotherapy and couples counseling are not effective with batterers. In fact, very often, they can be extremely detrimental to both the batterer and his partner. There are exceptional therapists who are trained in the area of trauma and intimate partner abuse, but too few are. Many are unable to accurately assess what is happening in the home between the partners and

64. Bancroft, *Why Does He Do That?*, 25.
65. Bancroft, *Why Does He Do That?*, 28.

with their children. Too often, the abused woman is viewed as the one with problems, not the abusive man.

Batterers are selfish and are very aware of their own feelings. It is their partner's feelings, children's feelings, and the feelings of others around him that he disregards. In therapy nonspecific for batterers, the main thrust is usually for the batterer to identify his feelings, and then to be forthcoming about them. A batterer has no trouble identifying his feelings and expressing them within the walls of his home. Therapy reinforces how important his feelings are and fuels the mentality of abuse. A batterer needs to be in a program specifically meant to help batterers.[66]

Couples therapy should be strictly avoided. An abuser does not consider his partner to be his equal, and that philosophy also exists when sitting in a therapist's office with his partner. Counseling in the context of improving a marriage (e.g., for better communication, creating intimacy, etc.) means that the partners need to recognize that they are equals in their relationship. The abuser does not recognize that both genders are equal.

A victim of abuse should not think that she needs to correct her behaviors in relationship to the cruelty she suffers. Too many therapists and counselors, including pastors, have told the victim that she needs to correct a certain behavior that the abuser finds annoying so they can get along better, and so that her partner will behave better. There are too many examples of pastors telling women they need to submit more or pray more, putting the blame on the victim and making her responsible for the problem and the fix. One woman told her pastor that her husband always wants to have sex in a way that could easily be described as abusive to her, and that he insists in spite of her objections. The pastor's advice was to tell her that she could not deprive her husband of his right to have sex with her and that she needed to bear it.

Believing that an abuser's behavior will change if the victim changes or behaves better is completely erroneous. How many times has an abused woman heard something like this from her abuser: "If you would just stop doing those things that push my buttons, I wouldn't hurt you." He is the one who needs to change his attitudes and behaviors.

When a woman tries to tell the couple's therapist what she is experiencing, she is often blamed by the therapist for wanting to put the fault on her abusive partner. Furthermore, he adds to the abuse she will suffer because she exposed him. On the way home after a couples therapy

66. Bancroft, *Why Does He Do That?*, 355.

session, with nine-month old Poppy in her car seat, Damon, while driving, screamed at the top of his lungs, over and over: "You just wait until I get you home! You had no business telling him what I did! Do you know how you made me look!?" And punish her he did.

## CULTURE, RACE, AND CLASS

Thinking that domestic violence occurs mainly within certain ethnic or socioeconomic groups is erroneous. In the United States, every racial and economic group has a high rate of domestic violence. Considering domestic violence worldwide, the US rate is neither the highest nor the lowest.[67] A clear predictor of the level of domestic violence in a given nation is the level at which women and men are viewed as equals. Nations with the lowest levels of domestic violence are those that espouse and practice equality. Restrictions on a woman's ability to be equally financially secure and a lack of equality in decision making in the home are two examples of aspects of inequality that take power away from a woman and leave her vulnerable.

Batterers across all cultures have similar fundamental characteristics, although the actual abuse or tactics or threats may vary. For example, an immigrant to the US in a domestic violence home may be told by her partner that he will send her back to their country of origin if she does not "behave." Or a woman in a wealthy home who is normally given a substantial allowance may have her funds terminated until she can "behave."

Courts, guardians ad litem, and child protective services can be swayed by culture and economic status, and often are. Thinking that certain cultures have more or less of a propensity toward violence in the home can lead to misguided recommendations to the court and the possibility of leaving women and children in a very dangerous environment. Court culture often leans toward underreacting to a domestic violence case when the parties are educated and have a good income.

## Warning Signs of Abusive Men

There are many warning signs of an abusive personality. Still, some abusive individuals may be difficult to recognize during the dating process. Abusive men know how to behave to be likable, so they start a relationship by

67. Bancroft and Silverman, *The Batterer as Parent*, 24, 26.

appearing affable, kind, and considerate to gain trust, and then turn abusive later. For this reason alone, getting to know a dating partner as well as possible is optimum, as eventually suspicions may rise as he reveals his true nature. While a prospective partner can watch for red flags and address specific behaviors, an abusive man may not exhibit all the behaviors at first or in any obvious way. Any history of violence is an excellent reason to either not start a relationship or to stop one. Such a partner will more than likely abuse future partners.

Since control is the foundation of the abusive man's behaviors, controlling behaviors may intensify as the relationship develops. For example, he may want to know who his partner has been talking with, why she did not call him back within a given time period, what her finances look like, how she spends her money, who she is with, and the like. Sometimes this control takes the form of pressure to become committed to him quickly, and he will find ways to isolate his partner, drawing her away from family and friends and keeping her from securing or maintaining a job or schooling. He will also sometimes control her time and the use of her vehicle, phone, and computer.

Verbal abuse and threats of violence may seem obvious indicators of an abusive personality, but when caught up in a relationship or operating out of fear, the abused partner will sometimes make excuses for individual occurrences and dismiss these warnings: "He was just tired" or "I made him mad." Any kind of abuse must be taken seriously, even so-called "playful" sex in which force is used. If a dating partner uses force, hits inanimate objects, drives too fast with the intent to scare his passenger, or maliciously hurts a pet, he is not only exhibiting controlling strategies, but is also trying to shock his victim into submission. He is showing her that she could be next, or that he is capable of harming her.

Jealousy is not love; love is not jealousy. But the two can erroneously be thought of as the same emotion. Jealousy is a lack of trust and is often the basis for using methods of control, when an abuser says the jealousy he exhibits comes as the result of how much he loves her. Other manipulative tactics include threats and comments such as: "I wouldn't do that to you if you didn't make me so mad!" or "If you love me, you will . . ." or "If you love me, you won't . . . ." Remember, an abusive man can be very charming as part of his deception and manipulation.

An abuser will blame others as a way of excusing his behavior and will frequently exhibit overactive sensitivity, expecting his partner to be sensitive to his emotional desires and act in the roles women have traditionally fulfilled. She is expected to "serve" him and is often viewed as inferior to him. In taking care of menial tasks such as cooking and cleaning, all must be done to his standards.

A victim of domestic violence must remember that she is not to blame for being in an abusive relationship. The fault rests solely in the abusive partner. Irrespective of the presence of red flags, the victim is not to blame for her situation.

## Ability to Change

For a batterer to change, he must view who he is honestly and with accountability and have the motivation to do so. His behavior comes from "learned attitudes and feelings of entitlement and privilege."[68] Change is a difficult and lifelong process for a batterer. Consequently, a very low percentage of abusers change their ways.[69] Psychotherapy, couples counseling, and anger management are not recommended, since the nucleus of an abuser's behavior does not rest in anger or feelings. Substance abuse programs do not help, since the batterer's foundational problem does not stem from drugs or alcohol. "Abusers are unwilling to be nonabusive, not unable. They do not want to give up power and control."[70]

A certified batterer intervention program may help, but only if the abuser is willing. The US National Institute of Justice did a meta-analysis (integration of results from various scientific studies) examining and rating two different approaches in batterer intervention programs: the Duluth model and the cognitive therapy model. The Duluth model uses a "feminist Psychoeducational approach with group facilitated exercises" and was "rated Effective for reducing recidivism . . . and Promising in reducing victimization."[71] The cognitive behavioral therapy approach focuses on identifying and changing thought processes that lead to abuse so as to provide the skills to control and then change behaviors.[72] The NIJ rated the

---

68. National Domestic Violence Hotline, "Is Change Possible in an Abuser?"
69. National Domestic Violence Hotline, "Is Change Possible in an Abuser?"
70. Bancroft, *Why Does He Do That?*, 75.
71. National Institute of Justice, "Batterer Intervention Programs Have Mixed Results."
72. National Institute of Justice, "Batterer Intervention Programs Have Mixed Results."

cognitive approach as yielding "No Effects" for both recidivism and reducing victimization.[73]

## Scriptural Encouragement

In general, women who are suffering within a domestic violence family are told they are stupid, less than, incapable, shameful, and more. These assertions are contrary to the truth of who a woman really is, which rests in what Scripture tells us.

The Bible shows us how precious all humanity is to our Lord, but here we will apply Scripture to women and children who have been mistreated. These women commonly have low opinions of themselves because of what they have been told and how they have been treated.

Genesis 1:27 tells us, "So God created humankind in his image, in the image of God he created them; male and female he created them." Each of us carries with us, every second of every day, the *imago Dei*, or the image of God. How precious it is that we are formed according to the image of Jesus. As we turn to our Creator, he will work in our life circumstances, conforming us more and more closely to that image of God, which he intended for us. Realizing that each of us bears the image of God means also realizing that, when someone is abusive, they are also showing thorough disrespect to that image within the victim.

The psalmist in Psalm 139:13–18 tells us that our beginning and end are known by God:

> For it was you who formed my inward parts; you knit me together in my mother's womb. I praise you, for I am fearfully and wonderfully made. Wonderful are your works; that I know very well. My frame was not hidden from you, when I was being made in secret, intricately woven in the depths of the earth. Your eyes beheld my unformed substance. In your book were written all the days that were formed for me, when none of them as yet existed. How weighty to me are your thoughts, O God! How vast is the sum of them! I try to count them—they are more than the sand; I come to the end—I am still with you.

We are God's creation, lovingly and magnificently made. Even in the very beginning of our existence, when formed in our mother's womb, we were known and loved. That love does not go away, regardless of our

---

73. National Institute of Justice, "Batterer Intervention Programs Have Mixed Results."

thoughts, our experiences, or our deeds or misdeeds. Out of that love, our Creator wants the very best for us. God's love for each of us is perfect and complete, and runs deep enough for him to have sent his Son to die in our place.

Joshua 1:9 tells us that, no matter where we go or what we experience, God is with us. "I hereby command you: Be strong and courageous; do not be frightened or dismayed, for the Lord your God is with you wherever you go." God is there during sleep and as the day progresses. The divine presence is with us in our disappointments, struggles, successes, questionings, happiness, weakness, and hurts.

None of us deserves to be treated poorly. All of us, in some way, bear the image of God. Controlling behaviors such as manipulation, physical and verbal violence, and withdrawal of positive emotions and care are treacherous and wrong. Do not believe the messages those behaviors send; rather, believe that God knows you intimately, loves you amazingly, and knows you were wonderfully made. Romans 8:38–39 tells us, "For I am convinced that neither death, nor life, nor angels, nor rulers, nor things present, nor things to come, nor powers, nor height, nor depth, nor anything else in all creation will be able to separate us from the love of God in Christ Jesus our Lord." There is truth we can believe about ourselves, regardless of our circumstances: each of us bears the precious *imago Dei;* the presence of God is always available; and Christ gives us divine and perfect love.

# 2

# The Batterer and Undermining

## Case Study

L ORI DECIDED TO LEARN how to do needlework early in their marriage. When Damon spied new yarn or pattern purchases, he threw them in the trash. She finally gave up what she thought would be a satisfying hobby.

Damon did not allow Lori to make a grocery list. Instead he would protest, "You should know what I need!" If she returned without something he wanted, Damon complained about her memory. He would then declare that she did not care about him, call her selfish, and send her back to the store.

Damon sneaked Poppy out of the house on many occasions. He often had her secured in the car before Lori realized he was taking her. Calling his phone rarely succeeded because he rarely answered it when she called him. When he did answer, he yelled and screamed at her for being a terrible mother. Lori sometimes succeeded in finding them at Damon's family cottage. One time, she found Poppy, at that time younger than eighteen months old, wandering in the road. Lori stopped and ran to her, and found a filthy child with a full diaper. When Damon saw Lori, he snatched Poppy away from her while explaining that he had to take Poppy away because she did not know how to be a good mother.

The day usually began with Lori caring for and playing with Poppy, doing household chores, and working at her studies. On the days Damon worked at home, he turned lunch time into an opportunity to undermine Lori. He would prepare Poppy's lunch, put it in front of her, and say, "See? Daddy cares more about you than Mommy because he fixed lunch for you. Mommy doesn't care about you because she didn't fix your lunch." He repeatedly scolded Lori in front of Poppy for terrible mothering. Even after their separation, Lori hurried to prepare Poppy's lunch before noon.

## Undermining Defined

Undermining lies at the root of nearly everything the batterer does to gain control. Cambridge University Press defines *undermine* as, "To make someone less confident, less powerful, or less likely to succeed, or to make something weaker, often gradually."[1] The Collins Dictionary states that to undermine is "to injure, weaken, or impair" usually "by subtle, stealthy, or insidious means."[2] One who is undermined finds their position and authority within the family weakened. This chapter's case study gives a good idea of what undermining looks like. The following list describes some demeaning ways one person can undermine another:

- Attack them physically
- Attack them verbally
- Lie about them
- Magnify their mistakes
- Make fun of them or laugh at their mistakes
- Make them feel their successes are unimportant
- Fail to encourage them or actually discourage them
- Prohibit them from engaging in activities or fulfilling a goal
- Limit finances
- Gaslight
- Brainwash

Through these behaviors, the batterer gives the intentional message that his partner's worth, philosophies, and beliefs are beneath his. Let us carefully consider gaslighting and brainwashing.

The 1930s play *Gaslight* was made into a movie in the 1940s, starring Ingrid Bergman as Paula Alquist and Charles Boyer as Gregory Anton. Gregory gradually dimmed the gas lights in their home. When Paula

1. *Cambridge Dictionary*, s.v., "undermine."
2. *Collins English Dictionary*, s.v., "undermine."

recognized that the lights were dimming, Gregory convinced her that she was imagining it. This led Paula to believe she was losing her mind and having difficulty knowing reality from falsehood. Gregory confined her to the house; after all, she was losing her mind. (Fear not: The movie has a good ending.)

When subjected to gaslighting, the survivor will begin to question herself, wondering if she remembered an event or conversation correctly. Gaslighting is a form of psychological abuse meant to confuse and control a survivor. The survivor may actually begin to question whether she is too sensitive, whether her partner actually hit her the night before, or whether she has a bad memory.

Brainwashing was identified more than fifty years ago by psychologist Robert Jay Lifton, who studied former prisoners of the Korean War and Chinese war camps. Lifton came to realize that these prisoners went through a three-stage evolution that "began with attacks on each one's sense of self and ended with an apparent change in beliefs."[3] The captors "introduced the possibility of salvation" after "breaking down the self" and then proceeded to "rebuild the self."[4] Brainwashing takes place in isolation, away from the influence of familiar people and situations. Other tools used are sleep deprivation and malnutrition, with real or threatened physical harm.[5]

> *Breaking Down the Self*
> Assault on identity: You aren't who you say you are.
> Guilt: You are bad.
> Self-betrayal: Agree with me that you are bad.
> Breaking point: Who am I, where am I, and what am I supposed to do?
> *Introducing the Possibility of Salvation*
> Leniency: I can help you.
> Compulsion to confession: You can help yourself.
> Channeling of guilt: This is why you're in pain.
> Releasing of guilt: It's not me; it's my beliefs.
> *Rebuilding the Self*
> Progress and harmony: If you want, you can choose good.
> Final confession and rebirth: I choose good.[6]

A general description of the three stages follows:

3. Sharecare, "How is Brainwashing Achieved?" para. 1.
4. Sharecare, "How is Brainwashing Achieved?" para. 1.
5. Sharecare, "How is Brainwashing Achieved?" para. 2.
6. Sharecare, "How is Brainwashing Achieved?" para. 4.

1. To break down the sense of self, the brainwasher attacks the target's beliefs over days, weeks, and months while also telling the target he or she is not who they believe they are (a daughter, a soldier, intelligent, etc.). At the same time, the target is shamed for any sins or perceived sins, which could be as simple as not sitting correctly. Then the target learns to denounce loved ones who share his or her former beliefs. Now the target can be saved from this terrible crisis by converting to another belief system.

2. Where a possibility of salvation presents itself, the brainwasher shows forbearance and even an emotional connection. This display of a sort of kindness gives the target a sense of relief. While the target feels guilt, she is unsure of the reason for her guilt until the brainwasher explains that her agony can be fully relieved if she replaces her beliefs with another belief system. Now, the target can get rid of her guilt by renouncing wrong beliefs.

3. To rebuild the self, the subject has to choose allegiance to the "good," defined as the new identity provided by the brainwasher.[7]

What does brainwashing have to do with domestic violence? The American Psychological Association *Dictionary of Psychology* defines brainwashing as "a broad class of intense and often coercive tactics intended to produce profound changes in attitudes, beliefs, and emotions."[8] A prisoner of war and their captors are enemies. But in a family situation, one expects love and support from others in the family.

> In a romantic relationship, the partners are supposed to be on the same side. It is reasonable to expect love, understanding, and compassion from your partner, and to want to offer that to them also. The relationship, unfortunately, creates a vulnerability to the coercive brainwashing of a malicious or self-centered partner. It is unexpected. It can sneak up on you.[9]

In order to exact control, an abuser will disallow his partner from making decisions and keep them sleep-deprived or malnourished, isolate them from family and friends, encourage the use of drugs and alcohol, exhaust them through the work expectations and childcare at home, manipulate

---

7. Layton and Hoyt., "How Brainwashing Works," para. 9, 10, 15.
8. *APA Dictionary of Psychology*, s.v., "Brainwashing."
9. Silvers, "Brainwashing in Abusive Relationships," para. 11.

them, create impossible rules and punishments (as Damon did when he expected Lori to know what he wanted at the store and prevented her from making a list), deny needed medications, humiliate through put-downs and name-calling, and more. These tactics align with brainwashing tactics. Trauma bonding occurs when an abuser makes his partner feel horrible and then becomes nice to her, consoling her. This "reinforces their attachment, even though the abuser was the original source of the suffering."[10]

Sometimes mind control compels a victim to return to her abuser after separation. The abused woman has been made to feel responsible for any troubles, so she blames herself. Her life has become so connected to the abuser's wishes that she sometimes feels lost without him.[11] But knowledge can be power: Those who understand how brainwashing works become less susceptible to it.

## Undermining Enacted

### UNDERMINING THE MOTHER DIRECTLY

We can look at the case study sections from the first two chapters to see some of the strategies Damon used to undermine Lori. We see that Damon did not support Lori when she had a miscarriage. She went to the hospital alone and underwent the difficult process with her doctor, when her husband should have also been present to support her. The bruising on Lori's legs made her friend question Lori's safety. To show Lori that he alone made decisions about who came into their home, after stating his disapproval, Damon raped her just before Lori's parents arrived. We can see him undermining Lori by narrowing her ability to access finances, putting into place schemes to keep her home, and berating her mothering skills. He even tried to use Lori's parents against her.

The tactic of gaslighting eventually makes a woman doubt her abilities, her memory, and her experiences. She begins to believe that no one would ever trust her version of events and conversations. How will she ever be able to leave if no one believes her?

The National Domestic Violence Hotline provides an excellent list of techniques that an abuser might use in gaslighting a survivor:

10. Fontes, "Yes, Abusive Partners Brainwash their Victims," para. 5.
11. Fontes, "Yes, Abusive Partners Brainwash their Victims," para. 6.

- Withholding: abuser refuses to listen or understand
- Countering: abuser questions the survivor's memory
- Blocking/diverting: abuser changes the subject or questions the victim's perceptions
- Trivializing: abuser dismisses victim's feelings as unimportant
- Forgetting/denial: abuser pretends to forget what took place and/or denies promises made[12]

## Undermining the Mother to the Children

Batterers will often specifically undermine the mother in her relationship to the children. As a result, the children learn aggressive and disrespectful behaviors toward their mother. Abusers will even keep the mother from exhibiting nurturing care toward the children, such as picking up a crying child, feeding the child, caring for a skinned knee, encouraging a sad child, etc. Thus, the children come to view the mother as the less responsible parent and the father as the better, more responsible one.

The case study in this chapter shows Damon verbally demeaning his wife and lying about Lori to Poppy. He threw away Lori's yarn and patterns and set her up for failure at the grocery store when he refused to allow her to make a shopping list. He shamed her if she forgot or failed to get him what he wanted, often in front of Poppy. When he gave Poppy her lunch, Damon told her that he cared for her, and Mommy did not, because he gave her lunch.

When Lori and Damon separated, Damon's tactics became more insidious. He engaged his lawyer, the guardian ad litem, the court system, and child protective services to demean Lori. Along the way he told Poppy that because Mommy is a bad mother she can mistreat or hurt her, thus attempting to use his daughter to hurt her mother. Finally, Damon continued to exhibit permissive parenting to help make him look like a good dad in the eyes of his children. We sometimes hear such a father called the "Toys R Us Dad" because of his permissiveness and gift-giving during the children's time with him.

12. National Domestic Violence Hotline, "What is Gaslighting?," para. 3.

## Scriptural Encouragement

Examples of people undermining others in an effort to gain control can be found throughout the Bible in all sorts of circumstances. King Herod, threatened by the birth of Jesus, directed that all babies in Bethlehem be killed so he might be rid of him. The Pharisees, who exhibited pride, arrogance, and hypocrisy, plotted to achieve the death of the Savior and sanctioned the lie the soldiers at the tomb told about the resurrection. Here we will address two other events in history found in the books of Ezra and Esther.

The account of Ezra takes place during the fifth and sixth centuries BC. King Cyrus of Persia commanded the Jewish people to return from exile to their homeland. He told them to go to Jerusalem and rebuild the temple. The Jews restored worship in Jerusalem. They rebuilt the altar and made burnt offerings. Next, they completed the foundation for the temple. At this time, the enemies of Judah and Benjamin asked to help rebuild the temple with them because they served the same God. They were told they could not help, so the non-Jewish settlers attempted to discouraged the people of Judah and make them afraid to continue building. Their enemies bribed officials to thwart the building plans, a tactic that continued until the reign of King Darius. Judah's enemies wrote a letter to King Artaxerxes complaining of the wickedness of the City of Jerusalem and reported that the residents would not pay their due in tributes or toll, which would reduce revenue. Consequently, the king forced the Jews to stop building until a decree was made.

Eventually, King Darius made a decree to find the orders of King Cyrus wherein he had commanded the Jews to rebuild Jerusalem. When they were found, Darius decreed that the Jewish people must complete the work. In addition, he said that anyone standing in the way would be punished. The Jewish people completed and dedicated the temple and were able to celebrate Passover. The Jews surely felt powerless and stifled as they were undermined in their efforts to rebuild the temple, but God had his way after all, and his people ultimately completed the work.

In the book of Esther, there is no mention of a deity, but there is an assumption that the Lord is behind these events that occurred in the fourth century BC. The story is set in the Persian capital of Susa, where King Ahasuerus is described as reigning over 127 provinces, from India to Ethiopia. Queen Vashti refused to appear at a celebratory feast upon the king's request, and so he decided to replace the queen and to declare every man the master in his own house.

In the citadel of Susa, Mordecai, one of the Jewish exiles, placed his cousin Esther in the king's palace with others chosen as candidates to be queen and told her to not reveal her Jewish heritage. King Ahasuerus made Esther the queen and held a banquet in her honor. In the meantime, Mordecai learned that two of the king's eunuchs planned to assassinate the king, so he told Esther, who told the king. The king had the eunuchs hanged.

King Ahasuerus then promoted a man named Haman above all the other officials, but Mordecai refused to bow down to Haman. This infuriated Haman, who began to plot to kill all the Jews in the kingdom. He reported to the king that the Jews had different laws and did not respect the laws of the king. Haman appealed to an agreeable King Ahasuerus to destroy all the Jews on one given day, young and old, men and women and children, and to plunder their goods. Haman planned to have Mordecai hanged. Mordecai, in his distress, sent word to Esther concerning the plan.

Esther then approached the king—a bold move, as she might have been rejected and punished for approaching the king without being summoned. She invited both the king and Haman to a banquet, which they attended. She also invited them to a banquet the next day.

That night, a reading from the book of records reminded the king that Mordecai had revealed the two eunuchs' plan to kill the king. Ironically, King Ahasuerus asked Haman what should be done to honor the man the king wants to honor and then followed his suggestions. The king directed that this person be dressed in royal robes, ride a king's horse, and wear a crown as his worth is extolled throughout the city. When Haman realized that the king wanted to honor Mordecai, he began to mourn, and his family and friends cautioned him concerning his future.

While at the second night's banquet, King Ahasuerus asked Esther what he could grant her. She said she wanted her life and the lives of her people to be spared, for she and her people were about to be annihilated. The king asked Esther who devised this plan, and she said, "Haman!" Thus, Haman and his sons met their demise on the gallows Haman had prepared for Mordecai.

The king told Esther to write an edict concerning the death of the Jews. The Jews were ordered to defend themselves, and killed 75,000 of their enemies. Mordecai instituted the Feast of Purim to commemorate the deliverance the Jews experienced from their enemies.

In both of these instances, the underminers attempted to thwart God's plan: the enemies of the Jewish people who stopped the building of the temple, and Haman, who set out to have all the Jews killed. King Darius settled once and for all the question about whether King Cyrus ordered the rebuilding of the temple, and decreed that obstructionists would be punished. What confidence Darius's actions must have given the Jews! And what confidence Esther and Mordecai's bravery gave the Jews living in King Ahasuerus's kingdom once Esther had revealed the undermining by Haman and stopped his plans! Ultimately, God had his way.

When undermined within a domestic violence context, women develop feelings of powerlessness, oppression, and low self-worth. They often lack confidence in their value because they are not treated with care, but subjected to intentional actions that hurt. Some women even get to the point of believing that they deserve to be treated poorly. No woman should be devoid of confidence or fail to expect others to treat her well. The Lord detests the sheer schadenfreude of the enemies of Israel, Haman, and the abuser in the home. The enemies of the Jews lied to get their way, tried to discredit God's people, and tried to convince others of their superior worth. In the same way, an abusive man will try to get his own way, discredit his partner, and try to convince others of his worth as he demeans his target. The opponents to the rebuilding of the temple, Haman, and domestic batterers share the traits of pride, and self-centeredness, arrogance, and a sense of entitlement.

God gives us many messages concerning our worth to him throughout Scripture. For example, Jeremiah 29:11 tells us: "For surely I know the plans I have for you, says the Lord, plans for your welfare and not for harm, to give you a future with hope." God's word provides encouragement for every woman in a domestic violence situation. God's plan is not for any woman to be maltreated or to experience physical or emotional shattering. His plans are for good, not harm.

The abuser makes the victim of domestic violence think she is powerless, but she truly does have power and resources. God knows all situations intimately and wants to help those who are suffering. Isaiah tells us in 40:29–31: "He gives power to the faint, and strengthens the powerless. Even youths will faint and be weary, and the young will fall exhausted; but those who wait for the Lord shall renew their strength, they shall mount up with wings like eagles, they shall run and not be weary, they shall walk and not faint."

3

# The Batterer and Incest

## Case Study

Poppy had her second birthday just before Lori and Damon separated, and Lori had just given birth to Rayne. They had separated after Damon committed assault and battery on Lori. During the first year of their separation, Poppy's behavior and words began to reveal sexual knowledge that a two- or three-year-old would not have known except through an experience or experiences with another, older person.

Lori enlisted the help of a therapist to support Poppy and to help her understand and work with Poppy. Periodically, Poppy offered descriptions of interactions with her father that concerned Lori and Deborah, Lori's mom. Sometime around Poppy's fourth birthday, she drew a stick-figure picture for her therapist and described what her father had asked her to do.

The therapist made a call to Child Protective Services and they launched an investigation. CPS conducted a video interview with Poppy, who did not divulge what she had revealed to the therapist (and her mother and maternal grandmother). On the way home, Lori told her that she was very brave and that she did a good job. Poppy responded by saying, "Sometimes it's easier to tell a story than to tell the truth."

## Child Molesters

Information based on research about child and teen sexual abuse helps adults to identify instances of sexual abuse in children, and specifically incest. While the "stranger danger" campaign in the 1980s helped increase vigilance to protect children, the idea that only strangers are dangerous is not the whole truth. In 90 percent of cases where children are sexually abused, the child knows and trusts the perpetrator.[1]

## GENERAL INFORMATION

According to the American Psychological Association, sexual abuse is "unwanted sexual activity, with perpetrators using force, making threats or taking advantage of victims not able to give consent. Most victims and perpetrators know each other."[2]

If the perpetrator acts on their sexual urges and experiences "significant distress or interpersonal difficulty as a result of their urges or fantasies" they may be diagnosed with a pedophilic disorder.[3] Often, the term *pedophilia* is used to refer to a psychological disorder that includes sexual feelings toward minor children. Specifically, *pedophiles* have a sexual preference for prepubescent children; *hebephiles* for children roughly between the ages of 11 to 14, or children crossing over into puberty; *ephebophiles* for those who have arrived at puberty, or 15 to 16 year olds; and *teleiophiles* for those 17 and older.[4] A person does not become a sexual offender in any of these categories unless they act upon their attraction by abusing someone or viewing child pornography. Collectively, these are known as *paraphilia*, or a "condition in which a person's sexual arousal and gratification depends on objects, activities, or even situations that are considered atypical."[5]

A perpetrator will generally use one of two different approaches to sexually abuse a child: situational or grooming. We often think in terms of a molester grooming a child or teen before engaging in abuse, but "the largest group of sexual abusers is referred to as 'situational abusers.'"[6]

With situational abusers, the child's age, gender, and appearance are not as important as their availability.[7] They take advantage of a situation whereby they have the likelihood of not being discovered. A child molester may use grooming to gain the trust of not only the child, but also those connected to the child, such as friends and family members. They use the

1. MassKids, "Who are the Abusers?," para. 1.
2. *APA Dictionary of Psychology*, s.v., "Sexual abuse."
3. *Psychology Today Diagnosis Dictionary*, s.v., "Pedophilia."
4. Bering, "Pedophiles, Hebephiles and Ephebophiles," para. 2.
5. *Psychology Today Diagnosis Dictionary*, s.v., "Pedophilia."
6. MassKids, "Who are the Abusers?," para. 12.
7. MassKids, "Who are the Abusers?," para. 12.

trust they gain to get close to their target. We are told that incest perpetrators usually use the situational approach, but grooming can also occur with incest.

Child molesters look and act just like the rest of us. Most abusers are family members, friends of the family, or those with access to children through schools, youth groups, after-school organizations, and more. The vast majority of sex offenders are heterosexual, and they represent all ethnic groups.[8]

MassKids provides a list of signs to look for in those who may molest children or teens:

- Prefers to spend time with children and teenagers who are not their children
- Does not seem to have adult friendships
- Finds ways to spend time alone with child or teen
- Does not respect verbal or physical cues to not hug, stroke, tickle, etc.
- Concentrates on a different child from time to time
- Does not respect the privacy of the child or teen
- Gives money or gifts for no recognizable reason or occasion
- Asks child or teen to have discussions surrounding sexual experiences or feelings
- Views child pornography[9]

Adults are not always the perpetrators of child and teen sexual abuse. "Sadly, children and teens are also involved in sexually offending against their peers or younger children, with 76.7% of male victims and 70.1% of female victims of child sexual abuse being victimized by other juveniles."[10]

## Batterers as Incest Perpetrators

Lundy Bancroft, in a shared chapter written with Margaret Miller, explains that domestic violence provides "an important risk factor for incest victimization" and that "roughly half of incest perpetrators" also batter the

8. MassKids, "Who are the Abusers?" para. 4.
9. MassKids. "Behavior Signs of Abusers," para. 6.
10. MassKids, "Who are the Abusers?," para. 22.

children's mother.[11] Sadly, too many children in these situations remain at risk when authorities or those assessing a domestic violence case view the mother as being untruthful or mentally unstable. They observe behaviors in the mother that result from the stress (fear, anxiety, depression, nervousness, etc.) of having an abusive partner and often erroneously conclude that she is the problem.

When those investigating a case believe the mother is lying about allegations of incest, the father often wins custody of the children. In fact, perpetrators will sometimes time their abuse to coincide with a custody dispute in order to discredit the mother. It has been demonstrated that "research has found that fathers are sixteen times more likely than mothers to maliciously fabricate allegations of child abuse."[12]

In domestic violence cases, children of batterers are 6.5 to 19 times more likely to experience sexual abuse by the batterer compared with non-battering parents.[13] Candace Lopez, the national sexual assault hotline director with the Rape, Abuse and Incest National Network (RAINN) states that "incest and domestic violence are intricately linked."[14] She explains that domestic violence is about power and control, which extends to the perpetrator's children, and that "girls are a higher risk of sexual abuse when there's domestic violence in the home."[15] When a woman's partner abuses her, the children in the family are at risk for assault, including sexual assault.

The batterer justifies his destructive behaviors through a sense of entitlement and the need for control—attitudes that can also lead to incest. According to a batterer's thinking, he owns his partner and children. They exist to serve him. Batterers and incest perpetrators share many traits. Bancroft lists many of these similarities:

- *Controlling*: Includes verbal and physical abuse as well as other means to control; uses increasingly forceful tactics when the abused does not comply.

- *Entitlement*: Victims are viewed as objects who are owned and whose purpose is to meet the needs of the self-centered abuser; the abuser believes he can treat his victims how he pleases.

11. Bancroft and Silverman, *The Batterer as Parent*, 86.
12. Child Abuse Solutions, *Fact Sheet*, 10.
13. Child Abuse Solutions, *Fact Sheet*, 3.
14. DomesticShelters.org, "When Incest Accompanies Domestic Violence," para. 2.
15. DomesticShelters.org, "When Incest Accompanies Domestic Violence," para. 9.

- *Exploitation:* Similar to entitlement, the abuser believes he can use family members for his purposes.

- *Denial and minimization:* They minimize or even deny their actions when caught.

- *Claimed loss of control:* Even though their actions necessitate forethought, they claim that any alleged incidents are due to a loss of control.

- *Claimed provocation:* Both groups claim that the victim(s) provoked them; for example, the incest perpetrator may say that the child seduced him, while the batterer claims that his partner pushed his buttons.

- *Grooming or seasoning:* He tries to build a good relationship with his victim, who may become attached to the abuser as the result of the positive experiences with him.

- *Positive public image:* Those outside the family usually do not view the abuser as one who would abuse his family because he presents as an agreeable person. He may even be active in his community or have a highly respected occupation.

- *Objectification:* They degrade their victims by depersonalizing them.

- *Sowing divisions within the family:* The abuser takes attention away from the abuse by sowing discord among family members.

- *Confusion of love and abuse:* Batterers will say they physically harm out of love; incest perpetrators will often characterize their abuse as intimate and loving.

- *Threats and imposition of secrecy:* Both types of abusers threaten the victim so he or she will not tell their secrets.

- *Manipulation:* They manipulate victims to remain in control; they manipulate both "individuals and systems" to escape accountability.

- *Discrediting of disclosures:* They make the victim the problem, claiming that the victim did not get what they wanted from the perpetrator, or that the victim is unstable.

- *Lack of mental health diagnosis:* In general, perpetrators do not have a mental health diagnosis; their behavior emanates out of "attitudes and belief systems."

- *High recidivism and resistance to change:* Without complete admission of wrongdoing and holding themselves accountable for their actions, change will not happen.[16]

A child sexual predator (nonfamilial) tends to prefer male victims. Often, a sexual predator violates children in an ongoing manner and will have many victims over time. Also, he is more likely to use force.[17] On the other hand, girls are at higher risk than boys from batterers who are incest perpetrators. The perpetrator "commonly has normal adult sexual interest and involvement that may co-occur with his offenses against a child" and usually has one or two victims over his lifetime, unlike the nonfamilial sexual predator.[18]

## Signs of Possible Sexual Abuse

Children will generally not reveal that someone has sexually abused them. Sometimes they think they are responsible, or perhaps the abuser has threatened them. Other times, a child is too young to have the vocabulary to describe what happened, which is particularly difficult in very small children. In other instances, protective adults do not interpret what the child reports as someone behaving inappropriately towards them: the child may merely complain, "I don't like being with Uncle Joe," or "Mrs. Kendall makes me feel weird." Sometimes other stressors cause the same behaviors.

MassKids lists some of the behaviors exhibited by children and teens who have been abused in this way:

- Fear of being in the care of a certain person or in the presence of a particular child
- Fear of certain places, such as showers, bedrooms, etc.
- Changes in behavior when a certain person is present
- Use of new words to describe genitalia or sexual behavior
- A new self-consciousness about genitals
- Sexual behavior inappropriate for the child's age
- Using other children, toys, or dolls to act out sexual behaviors

16. Bancroft. "Connection," para. 5–29.
17. Bancroft and Silverman, *The Batterer as Parent*, 87.
18. Bancroft and Silverman, *The Batterer as Parent*, 87.

- Having money or possessions for which you do not know the source
- Unable to provide details about activities during time spent with another adult or child
- Clinginess, anxiety, irritability, experiencing nightmares, bed-wetting, fear of the dark and inability to fall asleep, or other new fears and regressive behaviors
- Fear of having their mouth examined; sudden avoidance of touch with no injury present
- Changes in appetite[19]

Children will also sometimes reenact their abusive experience(s) through play, or even engage in age-inappropriate sexual behaviors with other children.

*Psychology Today* lists signs that a teenager may have been sexually assaulted:

- Atypical angry outbursts
- Decreased self-esteem
- Depression
- Anxiety
- Increased substance abuse
- Running away
- Suicide attempts[20]

If your child or teen exhibits any of these signs, or others which cause concern, guardians should find help to ensure the child's safety. If you are a child or teen who has experienced or is currently experiencing sexual abuse, contact the Rape, Abuse, and Incest National Network (RAINN), the largest anti–sexual violence organization in the US (find contact information in the appendix). Trained support specialists provide information, referrals, and advice.

19. MassKids. "Behavior and Physical Signs," para. 7.
20. *Psychology Today*, "Hebephilia," para. 7.

## Common Challenges of Sexual Abuse

The American Psychological Association provides further information concerning sexual abuse:

> Immediate reactions to sexual abuse include shock, fear or disbelief. Long-term symptoms include anxiety, fear or posttraumatic stress disorder. While efforts to treat sex offenders remain unpromising, psychological interventions for survivors—especially group therapy—appears effective.[21]

Often, we think of grief in connection with the loss of a loved one, but grief can take place in countless other types of situations. When someone has been sexually assaulted, they have lost a sense of control; the perpetrator has taken something from them without their permission. Moving through the grief process and regaining control both take time.

Sexual assault is *never* the victim's fault. Often, feelings of guilt and shame overwhelm the victim and stand in the way of healing. Victims need to understand that they have no reason to feel guilty and that, in healthy families, no one will judge them for what they have experienced.

Just because one does not fight the assailant or abuser, one cannot interpret this to mean consent, regardless of the age of the victim, the setting, or who the perpetrator is. Some courts have only just begun to understand that not fighting back when assaulted does not mean consent. Sadly, some courts still find in favor of a defendant accused of sexual assault because the victim did not try to defend him/herself. In reality, retaliation against the abuser sometimes makes the situation worse.

The phrase "fight or flight" does not adequately describe what happens to the sympathetic nervous system during stress. "Freezing in fear" is also a common response to distress.[22] We may speculate about what we would do if physically attacked, but we cannot know for sure what we would do until we experience the particular situation. Many who have been assaulted have said that they responded very differently than expected when faced with danger. Regardless of the response, a victim should never be made to feel shame or guilt.

With incest, the child or teen feels an additional betrayal because the treachery comes from someone with whom the minor should feel safe. A family-member perpetrator breaks the child or teen's trust. Everyone

21. *APA Dictionary of Psychology*, s.v., "sexual abuse."
22. Selby. "Why Didn't She Fight Back?," para. 18.

should feel loved, safe, and protected within the family, but abused family members do not. When incest is discovered, the non-offending parent will need to put aside their own feelings to provide support and protection.

## Scriptural Encouragement

Why do we experience such evil in this world? We live in a fallen world because "all have sinned and fall short of the glory of God" (Rom 3:23). Because all have sinned, the world is full of sin. Our lives are touched and sometimes altered by the sin around us. When someone hurts us, know that "The Lord is near to the brokenhearted, and saves the crushed in spirit. Many are the afflictions of the righteous, but the Lord rescues them from them all" (Ps 34:18–19). Concerning these verses, Ortlund tells us in the *ESV Devotional Psalter*: "For God has demonstrated that he is not a stoic God, a distant God removed from our frailties and distresses. In Jesus, God drew near. He entered into our broken-heartedness. The Lord Jesus knows what it is to be crushed in spirit."[23]

Through his grace, God restores what was lost, as the psalmist states: "From the depths of the earth you will bring me up again. You will increase my honor, and comfort me once again" (Ps 71:20b–21). Ortlund also provides an understanding that we can apply today to our trying circumstances:

> As difficulties pile up, as relationships sour, as hopes and goals fail to materialize, it is easy to throw in the towel emotionally and settle into cold-hearted cynicism. The psalmist, however, teaches us that pain is not meant to numb us and cause our hearts to withdraw; pain is meant to draw our hearts up to God. Adversity is not intended to diminish our hope in God. Adversity is intended to heighten our hope in him. We are brought to remember that God is all we have, and that he is enough.[24]

Fault, shame, and guilt should not be ascribed to the sexual assault victim. The difficult process of dealing with the hurtful memories and resulting emotions must be completed. Often, victims learn to fear relationships and ultimately have marital problems as the result of their experiences. For those who have been sexually abused, sex may seem dirty

---

23. Ortlund. *ESV Devotional Psalter* commentary on Ps 34.
24. Ortlund. *ESV Devotional Psalter* commentary on Ps 71.

and sinful. Rather, know that God views sex as a gift. It is something to be celebrated, not used for harm.

Healing is certainly possible for a victim of sexual assault. Be patient with yourself and allow the time to heal. Different people experience the healing process differently. A qualified counselor or therapist can most effectively help a victim through the journey toward wellness.

Lord, may we find relief in the comfort you give us and in the confidence we can have because of your unending grace, and may we find Jesus himself, as we pray for help through our trying situations, healing from our difficult experiences, and restoration of what was lost. Today we call on you, Lord, as no one needs to be alone in their journey.

## Fragile, Handle with Care

Waking up in a sweat
Her heart racing, the pulsing of blood running though her veins
She hears a train in her head
Taking in her surroundings, she assesses
She is in a safe place, no reason to fear
Barefoot she walks to the window and climbs out on the ledge
Breathing deeply, she watches the birds busy at work
The sun is rising and she drinks in the colors
The power of the early morning in nature
It is her medicine; only nature truly heals
So many years have passed since she lived in horror
Surviving and hiding and keeping secrets
She ought not to have done so, but she was just a kid
She wonders what it would have been like to always feel safe
Without a care in the world, to go after one's dreams
Backed by family, friends, and trustworthy people
How many years has she spent trying to forget
Hiding the pain and the shame and the guilt
Others had had their way, but not entirely
She became a warrior at such a tender age
A fighter, one who sees in the darkness
As though it were light outside
Just as the owl does
Silent in flight
Seeing the vermin crawling on the ground
A parallel universe existing in real time

Unable to focus, she used to detach and float away
Her imagination so vivid and real
Creating a place to run and hide within her mind
Sometimes up a tree
She learned she could escape from her anxiety
By creating her art and teaching others how
Who could she trust?
Why couldn't she speak about these things?
The power was not within her at the time
She longed to feel loved and safe so much
It sometimes felt as though she was having a heart attack
Her mind was trapped in a prison
Until one day, many moons later,
She came upon a child in the woods
The child was crumpled by a tree, sobbing and consumed
She leaned down beside her and gently spoke:
"Little girl, why are you crying?"
And when the child slowly turned her tear-stained face to look,
Their eyes met, and they both inhaled in wonder
Time stood still as the universe swirled around them
Embracing them in a warm breeze
And the scent of spring flowers
The woman reached out her hand and the girl reached back
Standing face to face, the woman, through tears of her own
Smiling wide, she told the girl
"I have found you; you are no longer lost.
I will never let go of you again.
I will protect you, and teach you, and keep you safe."
Together, they walked hand in hand, smiling
Their hearts felt light and clean
Their minds rapidly untangling
The woman hugged the child and she melted into her
Because she was her
The woman was healing her inner child
The age of pain and suffering was passing
Ushering into real time was peace and power
And a voice inside her head told her,
"I will raise you up above the ashes of your pain.
You have grown wise, your will to survive
will now turn to thriving."
For all of those who have felt the pain
Who have faced evil and prevailed
May the light of love and God shine in your hearts

There is a river whose maker is God
Go there and bathe in the healing waters
For there is much evil in this world
It exists in the minds and hearts of men
Who have lost their souls
For the want of lust and power
They seek the innocent to steal its very essence
They may have stolen yours, too
But you can find it in the river of life
Wash away the filth and come out clean
You are worthy to receive the gift of love
Of peace and of power over your own destiny
This life is yours
Let go of it all and reach for what you want
Let it be with a pure heart that you seek it
Not from anger and pain
You will get what you give
Don't accept any offerings that pollute your peace
Instead, create your own path
And make it beautiful and powerful
You will inspire hope and joy
Healing, and peace if you can do this
And you can . . .
"I think I can,
I think I can,
I think I can . . .
I knew I could,
I knew I could,
I knew I could."
I know *you can.*
—*Sarah Hale Folger*

# 4

# The Batterer during Separation and Divorce

## Case Study

W HEN LORI MADE THE phone call to 911 after being physically injured
by Damon, the separation between them began. Law enforcement
put a restraining order in place immediately, which prevented Damon from
contacting or going near Lori. For the next seven months Damon and his
lawyer challenged the restraining order and each month Lori and her lawyer tried to keep the restraining order in place. The judge lifted the order
after the seventh month because the court established a trial date for the
following month. The judge stated that he wanted the trial judge to make
the determination about whether to let Damon have ongoing contact with
Lori. Once the judge lifted the restraining order, Damon stepped toward
Lori in the lobby of the courthouse but Damon's lawyer prevented him
from approaching her.

In the meantime Damon's time with his two daughters were supervised
because of supported allegations with the Department of Social Services.
While she could not be certain, Lori suspected that someone in the court
had reported Damon to Social Services. In some states, when children witness a batterer physically abusing his partner, those children are considered
to be high risk for abuse. The court left the supervisory details to Damon's
mother, Nora.

After the Department of Social Services had concluded that the allegations were supported, Lori took Poppy and Rayne for a walk around the
neighborhood in their double stroller. A neighbor who had retired from
work in the court system as a victim's advocate came out to walk with Lori

and to see the children. When Lori told the neighbor that Damon had supervised visits with the children and why, the neighbor told Lori that it is usually the abuser who tries to engage Social Services first by making false accusations against his partner. Lori told her neighbor that Damon had already tried to engage Social Services against her.

At the first court appearance to determine if the restraining order would be kept in place, a few days after Damon's arrest, Lori's victim's advocate overheard Damon tell his lawyer that he would get full custody of the children because Lori is crazy and harmful to the children. He also told the court that Lori hit him, and that he did not touch her. Lori's medical reports told a different story. Her assigned victim's advocate said that Damon's mantra is used by many offenders in these circumstances.

During the time the police were at the house after Lori called 911, Damon's demeanor and speech were very calm. He cooperated completely, also telling the police that Lori had hit him. The attending law enforcement officers reported that Damon had obviously physically harmed Lori, given her condition and her description of other events. Additionally, when questioned separately, Damon told the police that he did not have a firearm, but Lori told them that Damon did have a gun and that she had hidden both the gun and the box of bullets weeks earlier. The police found both the gun and ammunition where Lori had stated. While Damon lied to protect himself and discredit Lori, he also discredited himself with law enforcement. They believed Lori's account of the event.

Before separation, Damon succeeded in convincing his mother and extended family that Lori had mental problems and difficulty parenting. Nora confronted Lori and told her that she just wanted Lori to love her son, Damon. Lori told Nora that loving her son would be easier if he did not mistreat her, and then proceeded to describe some of his behaviors. Nora clearly expressed disbelief in Lori's assertions, telling her that Damon would not behave that way. Lori then suffered the consequences when Damon's mother relayed the information she received from Lori to him. After one of the court appearances, a member of Damon's family yelled across the courthouse lobby in basso profondo voice, calling Lori a "bitch." Damon successfully convinced his family that Lori had lied about him.

Damon never stopped undermining Lori, even after they separated. In fact, Damon's tactics to discredit Lori to friends and family and to control Lori and the children became more insidious. He lied about Lori not only to his family and friends, but also to the children, to his lawyer, to the court, to the custody evaluator assigned by the court to investigate their case to determine parenting recommendations, to his therapist, and others, to discredit her. Damon accused his wife of Munchausen by Proxy, a mental illness in which a caretaker causes or makes up an illness in the person they are caring for. Lori's lawyer convinced Damon's lawyer that this accusation was a common tactic used by batterers, and that Damon would likely be discredited. Damon and his lawyer dropped the complaint, but that did not stop Damon from producing more lies and using other tactics to discredit Lori during the separation process.

## Separation and Divorce Defined

When a married couple separates, one or both of the parties decides that the couple will not live together. No legal action is necessary for this to happen unless the couple decides on a legal separation; the couple remains married. A divorce requires legal action and ends the marriage. If a couple wants space apart to determine what they want to do within their relationship, they may decide on a trial separation. When there is no expectation of continuing the marriage, a permanent separation results. When a petition for a legal separation is granted, a judge will order specifics about support, property division, child custody, etc. If the couple pursues a divorce, some or all of the separation details may remain in place, but some may change.

## Domestic Violence Divorce

With many divorces, discord and disputes between the parties prevent timely agreement on a final settlement. The term used for such a divorce is *high conflict* or *contentious*. These disputes can range from trivial matters to very serious ones. In one case, a judge told the parties they needed to stop quarreling over the Tupperware because a new set costs far less than their lawyers' time.[1] More serious matters include the family home; parenting arrangements, including custody; family financial assets; who pays the debts; who pays for the children's medical insurance; arrangements regarding schools and church for the children; and much more.

A high-conflict divorce or contentious divorce should not be confused with a domestic violence divorce. Although similar issues may be contested,

---

1. Spoken to a client by her lawyer.

confusing these very different situations does not do justice to the experiences of the woman and children involved and the manipulations and deceit of the abuser. High-conflict divorces may include some of the tactics used in a domestic violence divorce, but the behaviors, tactics, schemes, and aggressiveness employed by the batterer to discredit the mother and manipulate the children make a domestic violence divorce very different from most others.

## Behaviors and Strategies

A domestic violence perpetrator will use any scheme, up to and including homicide, and will maneuver to manipulate any system (e.g., court, education entities, law enforcement, etc.) or person to make them believe his partner is the problem.[2] The controlling schemes a batterer uses before separation look very much like the devices he uses after separation, but once he sees that his partner has the strength and wherewithal to leave him, he reinforces his resolve to regain and keep control. A batterer's abuses, manipulations, and lies increase, and he finds other ways to get control of and even physically harm his partner and children.

Those associated with any domestic violence family, whether as a professional or the next-door neighbor, should help keep the abused partner grounded in the truth. The batterer's need for control of not only his partner but also all those they are connected to will cause him to use different tactics to convince those who investigate, or simply observe his family informally, of his all-around decency and his partner's lack of ability and responsibility. When his controlling behaviors continue after they separate, it is termed *post-separation abuse* (PSA). Here we will review some of the most common strategies of the abuser post-separation.

### WITH HIS FORMER PARTNER

Often, an abuser will tell his partner that he will take the children away from her if she leaves him. He assures her that he will get full custody because everyone knows she is out of her mind and incapable of taking care of them. His efforts are focused on making others believe his assertions that demean his former partner. Damon certainly had his mother convinced,

2. Smith, Rita, "911: The Gateway to the Criminal Justice System."

and tried to convince law enforcement of Lori's guilt when they came to their home after Lori called 911.

The abuser will sometimes sue for custody of the children and may threaten to kidnap or kill them. These threats must be taken in earnest, as both do sometimes happen. Threats to kill the mother must also be taken seriously. When a batterer kills his children, they often do so as a means of violence against the mother.[3] A kidnapper may take his children out of the United States, as did a father a few years ago when he took his child to the Republic of Columbia. The child was recovered and the father lost custody in this case, but in many instances, the father does win custody.[4]

There have been cases where the batterer killed his children but left the mother alive, showing the extreme nature of his desire to control his situation and emotionally devastate the mother. In one recent event in a California church, a batterer shot and killed his three daughters and the church official who had agreed to supervise his visits with his children before shooting himself.[5] The mother is left with the unimaginable, heart-breaking loss of her children.

His tactics may also include economic abuse, including blocking her access to "bank accounts and credit cards or canceling them; ruining the target's credit; failing to follow through on needed (and sometimes court-ordered) payments" and sometimes even stealing the identity of his partner, or quitting his job so monetary support to the mother and children stops.[6]

After separation, "stalking, harassment, and emotional abuse often continue and may increase," as will the danger of homicide.[7] He might send harassing emails and texts or make annoying calls simply to inter-fere with the victim's peace. At other times he may hire an investigator or monitor her whereabouts with the use of an app. Some abusers sexually as-sault or coerce their ex-partners to have sex with them, and will sometimes "sextort" the victim with threats of molesting the children if she does not comply.[8]

---

3. Bancroft and Silverman, *The Batterer as Parent*, 75.
4. Bancroft and Silverman, *The Batterer as Parent*, 75.
5. Paybarah, "Mother of Children Killed by Their Father Said She Lived in Fear."
6. Fontes, "8 Common Post-Separation Domestic Abuse Tactics," para. 2.
7. Saunders et al., "Child Custody Evaluators' Beliefs," 21.
8. Fontes, "8 Common Post-Separation Domestic Abuse Tactics," para. 7.

## WITH THE CHILDREN

The abuse children suffer after separation can be as bad as before separation, and sometimes worse. The abuser will lie to the children, telling them that their mother bears the responsibility for the separation. A batterer will tell his children that their mother is crazy, a bad mother, incapable, or the like to make him seem like the better parent as he undermines the mother's parenting and authority.

After separation, he sometimes will make the children ask the mother to return to him (or let him return) to add pressure on the mother. When the court puts a restraining order in place, the father might explain how he will get in trouble if he tries to visit them at their house because Mommy lied to the people who are now making decisions when she told them that he hurt her. Through manipulations such as this, children will often blame the mother for the separation.

The batterer also tries to gain favor with the children by allowing them whatever they want, even when doing so is detrimental to them. This may involve offering special treatment (e.g., staying up late, eating cookies before dinner, not doing homework, etc.), or making promises that he may or may not keep (e.g., If you live with me, we will go to Disney).

After Damon's assault and battery trial and during the time he had a no-contact order he used Poppy to transmit messages to Lori. On one occasion, he told Poppy to ask Mommy if he could come for dinner. The abuser asking children to relay his messages to the mother is common. If a victim makes contact with her abuser when there is a restraining or no-contact order, she will likely find herself in physical and emotional jeopardy.

Sometimes the father will show favoritism toward one of the children, which causes a multitude of problems, sometimes long-lasting, with the other children. Perhaps a father prefers boys over girls or vice versa. When there are girls in the family and boys are favored, sometimes a sexist form of favoritism results; if girls are favored, a "romantic aspect in which the mother is in part replaced as the father's partner" results; or favoritism may shift back and forth.[9] Other abusers will intensify their abuse of the protective mother by abusing the children; still others are cunning enough to not abuse the children during separation in order to deceive a custody evaluator during the time a parenting plan is being decided upon and established.

9. Bancroft and Silverman, *The Batterer as Parent*, 78.

## With Family and Friends

When agreement and cooperation exist among family members that do not include the batterer, he is threatened by their capacity to control the outcome of the situation he has shaped. The batterer seeks to cause tension and discord within the family in order to strengthen his position. When the batterer pits family members against one another, attention is deflected from him onto those who disagree.

One of the manipulations used by a batterer is to narrow the contacts his victim has with family and friends, as Damon tried to discredit Lori to her parents. Because these efforts were not successful, he had to devise another plan: to make Lori think he had convinced her parents that she had mental problems. He had been working on his own mother before separation and had succeeded in making her believe that Lori had created the problems in their marriage. A batterer makes continued efforts to narrow the victim's circle of family and friends after separation while court officials and other authorities are making decisions related to custody and other matters, a task that usually includes interviewing friends and family. Her difficult circumstances, what she has experienced as a wife, and the abuses she sees her children experience all provide a rationale supporting his attempt to convince friends that something is wrong with her. Often a woman is left feeling isolated. During court proceedings after separation, Lori watched those who were once her friends present themselves in the courtroom to support Damon.

## With Professionals and Those in Public

How many times have we visited the grocery store and witnessed a parent dealing with their misbehaving child in a different way than we would have chosen? Perhaps we smile and (to ourselves) commend a parent for a great response to their noncompliant child. During separation, the batterer is generally very careful concerning how he behaves in public and with friends and family, as well as in front of the professionals who view and assess his abilities and behaviors with the children.

During separation and divorce, a variety of different professionals become involved in assessing the mother's and father's parenting and fitness: lawyers for both parties; judges; custody evaluators; individuals whom the custody evaluator interviews (doctors, teachers, family, friends, etc.); in some cases, a jury (only a few states allow for a jury and only under certain circumstances); and sometimes law enforcement. When the Department of Social Services becomes involved after an allegation is made against one or both of the parents, they investigate the parents and the situation to find out what has happened.

Professionals who do not have a thorough education in regard to domestic violence do not have the ability to make proper assessments concerning families affected by it. Too few are specifically trained or have the skill to identify and understand domestic-violence families and then make good decisions. The batterer has an edge if he can present well when others are watching. The abused woman is also aware that her abuser has the ability to sway others to his point of view and convince others of her deficiencies.

The mother usually presents as fearful, nervous, anxious, and sometimes angry because of what she and the children have experienced and the lack of understanding they have received. Parenting decisions made by professionals too often result in harm to the children, as fathers sometimes do win custody and mothers sometimes lose parenting time. Too often, Social Services and other professionals make wrong determinations, sometimes faulting the parent who tries to protect her children and making decisions that leave children at high risk for harm.

A batterer may be a highly respected person in the community. He could be anyone: a teacher, lawyer, judge, engineer, accountant, mechanic, business owner . . . anyone. An abusive man might volunteer in the community and raise funds for worthy causes, earning the respect of those around him. One man built his business from scratch, became a multimillionaire, and spent much time in community work. It was almost impossible for others to believe him to be the man his wife described. He made false reports to the police accusing her of abusing him and the children, to preempt the possibility of her reporting his abuse. When she eventually brought forth accusations, the court viewed the victim as bitter, and she lost not only custody, but also the ability to see her children. The father hired a full-time nanny and rarely spent time with the children.

## Scriptural Encouragement

When a woman is abused in her own home she feels trapped. Often, family and friends turn away; sometimes she does not have the ability to use her phone or computer without being monitored. Maybe she cannot continue her education or keep a job because he makes her quit, or she ends her career or education because she gets tired of being accused of having affairs with professors or people at work. When the couple has children, she cannot intervene when her partner mistreats them without experiencing severe repercussions. He demands that she must do this and must do that; she cannot do this and cannot do that. Her children may develop difficult behaviors as a result of watching and listening to their father and may learn to abuse her so they can earn the approval of their father. Observers, including professionals, may view her as the problem parent, or even crazy.

The abused woman is one whose partner has threatened her liberty and her peace. She feels completely removed from the way she thought she would be able to live her life. Nearly every choice and self-determination has been taken from her.

But there is good news! There is a place where abused women can experience liberty and peace. In his book *An Apologetic for Liberty*, Kevin S. Kookogey explains that true liberty comes from Christ. While one might have no freedom in one's physical environment, liberty can live deep inside each of us where no one can take it from us. While Kookogey does not specifically address domestic violence the application to domestic violence is clear:

> Any attempt by one created being to take advantage of, lord over, or subdue another created being is rebellion against God's order. . . ."[10]
> God created all of us and everything.[11]
> We walk with our neighbors in this world as equals to one another. One individual is not higher than another. Any efforts by someone to take away the freedom of another, fulfills a recognizable manipulation of the Devil's cunning work.[12]

While many Scriptures show us the true liberty we have in Christ, consider Isaiah 61:1 and Luke 4:16–21. Isaiah tells us:

> The spirit of the Lord God is upon me,
> because the Lord has anointed me;
> he has sent me to bring good news to the oppressed,
> to bind up the brokenhearted,
> to proclaim liberty to the captives,
> and release to the prisoners;

10. Kookogey, *An Apologetic for Liberty*, 21.
11. Kookogey, *An Apologetic for Liberty*, 14.
12. Kookogey, *An Apologetic for Liberty*, 31.

Consider the connection between Isaiah 61:1 and what Jesus says in Luke:

> When he came to Nazareth, where he had been brought up, he went to the synagogue on the Sabbath day, as was his custom. He stood up to read, and the scroll of the prophet Isaiah was given to him. He unrolled the scroll and found the place where it was written: "The Spirit of the Lord is upon me, because he has anointed me to bring good news to the poor. He has sent me to proclaim release to the captives and recovery of sight to the blind, to let the oppressed go free, to proclaim the year of the Lord's favor." And he rolled up the scroll, gave it back to the attendant, and sat down. The eyes of all in the synagogue were fixed on him. Then he began to say to them, "Today this scripture has been fulfilled in your hearing."

In Isaiah, we see that Jesus's anointing brings "liberty to the captives." In Luke, we see the fulfillment of this scripture. What was foretold in Isaiah we see fulfilled during the ministry of Jesus, as stated in Luke 4:21. God's rich inheritance, providing liberty to the captives, belongs to all who trust in Jesus. Liberty is your inheritance and mine to claim simply by reaching out and accepting this gift.

What does liberty in Christ mean? In Galatians 5:1 we are told, "For freedom Christ has set us free." We are told: "stand firm, therefore, and do not submit again to a yoke of slavery." In Matthew 11:30, Jesus tells us that his yoke is easy and not oppressive. Jewish law is a challenging yoke, as Paul tells us in verse 4: "You who want to be justified by the law have cut yourselves off from Christ; you have fallen away from grace." He says further in verse 6: "For in Christ Jesus neither circumcision nor uncircumcision counts for anything; the only thing that counts is faith working through love." The purpose of the law was to show humanity their sinfulness and need for a Savior. At the same time, we are not to use our "freedom as an opportunity for self-indulgence" as stated in verse 13. We have the freedom to follow Christ, guided by the Spirit, while living in the fruit of the Spirit (Galatians 5:22–23). We no longer operate under the burden of the law, but the freedom of grace frees us from the penalty and power of sin.

Be encouraged to connect with a community of believers who can affirm the truth that we have liberty in Christ, if doing so is not already a part of your life. Every time we hear a testimony of what the Lord provides through his grace, we are reminded that grace can set all of us free. Hearing how God's grace works in the lives of others increases our faith and reminds us of his presence and work in our own lives. Often, healing happens in community. In a Christian community one can have peace and assurance that in Christ there is liberty; in Christ, the source of true, lasting liberty, we find our freedom—a freedom that no one has the ability to take from us.

# 5

# Woman's Background, Health, and Decisions

## Case Study

G ROWING UP, LORI HAD a loving, caring family. Her parents were involved in their church, as were Lori and her brother and all four of them had many friends who were often at their house. Lori and her brother were taught traditional Christian values and formed their beliefs and morals through the lens of those teachings. Lori and her family were also very connected to their extended families. Holidays, birthdays, and other special occasions regularly called for dinner parties and happy celebrations.

But Lori's efforts to develop a safe and happy environment for her new baby met with a series of challenges. After Poppy had turned one month old, Lori left, taking Poppy to her parents' house because Damon could not be convinced that one of their dogs posed a danger to Poppy. The dog, Totter, had already bitten Lori and continued to show signs of aggression. Lori did not feel safe and believed that her baby could not be safe with Totter around. Damon claimed that his dogs were as important to him as his children, and removing one of them out would be just like taking his child away. A few days after Lori had left, she and Deborah took Poppy to see Damon for a visit so he could spend time with his daughter, and he agreed that the dogs would not be present. Nonetheless, he did not agree to give Totter to another owner or the shelter. So Lori went back to her parents' home with Poppy after the visit.

Another week went by and Damon called Lori to let her know that his uncle would take Totter and secure him when Poppy visited. But when Lori expressed some hesitation Damon said he had a gun in his hand and he would kill himself if she and Poppy did not return that day. Lori immediately collected her belongings, along with Poppy's, and drove the two hours back home. She then called Deborah at work and let her know what happened, and that she and Poppy returned home.

Later, after Lori and Damon had their second child, Rayne, and they began the process of getting a divorce, the court assigned a custody evaluator, Ms. Smith, to investigate and recommend a parenting plan. In one of the interviews with Lori, Ms. Smith asked Lori to describe why she had returned home after she left the first time. Ms. Smith told Lori in no uncertain terms that if Damon threatened to commit suicide she never should have gone back home. In the context of domestic violence, someone threatening to use a gun on himself likewise poses a danger to others. She told Lori that she should have called the police to check on him.

A few months before the police arrested Damon for assault and battery on Lori, he essentially killed Lori's rabbits. Lori kept them in cages in the backyard. One day, after pregnant Lori left the house with Poppy, Damon let the rabbits out of their cages and then let the dogs into the fenced-in backyard. When Lori came home, she saw the bloody rabbit remains on the ground. Damon angrily insisted that Lori, who was very upset, immediately clean up the mess.

During the weeks before Damon's year-long no-contact order ended, he emailed Lori. Lori called Damon's probation officer and asked if the terms of the no-contact order allowed for him to contact her in this way. The probation officer asked her to forward the email and told her with certainty that Damon had violated the terms of the order. Rather than recognizing Lori's fear, her lawyer told her he believed Lori had informed the probation officer about the email because she wanted to get Damon in trouble. Lori protested that she just wanted to keep herself and the children safe, because she believed that if she did not address the email violation, he would move another step closer. Her lawyer, with an aggravated demeanor, stated, "It certainly didn't look that way."

## Background

### GROWING UP

While many women who had caring, loving homes when growing up do get caught up in domestic violence, the risk for intimate partner violence

(IPV) is higher for those who had adverse childhood experiences (ACEs).[1] ACEs include witnessing domestic violence, or any type of violence, before age 17, as well as "abuse, or neglect . . . [or] having a family member attempt or die by suicide," and may be exacerbated by "aspects of the child's environment that can undermine their sense of safety, stability, and bonding such as growing up in a household with substance misuse, mental health problems, or instability due to parental separation or incarceration of a parent, sibling or other member of the household."[2] A PubMed.org report by Bensley et al., shows that "findings underscore the role of childhood experiences of abuse and of witnessing family violence in women's current risk for IPV, poor physical health, and frequent mental distress."[3]

## GROOMING

Many relationships that eventually become controlling and even violent begin as caring relationships that do not seem to hint at abuse. The process of moving from a positive, caring relationship to abuse is called grooming, a planned-out, "predatory tactic that is meant to build a deep emotional connection."[4]

In the beginning, the romance may include gifts, lovely sentiments, and warm and wonderful attention. She views the overwhelming attention as positive and perceives a strong, loving, and caring connection. He will endeavor to insert himself into her finances, social media, friendships, family, and other aspects of her private life, and at a time that seems right to him will begin to make her feel wrong, untrusting, and unloving if she objects. Here she begins to work to please her partner.

Remember that abusers generally try to make themselves look good to friends and family, to the point where it seems impossible to believe that he could be mistreating his partner. He begins to drop fewer and fewer understated negative comments about his partner's flaws. She becomes lonely and isolated as those who were close to her draw away.

First, she experiences what seems to be a genuine romance. The abuse escalates slowly, to the point that she does not easily recognize it because

1. Mair et al., "Adverse Childhood Experiences," para.1.

2. Centers for Disease Control and Prevention, *Preventing Adverse Childhood Experiences*, 7.

3. Bensley et al., *Childhood Family Violence History*, para. 3.

4. Fontes, "From Romance to Isolation: Understanding Grooming," para. 1.

she has become acclimated to it. "Grooming works by mixing positive behaviors with elements of abuse."[5] A manipulative, cruel partner thereby turns what seems to be authentic romance into abuse.

## Brain Connection

The experiences of an abused woman in a domestic violence situation may lead to both physical and mental harm. The National Institutes of Health tells us that "the national annual cost of medical and mental health care services related to acute domestic violence is estimated at over $8 billion."[6] They also tell us that "fifty percent of women seen in emergency departments report a history of abuse, and approximately 40% of those killed by their abuser sought help in the 2 years before death"; of those identified by police as victims of domestic violence, only one-third are identified as such in the emergency department.[7]

Domestic violence affects a woman's brain. Stress reactions release cortisol so an individual can stay on high alert during times of trauma or distress. When this happens, the part of the brain called the amygdala becomes activated. Traumatic stress overactivates the amygdala, which is the center for "emotions, emotional behavior, and motivation,"[8] and is known for processing fear. "In addition to its involvement in the initiation of a fear response, the amygdala also seems to be very important in forming memories that are associated with fear-inducing events" and also involves itself in anxiety, which is "the dread that accompanies thinking about a potential threat."[9] When traumatic events happen repeatedly, "fear responses become more intense" and "memories of traumatic events can become nightmares and flashbacks."[10] "When we are reminded of a trauma event or experience, the amygdala responds the exact same way it would if we were experiencing the trauma for the first time."[11] Consequently, an individual with this experience remains on high alert.

5. Samsel, "Abuse and Relationships: Grooming," para. 1.

6. Huecker et al., "Domestic Violence," para. 18.

7. Huecker et al., "Domestic Violence," para. 19.

8. Wright, "Limbic System: Amygdala," para. 1.

9. Neuroscientifically Challenged, "Know Your Brain: Amygdala," para. 3.

10. StoneRidge Centers, "Can Traumatic Stress Change Our Brains?," para. 7.

11. StoneRidge Centers, "Can Traumatic Stress Change Our Brains?," para. 8.

Traumatic stress also affects another area of the brain called the hippocampus, which keeps and recovers memories and also allows us to tell the difference between past and present experiences.

> Studies show that experiencing trauma and living with high levels of stress can decrease the volume of the hippocampus. This can make it hard for us to distinguish between the past and present. Because of this, even environments that remind us of traumatic experiences can cause fear, stress, and panic. Instead of the brain being able to easily create and store new memories, traumatic stress can keep old traumatic memories at the forefront of our minds, causing us to live in a constant state of hypervigilance and intense emotional reactivity.[12]

The prefrontal cortex helps us in "decision making, problem-solving, intelligence, and emotional regulation."[13] Traumatic stress affects the prefrontal cortex negatively and can hinder our ability to learn new information, manage logical thinking, manage emotions effectively, and solve problems.[14] In essence, any decrease of function in the prefrontal cortex also diminishes or ability to control fear.

Women in domestic violence situations continue to experience trauma even after separation and divorce because the abuser continues to produce difficult challenges and threats to provoke a continuing response. For some perpetrators, separation brings heightened abusive behaviors because of the loss of control.

We know constant stress causes both mental and physical problems. Too many health care workers address only the physical injuries presented by abused persons and do not address the underlying cause of the problems that create the injury. The medical community too often misses the mental injury inflicted upon women. Psychological (or emotional) abuse often leads to physical health problems such as ulcers, migraine headaches, high blood pressure, gastrointestinal disorders, fibromyalgia, nightmares and loss of sleep, and other complications. Given its prevalence, screening for domestic violence among those presenting at health care offices must become routine. Identification reduces incidences of injury, disease, and mortality.

---

12. StoneRidge Centers, "Can Traumatic Stress Change Our Brains?," para. 10.

13. Guy-Evans, "Frontal Lobe Function, Location in Brain and Damage," para. 12.

14. StoneRidge Centers, "Can Traumatic Stress Change Our Brains?," para. 11.

## Physical Health

### Physical Injury

Hitting, pushing, punching, or throwing someone, raping, strangulation, and other types of assaults can cause bruising, broken bones, bleeding, concussions, brain injuries, sexually transmitted diseases, and death. Other physical illnesses result from experiencing ongoing trauma. In the case of sexual coercion and rape, pregnancy can result. Physical harm also results from financial abuse or the withdrawal of food or other necessities from the victim.

An abuser may seem benevolent when he acts to relieve his partner of any financial responsibility or pressures her to quit a job if he is able to take care of her and the children. The result, however, is his complete control of the finances. She has to rely completely on the abuser for basic needs such as food, medication, toiletries, clothing, shelter, and more. He spends money, but she may not have the same ability, at least outside of a small allowance when he allows her to have one. He may go to lunch with coworkers or friends, but she does not have the ability to do so. She may have to ask permission to spend money on necessities. The victim is at the fiduciary mercy of the abuser. As a result, a woman may be forced to do without food, medicine, or other items required for good health, and may also be the case for her children.

Some abusers use food to control the victim. For health reasons, one client eliminated meat from her diet and substituted other protein foods. When the abuser saw these items in the refrigerator, he threw them in the garbage. Sometimes this tactic becomes so extreme that both the woman and the children suffer from exhaustion and malnutrition.[15] Victims who suffer from malnutrition develop serious medical concerns; children sometimes experience developmental delays and other serious health problems. During the time the abuser limits food for his partner and children, he does not limit what he allows for himself.

Strangulation is potentially lethal. Often strangulation is thought of as "choking," but death does not have to occur for this encounter to be called "strangulation."

> "Choking" refers to a blockage inside your throat, making it difficult to breathe. Strangulation is when pressure is applied from

15. DomesticShelters.org, "Forbidden Food," para. 20.

the outside, cutting off blood vessels and/or airflow in the neck, preventing oxygen from reaching the brain. This pressure can cause loss of consciousness in 5 to 10 seconds, and it can cause death in a few minutes.[16]

In "97 percent of strangulation attempts," abusers use "blunt force trauma."[17] Other than death, serious injury can result when someone has been strangled. There may be bruising, internal injuries, and even neurological damage resulting from oxygen loss. A lack of oxygen can cause memory loss, either temporary or permanent. There may also be "vision changes, ringing in the ears, swollen tongue, cuts and abrasions in the mouth, swelling of the neck, difficulty breathing, trouble swallowing, and other voice or throat changes," along with hoarseness and even seizures or other behavioral difficulties.[18] Strangulation also produces possible psychological injuries such as "PTSD, depression, suicidal ideation, memory problems, nightmares, anxiety, severe stress reaction, amnesia and psychosis."[19]

Law enforcement personnel use the following points to help survive if assaulted by strangulation:

- Try to stay calm.

- Protect your airway. If possible, try something called the "turtle shell technique" where you tuck your chin down and raise your shoulders up to help support your neck.

- Once released, try to escape from your abuser and call 911 before a second strangulation attempt is made.

- As a last resort, you can try collapsing and going limp, giving the impression your abuser succeeded, in order to hopefully release their grip.[20]

When someone has been strangled, they must find medical care where the provider understands the physical and psychological effects of strangulation regardless of whether outer visible signs are evident.

16. Clute, Penny, "The Law and You: Strangulation Always Serious," para. 3.

17. DomesticShelters.org, "Strangulation Can Leave Long-Lasting Injuries," para. 2.

18. Clute, Penny, "The Law and You: Strangulation Always Serious," para. 19.

19. DomesticShelters.org, "Strangulation Can Leave Long-Lasting Injuries," para. 3.

20. DomesticShelters.org, "Strangulation Can Leave Long-Lasting Injuries," para. 11.

## Suicide

The full extent of the prevalence of suicides related to domestic violence has not been established, but what has been uncovered creates concern and reason for further research:

- 25 percent of female suicide attempts result from domestic violence situations.

- Compared with the overall population, female victims of domestic violence have eight times the risk for suicide.

- 20 percent of pregnant female victims of domestic violence attempt suicide.[21]

Richard McKeon, PhD, the chief of suicide prevention at the US Substance Abuse and Mental Health Services Administration (SAMHSA), states that "survivors of intimate partner violence are twice as likely to attempt suicide multiple times . . . and cases of murder-suicide are most likely to occur in the context of abuse."[22] He points out that, traditionally, the mental health and IPV fields have worked separately on this issue, but SAMHSA has recently brought them together. Those working in suicide prevention can miss the signs of IPV, and those working in IPV miss the warning signs of suicide. Those who work in the field of domestic violence must not view perpetrators' threats to commit suicide as simply a form of manipulation. Those assertions pose a threat to not only the perpetrator, but also to the victim and the children. When the abuser threatens suicide he presents a great danger, putting both his partner and his children at high risk for homicide.

An abused woman may choose not to seek help because of embarrassment or shame. When she commits suicide, she transfers her shame to the abuser and to others in her life who did not provide help. Suicide may also be an act of retaliation and represent her last attempt to take her power back.[23]

---

21. Criminal Justice Research, "Female Suicide and Domestic Violence," para. 1.
22. Clay, "Suicide and Intimate Partner Violence," 30.
23. Criminal Justice Research, "Female Suicide and Domestic Violence," para. 3.

## DEATH

Sometime the abuser uses his own body (e.g., fists or feet) to kill his partner, or he may throw items at her, use items to pummel her, or throw the victim across the room or down the stairs. He may also use weapons such as guns. Just about anything can be used as a weapon. Between 2010 and 2017, "one million women in the US have survived being shot by an intimate partner."[24] "Some 47,000 women and girls worldwide were killed by their intimate partners or other family members in 2020. This means that, on average, a woman or girl is killed by someone in her own family every 11 minutes."[25] Sadly, the numbers are increasing.

How do we know when a batterer has the potential to kill his partner? Rita Smith has been involved in helping women in domestic violence emergency shelters for more than forty years, and is also a vice president for Domesticshelters.org and a senior advisor to the National Football League on policies involving domestic violence and sexual assault. In an interview with *A&E True Crime,* she described some of the red flags that might indicate that a person is potentially dangerous. One common red flag is that someone is "too good to be true" and seems to accelerate the relationship, pushing toward a deeply involved connection while exhibiting great charm.[26] The person will likely want to know all your connections, what you are doing at all times, what you like and do not like, and later, he will track or stalk his victim.[27] A partner is often capable of homicide if he exhibits a preference for sexual coercion or sexual violence. Those who initiate aggressive sexual encounters are "more likely to move to lethal actions," as are those who violate restraining orders or do so with increased frequency.[28]

The guardian ad litem assigned to Lori and Damon's case told Lori that she should not have returned to her house after Damon threatened suicide. Pet abuse or threats of abuse to a pet is another danger signal. The abuser seeks ultimate control through taking the life of his partner, his children, or the family pet, as Damon did to Lori's rabbits.

---

24. Kippert, "Warning Signs," para. 3.
25. UNODC, "Killings of Women and Girls," para. 1.
26. Kippert, "Warning Signs," para. 6.
27. Kippert, "Warning Signs," para. 7.
28. Kippert, "Warning Signs," para. 14.

Psychologist David Adams founded Emerge, the first batterer intervention program. He conducted research among thirty-one incarcerated men who had killed their wives and twenty women who had survived attempted homicide by an intimate partner and published the results in his book, *Why Do They Kill.* His "research concerned cisgender women in heterosexual relationships with cisgender male abusers," so it is uncertain whether "these findings apply to same-sex couples or women's violence against men or couples where one or both people are transgender."[29] Adams discovered that sex in those relationships that ended in homicide differed from sex in other domestic violence relationships. He saw the following four phases commonly occurring before an abuser kills:

- First phase: Sex happens fast and often
- Second phase: Frequent abuse, sex, and threats
- Third phase: Violence and control intensify
- Fourth phase: He blocks escape and kills her[30]

In the first phase, the man engages the woman in sex early, during their first or second meeting. He persuades her to have frequent sex, making it difficult for her to properly assess the relationship. In the second phase, if the victim tries to refuse, the perpetrator threatens and eventually engages in physical violence and jealous accusations. In the third phase, violence escalates, and he blames his victim while seeking ways to further control her. In the fourth phase, "violence, threats, and monitoring" escalate further, with sex becoming increasingly "violent and humiliating" to the point that about half of women will have terminated the relationship by this time.[31] The last stage includes homicide.

## Mental Health

Many aspects of domestic violence damage a woman's mental health. She is often disconnected from family and friends who may have been convinced by the abuser that he is the wronged party, or who simply do not know how to help, even when they see the abuse clearly. Too often, support is lacking from custody evaluators, the children's teachers, judges, social services,

29. Fontes, "4 Phases Before an Abuser Kills," para. 1.
30. Fontes, "4 Phases Before an Abuser Kills," para. 2–5.
31. Fontes, "4 Phases Before an Abuser Kills," para. 2–5.

and sometimes even her own lawyer and children. Lori experienced her lawyer's ignorance when he faulted her for asking the probation officer whether Damon's email violated his no-contact order.

When a woman separates from her abuser, she shifts from the fear of daily abuse and controlling behaviors to the fear of him attempting to control her and the children through his lawyer, the custody evaluator, and the court system. Sadly, the stigma attached to mental illness persists.

> Stigma arises from a lack of understanding of mental illness (ignorance and misinformation), and also because some people have negative attitudes or beliefs towards it (prejudice). This can lead to discrimination against people with mental illness. Even some mental health professionals have negative beliefs about the people they care for.[32]

A professional who had stopped working as a therapist and moved into education, explained that sometimes some of her colleagues made fun of their clients because of their mental illness. Mocking from those who should understand mental illness is unconscionable, unprofessional, and highly prejudicial. We do not make fun of those with cancer, diabetes, or a broken arm. A person is not their diagnosis, either physical or mental. The media, our friends or neighbors, and we ourselves need to gently correct and promote an accurate understanding to help remove the stigma. People with mental illness deserve the same acceptance as others who have physical ailments. "People with mental illness may also take on board the prejudiced views held by others, which can affect their self-esteem. They may feel ashamed or embarrassed. This can lead them to not seek treatment, to withdraw from society, to alcohol and drug abuse or even to suicide."[33] For those with a diagnosed or suspected mental illness, please be encouraged to seek treatment.

For a woman who dreads taking others into her confidence because of domestic abuse and the accompanying fear of being disbelieved, seeking help over possible mental health issues is even more daunting. Victims may find themselves ashamed of not only the abuse they experience, but also their symptoms of depression and other mental health issues. During the time when parenting decisions and child custody assessments are being made by custody evaluators and courts, victims are too often viewed with suspicion and disrespect because of their mental health issues—which are

32. Healthdirect, "Mental Illness Stigma," para. 8.
33. Healthdirect, "Mental Illness Stigma," para. 14.

often the result of the abuser's behavior. A protective mother may present as fearful, anxious, or angry, leading to misunderstanding the victim and her losing custody of the children.

Victims in a domestic abuse situation need to find a therapist well-versed in domestic violence, as they will have a much fuller understanding of the resulting mental health issues. "On average, more than half of the women seen in mental health settings are being or have been abused by an intimate partner."[34]

An abuser may assert control by withholding medical care so that the victim no longer has access to medication for physical and mental conditions, and no longer has someone to confide in. Even access to transportation can be taken away to prevent her from receiving care.[35]

## ATTENTION DEFICIT/HYPERACTIVITY DISORDER

A diagnosis of ADD or ADHD may affect how a woman views herself, making her vulnerable to relationships where she is abused. ADD is "a developmental disorder characterized by symptoms of inattention (such as distractibility, disorganization, or forgetfulness)."[36] "Attention-deficit/hyperactivity disorder (ADHD) is marked by an ongoing pattern of inattention and/or hyperactivity-impulsivity that interferes with functioning or development."[37] Those with ADHD experience the ongoing symptoms of inattention, hyperactivity, and impulsivity.[38]

Women with ADD and ADHD oftentimes come into adulthood with feelings of inferiority because they experienced challenges to learning throughout childhood. Because they have experienced ongoing correction in educational and social situations, they may come to consider constant correction by persons close to them to be normal. This leaves them extremely vulnerable to abuse. Consequently, when an abuser tries to make his partner feel inferior, his messages are easily received. Dr. Joan Teach, president of the Learning Disabilities of Georgia, explains:

34. Wheeler, "Loss of Agency," para. 4.

35. CHADD, "Finding Help for ADHD and Domestic Violence," para. 16.

36. Davis, "Medical Definition of Attention Deficit Disorder (ADD)," para. 1.

37. National Institute of Mental Health, "Attention-Deficit/Hyperactivity Disorder," para. 1.

38. National Institute of Mental Health, "Attention-Deficit/Hyperactivity Disorder," para. 1.

Many women affected by ADHD have absorbed the negative comments due to ADHD over their lifetime, such as "If you just tried harder" or "You're careless." Girls and women are frequently diagnosed later than boys and men. This means they have much longer in their lives when they don't know that ADHD is causing academic and social failures, time in which many develop the conclusion they are naturally failures and less capable than other people around them.[39]

The abuser will typically reinforce the victim's feelings of inadequacy.

## LOW SELF-ESTEEM

Emotional abuse is one of the many factors leading to low self-esteem. A victim may experience emotional abuse with or without physical abuse. Emotional abuse includes putting down the victim when alone or in front of others; demeaning her accomplishments; name calling; magnifying mistakes; threatening to harm her, the children, or their pets; making false accusations; blaming the victim for his abusive behavior; ignoring her; making unreasonable demands; making all the decisions; and much more. With these tactics, the abuser creates fear and further controls his victim by making her feel worthless. Further emotional harm is caused when support from family and friends is not received or there is a lack of understanding from custody evaluators, teachers, judges, lawyers, social services, and perhaps even her own children. Emotional abuse can cause low self-esteem as well as physical problems such as insomnia, headaches, asthma, and digestive issues.[40] Mental health consequences include anxiety, lack of trust, depression, and suicidal ideation.

## DEPRESSION, ANXIETY, AND POSTTRAUMATIC STRESS DISORDER (PTSD)

Common mental health diagnoses among victims of domestic violence are depression, anxiety, and posttraumatic stress disorder.[41] The traumatic stress a woman suffers in a domestic violence context changes the "brain's delicate chemical balance and structure."[42] These changes can be minor

39. CHADD, "Finding Help for ADHD and Domestic Violence," para. 10.

40. Kippert, "What is Emotional Abuse?," para. 11.

41. Wheeler, "Loss of Agency," para. 3.

42. StoneRidge Centers, "Can Traumatic Stress Change Our Brains?," para. 6.

(i.e., heightened sense of anxiety, impulsivity, and difficulty managing emotions) or severe (posttraumatic stress disorder) depending on the type of trauma.[43] Depression, anxiety, and posttraumatic stress disorder have distinct characteristics. The American Psychological Association (APA) defines depression as follows:

> A negative affective state, ranging from unhappiness and discontent to an extreme feeling of sadness, pessimism, and despondency, that interferes with daily life. Various physical, cognitive, and social changes also tend to co-occur, including altered eating or sleeping habits, lack of energy or motivation, difficulty concentrating or making decisions, and withdrawal from social activities.[44]

The APA describes anxiety as:

> An emotion characterized by apprehension and somatic symptoms of tension in which an individual anticipates impending danger, catastrophe, or misfortune. The body often mobilizes itself to meet the perceived threat: Muscles become tense, breathing is faster, and the heart beats more rapidly. Anxiety may be distinguished from fear both conceptually and physiologically, although the two terms are often used interchangeably. Anxiety is considered a future-oriented, long-acting response broadly focused on a diffuse threat, whereas fear is an appropriate, present-oriented, and short-lived response to a clearly identifiable and specific threat.[45]

The APA provides the following definition for posttraumatic stress disorder:

> A disorder that may result when an individual lives through or witnesses an event in which he or she believes that there is a threat to life or physical integrity and safety and experiences fear, terror, or helplessness. The symptoms are characterized by (a) reexperiencing the trauma in painful recollections, flashbacks, or recurrent dreams or nightmares; (b) avoidance of activities or places that recall the traumatic event, as well as diminished responsiveness (emotional anesthesia or numbing), with disinterest in significant activities and with feelings of detachment and estrangement from others; and (c) chronic physiological arousal, leading to such symptoms as an exaggerated startle response, disturbed sleep,

43. StoneRidge Centers, "Can Traumatic Stress Change Our Brains?," para. 6.
44. *APA Dictionary of Psychology*, s.v., "Depression."
45. *APA Dictionary of Psychology*, s.v., "Anxiety."

difficulty in concentrating or remembering, and guilt about surviving the trauma when others did not.[46]

PTSD and depression are sometimes confused with one another. "Depression is one of the most commonly co-occurring diagnoses in people
with posttraumatic stress disorder."[47] "Research suggests people with
PTSD are more likely to have depression. Likewise, individuals with depressive mood disorders are also more likely to experience more anxiety
or stress" and "people with PTSD may have greater anxiety around specific
people, places, or things."[48] Additionally, "people who have depression or
a depressive disorder are also more likely to have symptoms of an anxiety
disorder."[49]

Studies involving more than 36,000 people tell us that women living
in homes where there is domestic violence are doubly at risk of depression, and that the severity of the abuse is related to the intensity of the
symptoms of depression.[50] Mothers who are victims of abusive partners
have twice the likelihood of postpartum depression.[51] Abused women are
usually socially isolated and lonely, and therefore lack support. Therapists
can provide tools to help manage their clients' challenges, but real healing
requires a community of supportive and understanding people. Additionally, isolation creates a greater dependence on the abusive partner.

"The likelihood of abused women experiencing PTSD is seven times
higher than for those who have not been abused."[52] For an abused woman
who has PTSD, the continuing trauma creates a further challenge to recovery. After separation and divorce, the abuser will enlist help from others,
including those making decisions about child custody. He will generally
attempt to use the court system to try to control his target.

Even in the absence of depression, anxiety, and PTSD, an abused
woman's mental health can be affected in other ways by "difficulties with
being productive at work, school, with caregiving, establishing and engaging in healthy relationships, and adapting to change and coping with

46. *APA Dictionary of Psychology*, s.v., "Posttraumatic Stress Disorder."
47. Tull, "The Relationship Between PTSD and Depression," para. 10.
48. Holland, "PTSD and Depression: How are They Related?," para. 21.
49. Holland, "PTSD and Depression: How are They Related?," para. 24.
50. Promises Behavioral Health, "Domestic Violence and Depression," para. 2.
51. Promises Behavioral Health, "Domestic Violence and Depression," para. 2.
52. Walker, "How Domestic Violence Impacts Women's Mental Health," para. 3

adversity."[53] The victim experiences a loss of agency, or the sense of control over one's own life or the ability to know that one has the capacity to change or better one's situation. These feelings lead to a diminishing of the sense of self, a lack of meaning in life, and a lack of self-protection.[54]

## Bipolar Disorder

The National Institute of Mental Health defines bipolar disorder this way:

> Bipolar disorder is a chronic or episodic (occurring occasionally and at irregular intervals) mental disorder. It can cause unusual, often extreme and fluctuating changes in mood, energy, activity, and concentration or focus. Bipolar disorder sometimes is called manic-depressive disorder or manic depression, which are older terms.[55]

Bipolar disorder should not be confused with the normal ups and downs everyone experiences. In manic episodes, the feelings of happiness or irritability (being "up") coincide with a high activity level; depressive episodes, or feeling sad or hopeless, occur with a much decreased activity level.[56] Occasionally, bipolar disorder can appear in children, but it usually develops in teen years or early adulthood.[57]

Researchers believe that many factors can increase a person's risk, including genetics, chemical imbalances in the brain, and stressful triggers. These triggers may include "the breakdown of a relationship; physical, sexual, or emotional abuse; the death of a close family member or loved one," as well as "physical illness; sleep disturbances; overwhelming problems in everyday life, such as problems with money, work, or relationships."[58]

Research in the United Kingdom has found that women who are victims of domestic violence are three times more likely to experience depression, anxiety, schizophrenia, and bipolar disorder.[59] Consequently,

---

53. Wheeler, "Loss of Agency," para. 5.
54. Wheeler, "Loss of Agency," para. 8.
55. National Institute of Mental Health, "Bipolar Disorder," para. 2.
56. National Institute of Mental Health, "Bipolar Disorder," para. 3.
57. National Institute of Mental Health, "Bipolar Disorder," para. 4.
58. National Health Service (UK), "Causes—Bipolar Disorder," para. 6, 8.
59. Boseley, "Domestic Abuse Victims," para. 1.

"Victims of domestic violence are . . . at higher risk for developing bipolar disorder."[60]

## BATTERED WOMAN SYNDROME

Lenore Walker provides the criteria for identifying battered woman syndrome (BWS):

1. Intrusive recollections of the trauma event(s)

2. Hyperarousal and high levels of anxiety

3. Avoidance behavior and emotional numbing

4. Disrupted interpersonal relationships

5. Body image distortion and/or somatic or physical complaints

6. Sexual intimacy issues[61]

Avoidance behaviors evolve in an effort to get rid of difficult thoughts and feelings that appear as the result of trauma. These behaviors can include using drugs and/or alcohol, avoiding eye contact, burying emotions, daydreaming, isolating oneself, and more.

Battered woman syndrome is a subcategory of posttraumatic stress disorder. While "not all battered women meet all the DSM-IV-TR [*Diagnostic and Statistical Manual of Mental Disorders*, 4th Edition, Text Revision] criteria for PTSD," many do, and women who have BWS benefit from empowerment techniques and trauma treatment.[62]

BWS began to be recognized in the 1970s through the work of Lenore Walker, and is currently used increasingly as a defense in "homicide cases where a battered woman kills her abuser."[63] In most US states, women arrested for killing or injuring their partners may use BWS as their defense if they have exhibited the symptoms related to the syndrome and have experienced ongoing abuse.[64] According to Cornell University Law School, in court proceedings, "before expert testimony about Battered Woman's

---

60. Foy, "What is the Relationship between Domestic Violence and Bipolar Disorder?," para 5.

61. Walker, "Battered Woman Syndrome," para. 8, Table 1.

62. Walker, "Battered Woman Syndrome," para. 4.

63. Strucke et al., "Battered Woman Syndrome," para. 3.

64. Attorneys.com, "Legal Defenses for Battered Women," para. 4.

Syndrome becomes relevant . . . the party seeking to use expert testimony must establish that: (1) the victim is a battered woman and; (2) the jury would be aided by expert testimony to explain her behavior."[65]

A psychotherapist can be helpful in explaining the symptoms of BWS, the increased dependency of the victim on the abuser and the reasons she did not leave, and how the syndrome develops. This can provide the information jury members need to make an informed assessment of the abused woman's experiences and help them come to understand how she came to kill her abuser in self-defense. Understanding battered woman syndrome "helps to meet the legal burden that the woman had a reasonable perception of imminent (not immediate, but about to happen) danger. It is important to explain how the woman's fear and desperation are triggered when a new battering incident is perceived as about to occur."[66]

It is empowering for a victim to understand that an actual diagnosis exists for her symptoms, and that others also have had this experience. Engaging a mental health professional who has expertise in domestic violence is essential. In addition to helping an abused woman work through and heal from her experiences, a well-informed and wise therapist will help her through the stress of being challenged in court by the batterer.

## DISSOCIATION AND DISSOCIATIVE DISORDERS

First, let us define both dissociation and dissociative disorders:

> Dissociation is a disconnection between a person's thoughts, feelings, memories, behaviors, perception, and/or sense of identity. Nearly everyone has experienced dissociation at some time, with examples including daydreaming or zoning out while driving and not remembering the last few miles of highway ("highway hypnosis").[67]
> Unlike "normal" dissociation, dissociative disorders involve dissociation (an involuntary escape from reality) that interferes with a person's work and/or family life. Roughly 2% of the population is thought to experience a dissociative disorder, and it occurs across all ages, ethnic groups, and socioeconomic backgrounds.[68]

65. Strucke et al., "Battered Woman Syndrome," para. 6.
66. Walker, "Battered Woman Syndrome," para. 38.
67. Tull, "Links Between Trauma, PTSD, and Dissociative Disorders," para. 4.
68. Tull, "Links Between Trauma, PTSD, and Dissociative Disorders," para. 5.

The disorder has been diagnosed in about 2 percent of the population, but 7 percent of the population may have a dissociative disorder that remains undiagnosed.[69] Dissociation helps a person move through traumatic events such as accidents, violence, torture, military combat, or ruinous natural disasters, giving the victim the ability to survive and cope with the trauma experienced.

> Dissociative disorders usually develop as a reaction to trauma and help keep difficult memories at bay. Symptoms—ranging from amnesia to alternate identities—depend in part on the type of dissociative disorder you have. Times of stress can temporarily worsen symptoms, making them more obvious.[70]

"People who dissociate might:

- Seem distracted, not fully present
- 'Space out' while talking or working
- Do things on autopilot
- Seem dreamy or move slowly
- Say or do out-of-character things
- Have gaps in their memories or sense of time."[71]

"There are three types of dissociative disorders: Dissociative identity disorder; dissociative amnesia; and depersonalization/derealization disorder."[72] What used to be called multiple personality disorder is now called *dissociative identity disorder* and involves the existence of two or more "personality states" or identities. Symptoms include gaps in memory concerning daily events and past trauma events as well as personal information, and lead to a life of distress and challenges in "social, occupational or other areas of functioning."[73] *Dissociative amnesia* is common, but does not include normal forgetting. Here, one experiences "memory loss regarding important events or periods of time in a person's life."[74] *Depersonalization* refers to having the sense that one is outside their body watching events

69. Smith, "Dissociative Identity Disorder Facts and Statistics," para. 6.
70. Mayo Clinic, "Dissociative Disorders," para. 2.
71. Raypole, "5 Mental Health Issues that Could Trigger Dissociation," para. 4.
72. Wang, "What are Dissociative Disorders?," para. 3.
73. Wang, "What are Dissociative Disorders?," para. 8.
74. Tull, "Links Between Trauma, PTSD, and Dissociative Disorders," para. 7.

happening to them; *derealization* means that the person is somewhat re-moved from experiencing one's environment or surroundings.[75]

In reference to domestic violence, dissociation helps a person to live within a traumatizing situation without feeling overcome. Alison Miller recounts the story of one woman who managed to reduce her awareness of her husband's abuse in the "harmless portions" of his cycle, dissociate within the violent or abusive parts, and remove the danger of being with her husband from her consciousness when his behaviors were more positive. She eventually realized what she was doing and found a way to be more cognizant of the full picture of what was happening instead of only recognizing one part of the cycle at a time. This recognition helped her to leave.[76]

Children who develop a dissociative disorder to help cope with abuse will carry the disorder into adulthood unless they receive help. Consequently,

> Women with dissociative identity disorder (DID) are significantly more likely than other women to experience intimate partner violence. . . . Women with DID used coping strategies that were consistent with their diagnoses, such as switching and dissociating. These coping mechanisms reflect past self-preservation strategies that were developed in association with severe childhood maltreatment. Women with DID who experienced IPV sought to mitigate and safeguard themselves from danger using strategies they developed as maltreated children.[77]

## TRAUMA BONDING

When an abused person feels love and even sympathy toward the one abusing them, they have formed an emotional attachment called trauma bonding. This often happens when one or both parents of the abused partner were also abusive. As an adult, the victim brings their experience of a "repeated cycle of abuse, devaluation, and positive reinforcement."[78] Stockholm syndrome, a form of trauma bonding, describes the positive feelings toward their captor of a person being held captive.

75. Wang, "What are Dissociative Disorders?," para. 18–19.
76. Miller, "Intimate Family Violence: A Dissociative Family Dance," para. 8.
77. Snyder, "Women with Dissociative Identity Disorder," para. 1.
78. Raypole, "How to Recognize and Break Traumatic Bonds," para. 3.

In *Psychology Today*, Clayton explains trauma bonding as "a hormonal attachment created by repeated abuse, sprinkled with being 'saved' every now and then," and that trauma bonding in adulthood can result from childhood experiences because the brain has already wired itself to respond in this way.[79] The child has learned to view love in a context of abuse and neglect as normal because the brain equates the abuser with safety as well, since the abuser also offers relief from the abuse.[80]

When the abuser shows his victim relief from the abuse or shows kindness, the victim responds physiologically by releasing dopamine, which provides feelings of pleasure and strengthens the bond. Niceties provided by the abuser such as "apologies, gifts, or physical affection . . . serve as rewards that help reinforce the rush of relief and trigger the release of dopamine" and as a result, the victim continually tries "to make them happy to earn their affection."[81] Physical affection also creates the release of oxytocin, which makes us feel good, which can further strengthen the bond.[82]

An abused woman may feel trapped but want to make the best of the situation. She may want to believe the abuser's promises that the future will be better, and might continue to expect the partner to follow through with good behavior, even though he does not. She may focus on the good moments and the good parts of the person, defend the abuser, and not leave when others encourage her to do so. The vulnerability of an abused woman experiencing trauma bonding is not the result of weakness or mental illness, but is created by grooming and efforts by the abuser to gain the trust of the victim.

Just as the fault for the abuse falls on the abuser, the fault for trauma bonding does also. Although a history of trauma makes breaking the bond more difficult, doing so is not impossible.

## SUBSTANCE ABUSE

Drugs and/or alcohol can be used by a victim to cope with her experiences, but a woman can also be coerced into using substances by her abuser. An abuser can then sabotage her efforts to become well and even undermine her to authorities by calling out her substance use in a derogatory way,

79. Clayton, "What is Trauma-Bonding?," para. 1.
80. Clayton, "What is Trauma-Bonding?," para. 6.
81. Raypole, "How to Recognize and Break Traumatic Bonds," para. 28.
82. Raypole, "How to Recognize and Break Traumatic Bonds," para. 37.

such as complaining, "She's always drunk." Such actions will undermine a victim's efforts to convince the court that she should have custody of the children.[83] Here, we see another tactic the abuser uses to maintain control and to put the victim at a higher risk for abuse.

Substance abuse rates are higher among women who have experienced IPV compared with those who have not.[84] This fact "has been established through studies utilizing national or general community samples as well as samples of DV survivors in a variety of settings."[85] "Data available from four studies found that drug abuse prevalence ranged from 7% to 25% among women experiencing IPV."[86] Studies of women seeking alcohol treatment show us that 47–87% of those women have experienced violence by an intimate partner.[87]

## DISENFRANCHISED GRIEF

Disenfranchised grief is different from other types of grief in that it is grief that is not understood or supported, thereby protracting the emotional pain. We often think of the sadness after losing a loved one as a grief response. Society validates this. Many view grief as fitting into Elisabeth Kubler-Ross's five stages: denial, anger, bargaining, depression, and acceptance. Society places expectations on individuals, limiting the time and manner in which they will be allowed to grieve. Disenfranchised grief does not fit into these prescribed molds. "Widespread attitudes and beliefs contribute to disenfranchised grief."[88]

Kenneth Doka, a bereavement expert, explains that "disenfranchised grief refers to a loss that's not openly acknowledged, socially mourned or publicly supported," and it does not appear only when someone dies.[89] For an abused woman in a domestic violence family, many other circumstances

83. Rivera et al., "The Relationship between Intimate Partner Violence and Substance Abuse," 2.

84. Rivera et al., "The Relationship between Intimate Partner Violence and Substance Abuse," 3.

85. Rivera et al., "The Relationship between Intimate Partner Violence and Substance Abuse," 3.

86. Weaver et al., "Identifying and Intervening," para 6.

87. Florida Coalition Against Domestic Violence, "Exploring the Intersection," 10.

88. WebMD Editorial Contributors, "What to Know About Disenfranchised Grief," para. 6.

89. Cordoza et al., "The Importance of Mourning Losses," para. 2.

cause sadness and grief as well: fear of being judged, including the victim's resulting physical and mental health problems; loss of who they were before the abuse; regret for what they could have done with their life if they had not connected with the abuser; the death of a pet or pets; becoming disconnected from family and friends; court decisions; and even the end of their relationship with the abuser. When the woman's relationship has ended, there is relief and happiness, but negative feelings as well. She too often feels unsupported, leading to disenfranchised grief.

## Spiritual Health

One of the many ways for an abuser to exert control over a victim is to use her religious beliefs to shame or manipulate her. He may find ways to stop her from exercising her beliefs, make fun of her beliefs, or misconstrue the teachings of her faith to suit his controlling designs. The abuser will make himself the "god" in the relationship: what he declares to be truth carries more weight than the tenets of faith and God himself.

Regrettably, some Christian leaders who hold to theologies that restrict a woman's role in the church can provide even more fuel to an abusive partner's desire to control. The abuser makes his partner doubt her beliefs by belittling her, magnifies his own importance, and gains compliance.

Cultural and spiritual abuse entail similar tactics to control the victim. A person's sense of wellbeing and purpose can be directly tied to both cultural and religious beliefs. Abuses related to culture look very much like spiritual abuse: belittling one's beliefs; preventing practices common to those beliefs and denying the victim access to her cultural or religious community; causing the victim to violate cultural or religious obligations; and using the cultural or religious beliefs to silence the victim and to prevent her from reaching out for help.[90]

Often, abused women believe that God has abandoned them, and they will sometimes leave the church. Faith does not prevent troubles. We live in a fallen world. Members of the faith community need to reassure victims of God's love for them. The faith community, particularly church leadership, needs to avail themselves of proper, ongoing training so they are able to respond with wisdom and sensitivity to those in crisis because of both spiritual and cultural abuse.

90. National Domestic and Family Violence Bench Book, "Cultural and Spiritual Abuse," para. 2.

## Decisions

A woman will call 911 for help when she decides that her abuser has inflicted harm for the last time. Understanding how to handle the situation ahead of time will help immensely, not only at the time of the call, but also when the police respond. A victim can prepare herself by considering (1) how to manage the environment when the police arrive, (2) what information law enforcement is looking for, (3) and what information will help her get through this difficult experience. Both staying and leaving are accompanied by their own difficulties and safety issues.

### Report or Not?

### *Calling 911.*

Many fault a woman for not calling 911 when the abuser has hurt her, saying, "She couldn't have been too bad off if she didn't call 911." A woman who has not yet made an emergency call must not be found at fault. Anna Fagan of Genesis Women's Shelter & Support cites some of the reasons why women do not call for help:

- The victim may believe that calling will make the situation more dangerous or may determine that the safest action at that moment is to deescalate the abuse.

- Too often, when law enforcement arrests the abuser, the abuser receives only a "slap on the wrist," thus creating a more dangerous situation for the victim.

- The victim's ability to use the phone may be blocked, as well as her ability to leave the house and run to a neighbor's house.

- She may fear not being believed, and may even fear that the police will believe the abuser's false assertions and arrest her, especially if her wounds do not yet show but the abuser shows wounds from the victim's self-defense.[91]

Since approximately 80 percent of 911 calls come from wireless devices, be sure to provide the location of the incident immediately to the

---

91. Fagan, "Why Didn't She Call the Police?," para. 2–4.

dispatcher when making the call or precious time will be wasted.[92] Make an effort to remain as calm as possible, speak as clearly as you are able, and give the dispatcher as much information as possible. The responding officers do not want to approach the situation blindly, so the dispatcher will ask questions to help get that information. Also provide information concerning any children in the house and any escalation of abuse or threats. The dispatcher will not only ask questions in an effort to get all pertinent information, but will also be listening for what can be heard in the background (children, voices, screams, items breaking, etc.).

The dispatcher views an active silent call as one in which the caller cannot verbally communicate for some reason. Silence creates its own form of communication. In this case, follow the dispatcher's cues that will possibly provide necessary information (such as: press one if children are present, or press three if he has a weapon, etc.). Today, law enforcement should have the ability to receive calls from non-English speaking, hard-of-hearing, or deaf people.[93]

Finally, if at all possible, be the first to call 911. Abusers and other criminals also call 911 when they are involved in a crime to help remove any possible suspicions from them.

*Police Response.*

When the police respond to the 911 call, the victim will need to help the police identify the aggressor or perpetrator. Sometimes, the only visible wounds appear on the abuser because the victim has defended herself, or the abuser may inflict his own wounds to implicate the victim. The perpetrator can be very convincing in casting blame on the victim. Consequently, sometimes police arrest the wrong person; helping law enforcement identify the actual aggressor becomes essential.

Trying to remain as calm as possible, let the police know the circumstances that led to the call for help. Ask to be questioned outside of the hearing of the perpetrator and any children present. Let them know if there are any weapons and ammunition in the house and where they are located. Ongoing efforts by the abuser to control and exert power provide important information for the police. If the victim has been able to keep and hide

92. Moynihan, "911's Deadly Flaw," para. 2, 8.
93. New Jersey Division of Criminal Justice, "Handling a Domestic Violence Call," 2.

a journal and pictures of bruises and other wounds from previous incidents of battering, this is the time to produce it.

Because strangulation does not always leave visible marks on the neck, and because of potential internal damage when strangulation occurs, police will need to know if the abuser used this tactic so a medical examination can take place. Sexual assault is not always visible, so law enforcement will need to know if the perpetrator attacked in this way. Do not tidy up the house. Viewing the disarray (if any) will help the police make an assessment concerning what took place. Also, police may want to take pictures of the crime scene.

Remember to ask the police for a copy of the report and the report number in case an order of protection is pursued. Each member of law enforcement will be able to provide their name and badge number when asked.

### Mutual Abuse or Not.

Mutual abuse is when the two partners are equally abusive to one another, which rarely exists in domestic violence situations.[94] Abuse is never the survivor's fault. "The mutual abuse myth also supports the abuser's behavior."[95]

When police respond to a call and find that both parties are injured and admit to aggression against the other, both may be arrested, especially if mandatory arrest laws exist in that state. Describing the sequence of events to the police is vital, because one person may have been defending herself (as is usually the case), and police do not know what came before their arrival on the scene, so providing good information about the situation is essential.

Remain as calm as possible and explain what happened to precipitate the altercation and how you reacted. ("We had a fight" tells them nothing, but who started the fight does.) Provide your notes or journal and pictures if you have collected them.[96] At the very least, tell them that the current situation belongs to an ongoing pattern of abuse.

---

94. Thurrott, "Is Mutual Abuse Real?," para. 1.
95. Thurrott, "Is Mutual Abuse Real?," para. 2.
96. Thurrott, "Is Mutual Abuse Real?," para. 13.

## STAY OR LEAVE?

### *Staying.*

Some common reasons for staying are financial, threats imposed by the abuser (if you leave, I'll . . . ), the fear of being treated unfairly by the flawed legal system, trauma bonding, and the fear of judgment and disbelief by others. Sometimes a victim believes that what she experiences is common and without significance. After all, social media has the ability to make crime look normal (hence, the existence of rape culture). An abuser may use religion to justify his abuse and her obligation to stay. For the abuser, he feels the supreme loss of control if his partner leaves. Thus, he holds the reins even tighter and becomes more abusive when he thinks she will leave or she shows him her ability to leave (e.g., by calling 911, getting an order of protection, etc.).

Sometimes senior victims of partner abuse believe they must stay because of traditional ideas about marriage, while others may depend on the abuser for finances and care.[97] Those with disabilities may stay because they have difficulty accessing the court and other services.[98]

When a victim is ready to reveal her circumstances or when she decides she must leave, she will need a good, patient listener, and someone who will believe her. The listener must understand that it often takes time—sometimes a lot of time—for a woman to leave a domestic violence home. Staying takes courage. Leaving also takes courage.

### *Leaving.*

Leaving is possible even though doing so might seem impossible. Ensuring the safety and wellbeing of herself and her children provide her motivation. Preparation becomes the key to leaving.

A well-trained domestic violence advocate will help a victim leave her dangerous environment in the best way possible and will lead her to the resources in her geographical area. Resources include "shelters, counseling, lay legal advice, court assistance and support groups."[99] Domestic violence advocates also have the ability to help devise a safety plan specifically

97. DomesticShelters.org, "Barriers to Leaving, Part 1," para. 11.
98. DomesticShelters.org. "Barriers to Leaving, Part 1," para. 9.
99. DomesticShelters.org. "When it's Time to Go: Part 1," para. 3.

designed for a woman's life and situation and know how to keep such plans from the abuser. The websites WomensLaw.org and DomesticShelters.org will help to locate advocates and shelters. If you cannot find one online where you live, contact the National Domestic Violence Hotline at 800–799-SAFE (7233). Often women believe they cannot leave because they do not have help or the necessary information. If you know someone who needs help in leaving her situation, give her the good news that she can find an advocate and guide her with the information to do so.

Victims benefit by thinking ahead about where they will go after leaving. Mentally rehearse ways to leave the house in case the abuser is home. If possible, safely remove weapons from the house. Leaving when the abuser is out of the house is a safer way to leave, but a woman may find she has to leave when he is home.

DomesticShelters.org and WomensLaw.org have a list of items to pack and have ready if at all possible. Some women find the right opportunity to leave and do so without having packed anything at all. If a bag is packed ahead of time, put it in a good hiding place where it can be grabbed quickly. Keeping the getaway bag at a trusted friend's or neighbor's house works better. The following list includes children's items, items for immigrants, pet particulars, and other articles that may be needed:

- Spare car keys and passport(s) (your driver's license is likely in your wallet or purse that will go with you).

- Since the abuser may track where you are through credit card usage, or may cancel them, take enough cash for forgotten incidentals, transportation, food, and lodging for a few nights. Sometimes saving cash little by little helps if time allows.

- Work permit, green card, or immigration papers.

- Enough changes of clothes for a few days for you and the children.

- Infant formula, diapers, and wipes.

- Familiar items for the children for comfort; if duplicates are available, pack the duplicate.

- Pet food, vet records, and leashes.

- Medications and vitamins for you, the children, and any pets taken.

- Important documents or copies: children's birth certificates, social security cards, school records, immunizations, pay stubs, bank account information, marriage license (if possible, take the original), will, mortgage papers, lease agreement, insurance information.

- Order of protection.
- Evidence such as a journal, photos, police records, medical records.
- Cherished personal items such as photos, jewelry, Aunt Mindy's crystal vase, etc.[100]

Regardless of whether a victim leaves in an instant or whether she planned her exit ahead of time, leaving is often one of the most dangerous times. Exiting does not mean she simply walks away and experiences the freedom she wants. Getting an order of protection will help keep her and the children safe. Particularly if they have children together, his presence in the family's life will continue and his tactics to control will become stronger, often using the court system to control and punish her.

Survivors can find support from an understanding family member, a shelter, or an advocate. A support person can help her remember what she experienced with her partner, why she left, his empty promises to change or get better, and the health and safety issues impacting not only her, but also the children. Nonetheless, the decision belongs to the victim, and an advocate must let her know of their ongoing commitment to offer support.

## Scriptural Encouragement

An abuser who wants to use Scripture to control his partner will find many to twist in his favor—Scriptures that even some scholars of theology have interpreted poorly or inadequately. Some theologians have incorporated into their understanding of the Bible's message the influence of ancient pagan philosophers, the experience and influence of their own culture, or personal bias. Sometimes understanding what Scripture tells us means looking at the original Hebrew and Greek. While knowing the original language provides a solid start for translation, understanding the culture in which a document was written is also necessary to determine the meaning and intent of the original writer.

The philosophies of Plato and Aristotle (Plato's student) depict a world ordered according to a hierarchical pattern, and their school of thought profoundly influenced early theologians. Both Plato and Aristotle espoused

---

100. DomesticShelters.org., "When it's Time to Go: Part 1," para. 6.

a low view of women. In Plato's *Laws*, he explains where women fall in the hierarchy:

> Now better men are the superiors of worse men, and in general elders are the superiors of the young; wherefore also parents are the superiors of their off spring, and men of women and children, and rulers of their subjects; for all men ought to reverence any one who is in any position of authority, and especially those who are in state offices.[101]

In *On the Generation of Animals*, Aristotle describes women as inferior:

> For females are weaker and colder in nature, and we must look upon the female character as being a sort of natural deficiency. Accordingly while it is within the mother it develops slowly because of its coldness (for development is concoction, and it is heat that concocts, and what is hotter is easily concocted); but after birth it quickly arrives at maturity and old age on account of its weakness for all inferior things come sooner to their perfection or end, and as this is true of works of art so it is of what is formed by Nature.[102]

Aristotle also views humanity as hierarchical: "Not only did Aristotle find a kind of hierarchy or sophistication from plants to animals to humans, but he also saw a similar hierarchy amongst slaves, women, and men."[103]

Sadly, Plato and Aristotle strongly influenced early theologians, including Augustine and Thomas of Aquinas respectively. "St. Augustine's christianization of Plato along with St. Thomas's christianization of Aristotle carried through the Middle Ages to the present day with the resulting erroneous theology of women."[104] In *Timaeus*, Plato theorizes about "the subordination of the lesser gods (easily compacted and transferred onto the Son and Holy Spirit, when later transferred to Christianity) and the reduction of women to reincarnated failed men being offered a second chance to 'live justly.'"[105]

Another erroneous theological teaching is that hierarchy is present within the Godhead. In *Christian Egalitarian Leadership: Empowering the Whole Church according to the Scripture*, William Spencer explains the

---

101. Plato, *Laws*, Book XI.

102. Aristotle, *On the Generation of Animals*, Book IV, Part 6.

103. Dimock, *Christian Egalitarian Leadership*, 92.

104. Dimock, *Christian Egalitarian Leadership*, 106.

105. Spencer, *Christian Egalitarian Leadership*, 64.

intentions God had for both Adam and Eve, and the rest of humanity, before the fall, and then what happened after the fall.

First, we find God's intention for humanity in Genesis 1:26–27:

> Then God said, "Let us make humankind in our image, according
> to our likeness; and let them have dominion over the fish of the
> sea, and over the birds of the air, and over the cattle, and over all
> the wild animals of the earth, and over every creeping thing that
> creeps upon the earth." So God created humankind in his image,
> in the image of God he created them; male and female he created
> them.

We see that God's original intention for Adam and Eve and the rest of humanity included filling the earth, subduing it, and having dominion ("let
them" rule) over all of it. God intended dominion, or ruling, to take place
as the result of women and men working and ruling together cooperatively
and as equals, serving one another. They were not to rule over each other.[106]

But the fall compromised this joint rule. After the serpent tempted
Eve to eat from the tree of the knowledge of good and evil, God punished
the serpent for being deceitful and tempting Eve. Then he pronounced his
penalties for Adam and Eve. Genesis 3:16 describes Eve's penalty: "Yet your
desire shall be for your husband, and he shall rule over you." Spencer provides many different translations of the Bible to show their similarities and
differences in translating this phrase.[107] Some say, "he shall rule over you,"
or "he shall rule over thee." Others say, "he will be your master," "he will
lord it over you," or "you will be subject to him." The New Living Translation and English Standard Version give us, respectively: "And you will
desire to control your husband . . ." and "Your desire shall be contrary to
your husband . . ." These versions:

> choose to add an interpretation to the Genesis 3:16 explanation,
> suggesting the woman has a different objective in mind than sim-
> ply desiring her husband: she herself will now be turning toward
> oppression, desiring to control him by acting contrary to the man
> and, as a result, he will have to rule over her to keep her in line.[108]

Spencer further explains:

---

106. Spencer, *Christian Egalitarian Leadership*, 75, n. 33, as found in Assohoto et al.,
*Africa Bible Commentary*, 11.

107. Spencer, *Christian Egalitarian Leadership*, 76.

108. Spencer, *Christian Egalitarian Leadership*, 78.

there is no adverb for "contrary" or infinitive for "to control" either in the Old Testament Hebrew original or in the Septuagint translation of Genesis 3:16 (17). So, no grounds exist for putting these words in. To do so is adding an object not in the text to make the woman's action bad and, therefore, an excuse for her coming oppression. And, neither of the nouns in Hebrew or in Greek for "turning" in itself contains "contrary" or "to control" to signify a rebellious aspect to the woman's yearning or desire in turning toward her husband.[109]

The Septuagint, a Greek translation of the Old Testament used in the first century, uses the word *kurieuo,* which means "lording it over someone." This describes what "the fallen man would do to the fallen woman now," and "describes the lamented state of domestic abuse, which was a condition God never wanted for humanity."[110] God was not giving a command to lord it over Eve, but rather, predicting what would now happen because of the sin that had tainted the relationship between husband and wife.

From the very beginning of Creation, God planned for husband and wife to love and esteem one another. Sin ruined the original magnificence of their relationship. As redeemed people, we should consider God's original plan and the ideal relationship between wife and husband as our model. As Paul points out in Ephesians 5:32, this relationship is deeply meaningful as he views Christ's relationship with the church as our example. Through Christ's sacrifice, we are meant to live redeemed lives and to leave sinful patterns behind.

Ephesians 5:21 clearly states that we are to submit one to another: "Be subject to one another out of reverence for Christ." But verses 22 and 23 may raise questions, especially in view of verse 21: "Wives, be subject to your husbands as you are to the Lord. For the husband is the head of the wife just as Christ is the head of the church, the body of which he is the Savior." Spencer's explanation cannot be improved upon as he explains the cultural context of these verses that many ignore when applying them today:

This advice is being made to a largely Gentile church, that its cult of Artemis was run by women, now presumably newly converted to Christianity and not being permitted to lead with such a toxic background that needed to be completely revamped, rather than

109. Spencer, *Christian Egalitarian Leadership,* 79.
110. Spencer, *Christian Egalitarian Leadership,* 79.

the Ephesian church being filled with Jewish women already conversant with the Torah and the prophets, or that "head" in Gentile understanding means origin or source, so that honoring one's source is what Gentiles would understand, but just taking the passage completely out of context, still nowhere within it is a statement made specifying that, just as the Son fully submits unilaterally to the Father, should women submit unilaterally to the men. Instead, the submission the passage deals with for women concerns honoring their husbands, and husbands caretaking their wives. Wives are not being told [to] be like the Son of God. No reference to the Trinity is being made for such an interpretation is gender-bending eisegesis.[111]

Here we see the inference of a hierarchical Godhead when hierarchy does not exist in the Godhead; a less-than-adequate interpretation for the word "head"; and a lack of consideration for the cultural context—all leading to misunderstanding.

Luke 22:25–26 offers further confirmation that what God spoke to Eve after the serpent's temptation produced compromised a prediction: it was neither a command, nor what God thought should happen from the moment of the curse up until today. Jesus told the disciples that they are not to lord over one another: "But he said to them, The kings of the Gentiles lord it over them; and those in authority over them are called benefactors. But not so with you; rather the greatest among you must become like the youngest, and the leader like one who serves." We are not to "lord it over" anyone, but to serve one another as we live a Christ-redeemed existence.

Genesis 3:16 is one of the most common Scriptures used to diminish a woman's role in the church and in life in general, and the one Scripture that may set the stage for other misunderstandings as we form our theology. A woman's God-given worth and abilities should not be diminished by anyone, whether in the home, the church, the marketplace, or elsewhere. To do so ruins God's plan for her, the community, and the church, and provides rich fodder for abuse, and even violence, when someone twists the meaning of Scriptures and then uses them to control or demean.

---

111. Spencer, *Christian Egalitarian Leadership*, 68 n. 29.

# 6

# Woman as Parent

## Case Study

WE SAW AN EXAMPLE of Damon's selfish parenting when he let toddler Poppy run around the cottage without supervision while he sat on the lake's edge with his friends, and again when he let Poppy watch videos all day to occupy her so he could do what he wanted.

However, when the court-appointed evaluator did her investigation of the family for parenting recommendations, her report stated that Damon showed himself to be a good father. She provided examples of how he engaged now almost three-year-old Poppy, listened to her, and watched her. She stated in her report that Poppy displayed a good connection with her father and that her behavior showed good engagement with him. The evaluator reported that she was aghast at Lori's mothering, saying she was uncomfortable and nervous in her role as mother, and that in all her years as a custody evaluator she had never experienced any parent this ill at ease with her own children. Consequently, the father should be given liberal parenting time. The court followed her recommendation.

In preschool and elementary school, Poppy often returned home to Lori acting out with loud and long temper tantrums and saying hateful things to her mother. Poppy and Rayne's play therapist told Lori that Poppy had to behave well when with her father and that she had to maintain control of her emotions and behavior because she felt the need to protect both herself and Rayne. She had tremendous emotions bottled up inside her and waited until she got home to release them, where she knew she would be safe. The therapist called Poppy's management of the situation with her father as "getting along through terror."

When Poppy and Rayne became teenagers, they decided they did not want any more of their mother's rules and boundaries. They made the decision to live with their father. After this Damon made his daughters' time with their mother difficult, messaging Lori that they did not want to see her and telling her that their daughters were afraid of her. When Lori tried to send her daughters presents or money, Damon intercepted the mail and did not allow the girls to receive their gifts from her. In a telephone call to her mother, Poppy stated that Dad's live-in girlfriend had told both her and Rayne that their mother was treacherous and to stay away from her.

## Parenting Styles

An overview of the four main parenting styles will be helpful in understanding the woman as parent when she is caught in a domestic violence situation. These descriptions are based on the work begun by psychologist Diana Baumrind in the 1960s and refined by E. E. Maccoby and J. A. Martin in the 1980s. They are: authoritative (or democratic), authoritarian (or disciplinarian), permissive (or indulgent), and uninvolved (or neglectful). Baumrind discovered a correlation between parenting style and the child's behavior, which in turn affects the child's development and outcomes.[1] A parent may not fall exactly into one of the four main parenting styles, but may at different times act outside the style they generally use. At other times, parents evolve over time and change their style based on experience.

### AUTHORITATIVE PARENTING

Children receive warmth and responsiveness through authoritative parenting. Parents expect achievement and the development of age-appropriate maturity, and work with their children through affection, encouragement, and validation. "These parents set rules and enforce boundaries by having open discussions, providing guidance, and using reasoning," but do not try to extract expected behaviors through coercion.[2] In general, children of authoritative parenting have better mental health outcomes, better self-esteem and social skills, do not tend toward violence, have more independence, and are happier and more content than those children who

1. Li, "4 Types of Parenting Styles," para. 3.
2. Li, "4 Types of Parenting Styles," para. 15.

experience other parenting styles.[3] In general, research has shown that authoritative parenting leads to the best overall outcomes for children.

## Authoritarian Parenting

Parents who engage in authoritarian parenting make strong efforts to control their children, even through harsh punishment. Both authoritative parenting and authoritarian parenting demand high standards, but the difference rests in the approach to the child. Authoritative parenting says, "Let's talk about why it's important to do your chores and how we can think together about how to make this happen." Authoritarian parenting says, "You need to do chores because I said so." An authoritarian parent uses coercion to get their child to respond the way the parent desires. These parents consider any questioning by the child as back talk while authoritative parents consider questioning by a child as the beginning of a fruitful conversation.

Authoritarian parenting often results in children having an unhappy disposition. They have less of a sense of security and lack independence. In general, children from this style of parenting do not exhibit social maturity, have poor academic performance, do not engage in good coping skills, and have higher rates of substance abuse.[4]

## Permissive Parenting

Permissive parents have low expectations with few rules and boundaries. At the same time, they do not always enforce the rules they do make. They are "warm and indulgent."[5] Consequently, these children do not possess a good ability to follow rules or engage in good self-control, and exhibit social immaturity and egocentrism.[6]

3. Li, "4 Types of Parenting Styles," para. 22.
4. Li, "4 Types of Parenting Styles," para. 28.
5. Li, "4 Types of Parenting Styles," para. 30.
6. Li, "4 Types of Parenting Styles," para. 31.

## Uninvolved Parenting

Uninvolved parenting is also known as neglectful parenting. Parents who engage in this style provide the physical essentials such as food, clothing, and shelter, but little else beyond those basics. "These children receive little guidance, discipline, and nurturing from their parents. And oftentimes kids are left to raise themselves and make decisions—big and small—on their own."[7]

Uninvolved parenting does not always happen intentionally. A parent may have experienced the same style from his or her own parent(s), or perhaps experienced parental abuse. A parent may be preoccupied by their own special interests, work, or stressors, such as financial, health, or other concerns.[8] Sometimes emotional detachment becomes neglect and even rejection. Correction of the child generally happens only when the child infringes on the parent in some way.

Children who experience this kind of parenting may learn how to take care of themselves, but they do not experience love, nurturing, discipline, and boundary setting. Children who do not receive positive attention and nurturing do not have healthy self-esteem. Because of a lack of engagement at home, they do not have the social skills to connect well with others or to do so with confidence. Children learn through parental engagement, discipline, and boundary setting. They also learn social skills by watching the adults around them and through their parents' correction and encouragement—for example, "Share your toys with Bobby and he will want to share with you!" Neglectful parenting leads to high rates of mental health difficulties, delinquency, substance abuse, impulsivity, and subpar emotional regulation.[9] Uninvolved or neglectful parenting leads to the poorest results in children compared with the other parenting styles.[10]

## Cultural Considerations

Children in different cultures may respond differently to the various parenting styles. But those who grow up in families where the parents neglect their children or remain uninvolved all have difficulties, regardless

7. Higuera, "What is Uninvolved Parenting?," para. 5.
8. Higuera, "What is Uninvolved Parenting?," para. 7.
9. Li, "4 Types of Parenting Styles," para. 35.
10. Li, "Uninvolved Parenting," para. 30.

of culture.[11] Depending on the culture, the authoritative style of parenting does not always have the best educational outcomes. As an example, African American children whose parents use the authoritative style of parenting usually do not perform well educationally if they do not also have peer support, and Asian American students whose parents use the authoritarian style perform better in school when they also have peer support.[12] Among children and youth of color, authoritative parenting is not necessarily associated with better academic outcomes even though authoritative parenting is associated generally with better child outcomes. Additional research may reveal more as children's individual personalities and other differences are considered.

## Mother's Challenges

### Challenges from Abuser

#### Pre-Separation.

The batterer's main parenting style must be considered before examining the mother's style, because the relationship between the mother and children is often compromised because of the father's abuse.

Regardless of the parenting style predominantly used by abusive men, the children also experience abuse when their mother is abused. They may witness their mother's abuse through their eyes or ears, or may experience the aftermath when they see their mother's fear or emotions. The knowledge that their mother has been hurt hurts them as well. Financial abuse hurts children when the mother's ability to pay for school trips, clothes, dance lessons, or food stops or becomes less predictable.

Batterers tend toward the most inflexible form of parenting, the authoritarian style, but some researchers have shown that abusers tend to also use permissive parenting.[13] Abusive men want control, so the authoritarian style of parenting is a logical choice when they believe that insistence on obedience brings them under control.

Abusers also tend to be under-involved in their children's lives, sometimes believing that their "domain" includes authority over the children,

11. Higuera, "What is Uninvolved Parenting?," para. 20.
12. Li, "4 Types of Pareneting Styles," para. 44.
13. Bancroft and Silverman, *The Batterer as Parent*, 30.

but that the task of caring for the children belongs to the mother.[14] The batterer's self-centeredness means he wants attention paid to his successes, ailments, and frustrations, including those he expresses to the children about their mother not living up to his expectations.[15]

The batterer may try to control how the mother will mother by acting as the decision maker regarding reproduction and contraception, childbirth, or breastfeeding. He may also realize he is no longer the focal point when they have children, and will attempt to take the mother's attention away from them, often making her ignore them when they need attention.

Within domestic violence families, parentification happens when children perform adult duties such as laundry and making meals, and even provide emotional support, such as mediating disagreements or providing encouragement. Parentification can take place child to child, child to parent, or both. Caroline Tunkle provides a concise analysis of parentification within a domestic violence context based on research involving twenty-five young adults who were exposed to father-mother domestic violence:

> Analysis identified five main parentified roles: intervening to protect mothers from violence, serving as mother's emotional support system, shielding siblings from violence and conflict, caring for siblings' daily needs, and managing parents' health and well-being. The young adults carried out these roles for various reasons including protecting their mothers and siblings from their fathers' use of physical violence, feelings of obligation or due to a parent approaching them. Though parentification was common throughout these participants [sic] experiences, variations identified depended on the DV context.[16]

Parentified children fulfill these roles because of fear of their father's violence, or to protect their mother and siblings, or to bolster their mother's mental and physical health.[17] They fulfill the emotional role by being the mother's "support system or confidante" and fulfilling siblings' daily needs.[18] In this chapter's case study, Poppy felt the need to protect her sister when they were with their father.

14. Bancroft and Silverman, *The Batterer as Parent*, 32.

15. Bancroft and Silverman, *The Batterer as Parent*, 35.

16. Tunkle, "Parentification," 2.

17. Tunkle, "Parentification," 32–33.

18. Tunkle, "Parentification," 32.

In order to hurt the mother, the abuser will mistreat the children and even endanger or neglect them. To keep the mother "behaving" according to his rules, the abuser will threaten to harm the children or take them away if she does not comply.

## Post-Separation.

An abuser often blames the mother for the separation, telling the children that she is responsible for him not being able to live at home. This further tears down the bond the children have with their mother.[19]

An abuser will act involved and caring when the court assigns a custody evaluator to investigate and make decisions related to custody and parenting plans. We saw how Damon moved from uninvolved parenting to involved parenting in the presence of the custody evaluator, acting like a good father for the sake of appearances. A victim of abuse will likely show anxiety and nervousness, as Lori did. It is common for an abuser to call Child Protective Services to make false complaints against the mother. When he sees the opportunity to gain public recognition for great fathering, he takes the opportunity to act in such a way that others will admire his attentive and engaged parenting.

When he has the children alone at home, his parenting looks very different. Friends, sometimes extended family, professionals who attend the children (e.g., teachers, doctors, etc.), and professionals who assess the family do not view the full picture of the abuser's parenting. Some professionals do not go deeper than a surface-level assessment of the father's parenting, saying something similar to: "The children get along very well with their father and he is very good with them, so I fail to see the problem."

All these challenges to a mother's parenting often lead children to emotionally disconnect from their mother, as they

> tend over time to absorb the batterer's disrespect for their mother, which can lead them to feel superior to her and ashamed to be connected to her. Furthermore, they may have well-founded fears that the batterer will retaliate against them with verbal abuse or violence if he sees them as allied with their mother.[20]

19. Tomison, "Exploring Family Violence," 8.
20. Bancroft and Silverman, *The Batterer as Parent,* 70.

The children also may want more permissive parenting. Dad will likely not have a curfew or other expectations regulating the children's social life; he will likely not have boundaries in respect to eating habits; he will likely not have expectations governing academics and bedtime, etc. In their teen years, Poppy and Rayne gravitated toward permissive parenting and chose to live with their father, who then had a greater opportunity to separate them from their mother, both physically and emotionally.

## CHALLENGES FROM CHILDREN

### Pre-Separation.

When a father abuses a child's mother, the relationship between mother and child may become compromised. When the batterer abuses the mother, he undermines the mother's authority. The abuse signals that Mom must deserve the treatment he gives her. If yelling and talking back at Mom and pushing her around is appropriate for the father, why would it not be appropriate for the children? Sometimes the batterer will reward the children when he sees them mistreating their mother. At other times, the children report to the father how they mistreated their mother while he was absent to seek out that reward.

The abuser will devise different ways to undermine the mother deliberately. Perhaps he will overrule her, becoming either more lenient or even more restrictive. Often abusers try to keep children close to minimize their conversations with others about what happens at home. Or perhaps he will speak in an accusatory way about the mother, such as calling her an alcoholic when she is not, calling her stupid when she is intelligent, or mockingly laughing at her. And the list grows.

The abuse leaves the mother depressed, withdrawn, and sometimes not as responsive to the children. They view her as disheartened and unable to succeed in stopping the violence or the verbal onslaught of insults, name-calling, and blaming.[21] They may come to believe that she deserves such treatment, especially when authorities fail to hold the abuser accountable. His abuse becomes the primary means of undermining the mother.

21. Bancroft and Silverman, *The Batterer as Parent*, 57.

*Post-Separation.*

Undermining post-separation becomes a retaliatory act, because the victim has shown the abuser that she knows how to leave her cruel situation. Now he is interested in gaining custody, not because he wants time with the children and to care for them, but because he wants to further extend his control of the mother. A part of his retaliation is to use the children against the mother. He may choose permissive parenting, allowing the children to do what they want, eat what they want, go where they want, and say what they want. He will let the children do things he knows their mother will not allow. When they return home, they return not only to mom, but to the healthy rules and boundaries she expects the children to adhere to. They cannot eat what they want, stay up as late as they want, or forget to finish their homework. Children will then often act out toward the mother, and the abuser will claim that she cannot control her own children.

## Mother's Parental Navigation

*Pre-Separation.*

After a violent incident with the perpetrator, the mother will probably experience "shock, rage, and fear and may be experiencing posttrauma symptoms such as nightmares, flashbacks, or depression. Thus, the children may find her cold and withdrawn, short-tempered, and emotionally volatile."[22] As the children witness these behaviors, their belief that their mother deserves her abusive treatment is reinforced. Mom cannot display playfulness or cheerfulness with the children because of her stressful experiences, so Dad is more fun. Teenagers may take on the abusive language of the batterer toward their mother, or they may believe they need to side with her in order to provide support because she does not have the competence or maturity to defend herself.[23] Some may physically harm the mother. One client recalled how her son verbally and physically abused her, hitting and pushing her, using the same angry words against her that his father used.

The mother needs help to understand why her children behave in difficult ways, and she needs the tools to regain her rightful authority.

22. Bancroft and Silverman, *The Batterer as Parent,* 58–59.
23. Bancroft and Silverman, *The Batterer as Parent,* 59.

Protective mothers need help to identify non-physical means of discipline to use in response to these confrontations.

Because abused mothers focus their attention on appeasing the abusive partner, she can sometimes neglect the children.[24] In the process of trying to protect herself, she also tries to protect the children. Too often, the onus falls on the mother to keep everyone safe. She is viewed as the one responsible for attending to all the children's needs, so she is the one blamed for any neglect.

### Post-Separation.

Now the victim finds herself on high alert for lies and accusations that the batterer may bring to the court through his lawyer. She is also alert for threats to contact Child Protective Services with false accusations to discredit her and gain custody. When the custody evaluator investigated the family to evaluate parenting, Lori displayed nervousness and anxiety as the evaluator viewed her time with the children. This is normal for an abused woman who lives under daily threats toward herself and her children. The victim knows that investigators too often make judgments about their situation without having the full picture.

## Navigating Social Services

Threatening to call Child Protective Services is a common way for abusers to try to control their victims. After separation, many abusers will call CPS and file a report to show the victim that they still have control. Abusers will lie about the mother and often succeed in initiating an investigation, which makes real his threats to take the children away.

Child Protective Services can be helpful, but they can also be a detriment. Sometimes they offer helpful services such as providing home supplies, therapy for children and adults, and educational and job helps. If they properly assess the family situation, they may compel the abuser to participate in a batterer's program. Other times, they do not make a proper assessment. There are times when they do remove children from the home, but overall, "they are more the exception then the norm."[25]

24. Tomison, "Exploring Family Violence," 7.
25. Bancroft, *When Dad Hurts Mom*, 173.

Social workers need to not only show respect for the people they interview, but also take the time necessary to gather all the pertinent information. Again, as we say in our family, "This is not fast food!"

Those who investigate any family experiencing domestic violence need the ability to assess for domestic violence and understand the family dynamics. The mother may need to have an advocate with her who understands the history of the family and who is able to help describe her situation. An advocate can help explain more fully what the victim has experienced and provide a more clear understanding when the victim finds it too difficult to talk about her situation, perhaps because she is unsure whether they will believe her, whether they will understand what she is going through, whether they will have respect for her race, culture, or class, or whether they will reach a fitting conclusion. A call to CPS puts additional stress on the victim especially when she has a history of mental health or substance abuse problems, but she can still reach a good outcome. When a victim learns about the report, she can make a call to CPS to let them know of her willingness to speak with them and to inform them of any threats by the abuser and when they were made. The importance of journaling has been mentioned before, and having done so will allow her to relate what was said by the abuser and when. This allows CPS investigators to understand what she is doing to protect her children and that she is doing her best. If a separation has already occurred, she can help the investigator understand that doing so became necessary to protect not only herself, but also (or especially) the children. Children who witness the abuse of their mother are also being abused, whether or not the abuser has directed harm toward the children.

As intrusive as it feels to have a social worker involved with the family, many positive outcomes are possible. If a mother has been isolated, the involvement of CPS breaches that seclusion. A mother may receive badly needed services and helps; her partner may be held accountable for his actions toward the mom and the children; her abuser may receive the services he needs; and, ultimately, the involvement of Social Services may help her leave the abuser at the right time.[26]

26. Bancroft, *When Dad Hurts Mom*, 193.

## Scriptural Encouragement

Mothers try to do their best for children while the abuser uses his tactics of control. Parenting is hard, and even harder when violence exists in the home. A victim's focus on staying safe and protecting her children may take energy away from other nurturing aspects of being a parent. Poor mental or physical health and the need to continually navigate difficulties created by her abuser take a toll. It helps to have sound principles for parenting already "planted" in one's head so one can recall them in the more difficult moments of child rearing and avoid an inappropriate response.

Awareness is often the impetus to seek help. For example, a victim preoccupied with protecting herself and her children may not fully recognize that the children are missing the more nurturing side of parenting. Or perhaps a mom lacks confidence in her own good-sense parenting ideas because of the father's insistence on how she must discipline the children.

What does the best parenting help look like, and how does one determine which style is best for the family? Research can tell us which style of parenting provides the most benefits to children globally, but not necessarily for a specific family or in a given culture. We may know and consult with parents who have already raised children successfully. Thoughtful and caring parents have a lot of wisdom to impart and can provide a lot of encouragement. Ultimately, the best way to determine how to parent most effectively is to gain information about parenting and ask for wisdom from the one perfect parent: our heavenly Father.

In 2 Corinthians 6:18, we are told that God will be our father: "and I will be your father, and you shall be my sons and daughters, says the Lord Almighty." As our parent, God provides instruction and involvement. Psalm 25:12 says, "Who are they that fear the Lord? He will teach them the way that they should choose." Through instruction, our heavenly parent gives us boundaries, explaining what we should do and what we should not do and offering a clear understanding of both, often explaining both good and bad consequences. As parents, we need to provide our children instruction, and they need to see we have unwavering interest in them through that instruction and involvement.

When parents give children boundaries at home, the children are able to more easily navigate the world around them at home, school, and work. Parental boundaries allow children to feel safer and more secure. Predictability implies that there are certainties in life and prevents anxiety. Likewise, knowing God's rules helps people of all ages know how to better navigate the world around them. The Bible provides insight for all life events, from how to handle offenses from others to how to experience a successful marriage.

Our Lord gives us sacrificial, everlasting love and offers forgiveness. Psalm 103:12 tells us that "as far as the east is from the west, so far he removes our transgressions from us." Hebrews 8:12 does as well: "For I will be merciful toward their iniquities, and I will remember their sins no more." We often quote John 3:16 as a verse that encapsulates the love available to all of us and the sacrifice made because of that love: "For God so loved the world that he gave his only Son, so that everyone who believes in him may not perish but may have eternal life." As we parent, we love our children, sacrifice for them, and forgive them when they make unhealthy, damaging decisions or do things they should not. Loving our children means we will teach them, involve ourselves in their lives, sacrifice for them, and forgive them. Every attribute of God shows us a quality that leads to good parenting.

Those in the church can be encouraged to spend time with children who live in homes where domestic violence occurs or has occurred. We do not always know what a family experiences at home; consequently, we may not recognize which families could benefit from our help. But those who have identified such a family can provide the blessing of giving time and a period of relief to the children as well as to the protective mother. Doing so provides the children with an example of healthy family living and a respite for a mother who is trying to manage protecting the children while keeping the abuser appeased. Knowing they are in safe, loving hands for a time gives her a precious gift.

7

# Women, Children, and Court Culture

## Case Study

A FTER ALMOST THREE YEARS of continual court appearances, a court-approved parenting plan was finally approved. During this time, Lori struggled with Damon's lies about her, about the children, and about her ability as a mother. He lied to his lawyer, the guardian ad litem, and the judge, both face-to-face and in the form of motions in which Lori and her parents were defamed. Lori's main concern was to keep her children as safe as possible. Damon's main concern was to gain control of the children, which would show Lori who truly had control. But the final parenting plan did not keep the children safe. As Lori and Damon stood with their lawyers in the courtroom as the judge announced the final court order, Lori's face fell in fear and disappointment and Damon displayed an angry expression. The judge said, "I know I've made the right judgment when both parents are upset with the decision."

Lori immediately felt fear for her children and foresaw many more struggles ahead with Damon because he had been granted liberal parenting time and shared legal custody. Damon's anger came from his desire for more control. Throughout the long process of waiting for the final court order, Lori kept hearing from the guardian ad litem, the lawyers, and the judge that the top priority was the best interest of the children (known as BIC in the court system).

Lori believed that the court had failed her, and especially her children, in their so-called attempt to prioritize BIC. A later court order was needed to address Damon's hostility toward Lori when they met to hand the children over to one another, requiring that both parents stay a good distance

# Women, Children, and Court Culture

## Case Study

A FTER ALMOST THREE YEARS of continual court appearances, a court-approved parenting plan was finally approved. During this time, Lori struggled with Damon's lies about her, about the children, and about her ability as a mother. He lied to his lawyer, the guardian ad litem, and the judge, both face-to-face and in the form of motions in which Lori and her parents were defamed. Lori's main concern was to keep her children as safe as possible. Damon's main concern was to gain control of the children, which would show Lori who truly had control. But the final parenting plan did not keep the children safe. As Lori and Damon stood with their lawyers in the courtroom as the judge announced the final court order, Lori's face fell in fear and disappointment and Damon displayed an angry expression. The judge said, "I know I've made the right judgment when both parents are upset with the decision."

Lori immediately felt fear for her children and foresaw many more struggles ahead with Damon because he had been granted liberal parenting time and shared legal custody. Damon's anger came from his desire for more control. Throughout the long process of waiting for the final court order, Lori kept hearing from the guardian ad litem, the lawyers, and the judge that the top priority was the best interest of the children (known as BIC in the court system).

Lori believed that the court had failed her, and especially her children, in their so-called attempt to prioritize BIC. A later court order was needed to address Damon's hostility toward Lori when they met to hand the children over to one another, requiring that both parents stay a good distance

109

from each other. As a result, grandparents facilitated the exchanges and the parents stayed in the doorway of the house or in the vehicle.

Soon after the judge devised the final parenting plan, Lori took Poppy to her regular appointment with the therapist. Poppy, crying and screaming, refused to get out of the car to walk into the building. She told Lori she never wanted to see this therapist again. Lori asked if she wanted to see another therapist and Poppy responded affirmatively. After more research and interviews, Lori located another therapist for her daughter. Poppy seemed to enjoy her time with the therapist and looked forward to those weekly visits until a few months later, when, again, Poppy refused to get out of the car. In tears, Poppy reported that her father was angry with her because the therapist called him and said that she had told her bad things about him in one of her sessions. Lori could not help Poppy understand that her therapist would not do such a thing, and that maybe Daddy made a mistake. Later, the therapist explained to Lori that an abusive father will often try to sabotage their child's relationship with a therapist to protect himself.

The court order giving Damon liberal time with the children and shared legal custody set the stage for many years of Damon's efforts to control and manipulate Lori and the children, often using the court system to do so.

## Court Culture Described

Court culture stems from the beliefs and behaviors of judges, those acting in behalf of the court (e.g., guardians ad litem, Social Services, etc.), and court administrators who influence how legal rulings are implemented. Court culture incorporates its own philosophies and ways of doing business and operates differently than our overarching culture. Because humans have many frailties, every workplace has challenges and needs for improvement. The court system is no different. Those working within the courts who deal with domestic violence cases need to become more knowledgeable about domestic violence. In particular, they should be educated about the potential repercussions of a bad decision, including potential harm to mothers and children. Law schools, seminaries, psychology training, police academies, counseling courses, and more are often woefully lacking in instruction and training in the area of domestic violence and rarely reach the depth of knowledge needed for professionals and officials to perform their future jobs adequately.

Individuals working in the court system as lawyers, guardians ad litem, judges, and others need to be aware of their own flaws, biases, prejudices, and knowledge gaps, and how these can affect people's lives. Court decisions in a domestic violence case can create great adversity for the protective parent, but those decisions also adversely affect the children, and sometimes do more harm to the children than to the protective parent.

Individual responses from those associated with the court, whether by a judge, investigator, or others, can also have a great impact. Sometimes these comments appear unfair, like the judge's remark when both parents showed disappointment over his decision. In another example, the mother of an abuse victim attended court as a support to her daughter. The mother followed her daughter's lawyer's advice concerning how to present herself in court: how to dress, how to sit quietly, how to behave, etc. Suddenly, part way through addressing her daughter's case, the judge looked straight at the mother, pointed at her, and said, "And I don't want to see that woman in my courtroom again!" When the daughter questioned her lawyer about why that happened, the lawyer said that there is nothing to be done about it, and to just mind the judge.

The court officials may also believe common myths concerning domestic violence. Trying to persuade the court otherwise often leads to disappointment. A common saying comes to mind: People don't know what they don't know. Too often, the court does not want to know what they do not know.

A significant part of the problem stems from the differences between family law and domestic violence law. Too often, family law overrides domestic violence law and enacts unsafe decisions for the protective mother and the children. Farney and Valente, in their 2003 article in the *Juvenile and Family Court Journal*, explain the intersection of family law and domestic violence law and explain why the courts often discount domestic violence in their decisions. They cite six assumptions for both types of law, show how these assumptions conflict, and explain how the ultimate decisions made by the court tend to often place domestic violence victims and their children at risk:

1. Domestic violence law assumption: Physical threat or harm, including emotional and financial abuse must be taken seriously; family law

assumption: Domestic violence is not a factor if serious bodily harm or an imminent threat is lacking.[1]

2. Domestic violence law assumption: "Granting custody or visitation to the abuser can place both the domestic violence survivor and child in danger"[2]; family law assumption: "Evidence of emotional abuse or violence toward intimate partners may be irrelevant to the issue of someone's fitness as a parent."[3]

3. Domestic violence law assumption: "Obtain structured agreements and schedules through the court process to avoid contact or negotiation for the abused party; do not mediate"[4]; family law assumption: Parties have the responsibility of determining a mutual agreement, as any party unwilling to do so is considered "unfriendly."[5]

4. Domestic violence law assumption: "Creativity and persistence are important to outcomes that will not further opportunities for control, harassment, or abuse"[6]; family law assumption: It is punitive to deny an abusive parent custody or contact with the children.[7]

5. Domestic violence law assumption: The different forms of relief must, together, include plans that prevent the abuser from using "financial, property, or decision-making power to harm the survivor and the children"[8]; family law assumption: Domestic violence is an irrelevant issue because it is outside family law, and using "more than one remedy is viewed as strategic litigiousness."[9]

6. Domestic violence law assumption: "Hold abuser accountable; enforce orders and respond to violations quickly and consistently"[10]; family law assumption: "The victimized party has the responsibility for making the order and the relationship work."[11]

1. Farney and Valente, "Creating Justice Through Balance," 40.
2. Farney and Valente, "Creating Justice Through Balance," 41.
3. Farney and Valente, "Creating Justice Through Balance," 41.
4. Farney and Valente, "Creating Justice Through Balance," 41.
5. Farney and Valente, "Creating Justice Through Balance," 41.
6. Farney and Valente, "Creating Justice Through Balance," 42.
7. Farney and Valente, "Creating Justice Through Balance," 42.
8. Farney and Valente, "Creating Justice Through Balance," 43.
9. Farney and Valente, "Creating Justice Through Balance," 43.
10. Farney and Valente, "Creating Justice Through Balance," 43.
11. Farney and Valente, "Creating Justice Through Balance," 43.

Conflicts between domestic violence law and family law lead to a court culture that continues to put victims of abuse and children at risk.

## Court Professionals' Preparedness

### LACK OF DOMESTIC VIOLENCE EDUCATION

In Lori's case, the best interest of the children was not upheld because the lawyers, the guardian ad litem, and the judge were abysmally ignorant concerning domestic violence. Some protective mothers lose custody of their children, some lose all parenting rights, and others lose the ability to have any time with their children. To properly address domestic violence cases, in-depth education and ongoing instruction are needed. Protective mothers and those who work in the domestic violence field fully appreciate those court agents who do have the necessary knowledge about domestic violence. However, there are too few of them to serve the large number of domestic violence cases.

Too many lawyers, guardians ad litem, mediators, and judges who deal with family law and parental recommendations for the court lack the tools necessary to fulfill the job at hand. Comprehensive understanding and full knowledge of domestic abuse must be found in their "tool box." Doctors and nurses cannot do their jobs if they do not have a stethoscope; a draftsperson cannot do the job if there is no pencil; a mechanic cannot perform work without a proper wrench; a chef cannot prepare food without a culinary knife. Neither can judges, lawyers, mediators, nor custody evaluators do their jobs without fully understanding domestic violence issues.

> Attorneys routinely spend enormous amounts of time and energy to learn about technical and scientific areas of knowledge when they seek to help their clients in cases involving medical issues, accident cases or criminal issues, but have never made a similar effort to understand domestic violence even when they handle dozens or hundreds of these cases.[12]

Given the high percentage of couples for whom domestic violence is the reason for divorce, any professional involved in family law and custody recommendations should invest in the time needed to fully understand their subject matter. A study of reasons for divorce involved fifty-two participants who had also participated in a Prevention and Relationship Enhancement

12. Goldstein, "How Can Protective Mothers Find a Good Attorney?," para. 2.

Program (PREP) while engaged to be married. Findings revealed that 23.5 percent claimed domestic violence as their reason for divorce.[13]

The 1995 Family Violence Project reported that "training of family law attorneys on domestic violence is low, [and] the quality of representation provided to battered mothers is often inadequate."[14] Not only does the lack of domestic violence training leave battered women and their children in unsafe situations, but also without the justice they deserve. Those who handle domestic violence cases must be able to identify them as such and learn how to best handle related custody and parenting decisions.

## MEDIATION

Court mediation provides a way toward settlement in divorce cases, relieves the court's time and schedule, and helps couples arrive at a mutual agreement. As a neutral third party, the mediator helps couples come to an agreement concerning issues such as division of property, custody, and parenting of children.

Intimate partner violence complicates the mediation process significantly. A good outcome hinges on whether the mediator has sufficient domestic violence training; whether the mediator can identify intimate partner abuse; victim protection before, during, and after sessions; and whether the outcome is fair to all parties.[15] A batterer often becomes more abusive after separation and divorce, so he could make threats related to what happens in the mediation room. In mediation, women often agree with what the abuser wants to protect herself and her children.

The National Institute of Justice funded a study that involved 965 couples who engaged in mediation in Pima County, Arizona, to resolve "custody and parenting disputes."[16]

> Based on a semi-structured clinical interview with each of the parents individually, mediators identified intimate partner violence in 59 percent of cases based on the clinical interview. The researchers concluded that mediators identified many, but not all, cases of self-reported intimate partner violence and suggested that classification based on a nonsystematic, semi-structured interview may

13. Scott et al., "Reasons for Divorce," para. 15.

14. Bancroft and Silverman, *The Batterer as Parent*, 122.

15. National Institute of Justice, "Mandatory Divorce Custody Mediation," para. 2–3.

16. National Institute of Justice, "Mandatory Divorce Custody Mediation," para. 3.

not be the best method for identifying intimate partner violence. They further found that safety accommodations were provided most frequently for those participants who specifically requested it and that only about 19 percent of all couples received at least one accommodation, despite a much higher prevalence of intimate partner violence overall.[17]

The study also found that, in the cases where there was intimate partner violence, there was a much lower likelihood of custody agreements, and mediated agreements "rarely restricted parenting or contact between parents."[18]

## Bias against Women

### Gender.

Our decisions can be skewed as the result of beliefs and attitudes we hold, whether or not we realize it. In domestic violence cases, blaming the victim is commonplace and often viewed as valid:

> The beliefs held by many custody evaluators—that domestic violence is irrelevant to custody, that women often make false allegations of abuse, that a father's parental rights are the most important consideration, and that victims are partially responsible for their own abuse—may be explained by gender bias and certain other cognitive biases that cause victim-blaming. These biases are evident in the beliefs they hold and are often influenced by their lack of knowledge about domestic violence and victimhood. The biases then affect the recommendations that evaluators make.[19]

Stereotypes about women often lead people to mistrust their accusations, which can lead to blaming the victim and even punishing her for those accusations. Even today, there are those who believe that there are times that abuse of a woman is justified. Not that long ago, the law supported the husband striking his wife.

---

17. National Institute of Justice, "Mandatory Divorce Custody Mediation," para. 3.
18. National Institute of Justice, "Mandatory Divorce Custody Mediation," para. 5.
19. Perrin, "Overcoming Biased Views of Gender and Victimhood," 167.

## *Mental Health.*

Evaluators often have a low view a woman's ability to parent when the evaluator observes a woman's demeanor and behaviors, which result from fear, anxiety, depression, PTSD, or anger stemming from the abuse. Her angst becomes compounded when court process and decisions have the potential of putting her and her children at risk. An abused woman also fears not being believed; indeed, often those evaluating her, her abuser, and the children do not believe her assertions. A custody evaluator may interpret these behaviors as indicators of inferior parenting, but they are more likely the results of the abuse she and the children have suffered, fear of not being believed, and fear of the court's eventual decisions. Too many erroneously believe that standard personality or psychopathology testing is adequate in potential domestic violence cases.

## *Parenting.*

Bancroft et al., show that there are discrepancies in how court professionals assess good parenting in the mother and then in the father, generally holding the mother to a much higher standard. Women's parenting evaluations usually rest on "their actual history of performance as parents and father's . . . on the basis of their expressions of emotion and their stated intentions for the future."[20] Also, custody evaluators tend to hold women accountable for not protecting their children from an abusive parent rather than holding the abusive parent accountable for the abuse.[21] Too often, assessors view a father's parenting as good if he simply wants to spend time with his children.

## Suppositions and Misconceptions

### *Domestic Violence is Irrelevant when Determining a Parenting Plan.*

In the mid-1700s, *Blackstone's Commentaries on the Laws of England* described domestic violence law as one where a husband had the right to keep his wife in line in the same manner he would "correct his servants or children,"[22] including beating. From there, we move to the early 1800s to

20. Bancroft and Silverman, *The Batterer as Parent*, 121.

21. Bancroft and Silverman, *The Batterer as Parent*, 121.

22. Farney and Valente, "Creating Justice Through Balance," 38 n. 26.

the case of *Bradley v. Mississippi*, where "husbands could beat their wives with a rod or stick as long as the instrument was less than the diameter of the base of the husband's thumb."[23] In the latter half of the 1800s, the idea of men correcting their wives evolved into the understanding that women should submit to domestic violence, as they may "improve," but excessive force leading to permanent injury was not acceptable.[24] During the feminist movement of the 1960s and the battered women's movement of the 1970s, public opinion was that family members needed to be "free from abuse" and that abusers should be punished.[25]

Nonetheless, today, many judges, guardians ad litem, and lawyers do not view domestic violence as relevant when formulating a parenting plan. The courts too often view domestic violence cases as ones where both parties need to work cooperatively to resolve their issues. But cooperation requires low conflict and effective communication.

Because a batterer's abuse and efforts to control do not stop after separation or divorce, a parenting plan must include safety measures for both the mother and the children. If the abuser harmed the children before separation or divorce, the abuse will not stop afterward. If an abuser has access to his children without supervision, he will likely use them to show the mother that he still has control.

We have learned that just because a child does not show fear or anxiety when with the abusive parent, that does not mean they are safe or even comfortable being around that parent. Trauma bonding can create an illusion of a loving relationship. Or the child may be on their best behavior in order to stay safe or earn their father's favor. Outward appearances do not reflect the reality of continuing domestic violence.

The courts may view a separation as a cure for the children's difficulties. After the parents separate, however, the children do not automatically bounce back from the psychological and physical problems caused by the bad experiences they had when their father and mother lived together. Seeing and hearing their mother being abused has the same impact as if they were themselves "directly physically or sexually abused."[26] As they grow into adults, they will have a higher risk for health problems and violent crimes.[27]

23. Farney and Valente, "Creating Justice Through Balance," 38 n. 27.
24. Farney and Valente, "Creating Justice Through Balance," 38.
25. Farney and Valente, "Creating Justice Through Balance," 38.
26. Domesticshelters.org, "5 Myths," para. 9.
27. Domesticshelters.org, "5 Myths," para. 9.

Separation also does not prevent a child's ongoing abuse from their father when he has unsupervised parenting time.

### *Domestic Violence Allegations are False or Overstated.*

Too often, people make judgments about others' situations without knowing the facts and considering the evidence. Victims of abuse can be revictimized through others' bad judgments or misunderstandings about the actual situation. Those unfamiliar with the dynamics of domestic violence may ask questions such as, "If Jack abused her, why didn't she call the police?" "Why has she decided to complain now if this has been going on for years?" "Why didn't she leave?" Others may claim that abused women falsely accuse the abuser of harming her and/or the children in order to discredit him and gain an advantage in court cases. The reality is that false allegations from a woman are very infrequent (less than two percent), whereas false allegations from an abusive man are considerably more frequent (abusive men are "16 times more likely to make deliberate false reports").[28] Women are more likely to keep their abuse to themselves and not reveal the experiences they have had with the abuser.[29] It is far more common for a woman to lie to conceal abuse than to fabricate a story that she has been abused.

### *The Victim is also Responsible for the Abuse.*

Claiming that a victim is at least partially responsible for the abuse contains echoes of archaic domestic violence laws: "If she would submit more to her husband, he wouldn't have to keep her in line." Uninformed faith leaders still tell women that they just need to submit more to their abuser, and sometimes they are told to pray harder because they may not be praying hard enough. One abuse victim's pastor told her that she needed to submit to her husband's desire for sexual contact in ways that also physically hurt the victim.

To say that a victim is also responsible for the abuse plays into the hands of the abuser, who often will tell the victim that she is responsible because of something she said or did. The victim does not "make" the abuser

28. DomesticShelters.org, "Do Survivors Lie?," para. 9.
29. DomesticShelters.org, "Do Survivors Lie?," para. 8.

harm her or the children. He is responsible for his actions; the victim does not bear any responsibility for the abuse.

### Children Need the Father's Involvement.

Domestic abusers use control, including intimidation, as the foundation for how they treat their wives and children. They not only lack empathy, but also nurturing qualities and a recognition of their children's needs. In these situations, a role reversal often takes place, where the children believe that they are responsible for taking care of their father.[30]

An abuser is a poor role model. Children need to be able to look up to the adults in their lives and imitate good attitudes and behaviors. Domestic abusers do not model a caring, cooperative, or empathetic attitude. Many of the tactics used against the mother they also use with their children: threats, manipulations, lying, making false promises, and more.

Abusive men generally use the authoritarian style of parenting. For an abuser, excessive amounts of harshness and rigidity are common.[31] They may expect obedience from children without the nurturing element of helping them to understand why the behavior is important. This type of parenting can become dictatorial and hurtful.

Abusive fathers also use their time with the children to discredit their mother and try to harm their relationship with her. The father's connection with the children allows him to use them against the protective mother. He may use them to pass messages to her, finding out where she has been and where she is going, and generally to stay in the life of the mother in unfavorable, threatening, and harmful ways.

When a father has abused his children directly, they are at very high risk for abuse after separation when he has them in his custody. Even when children's physical safety is not in jeopardy, their emotional and developmental wellbeing is at risk.

### Misunderstood View of Mother.

Because of the mental health issues that develop in abused women, they often do not present a good appearance in court. A woman may dissociate,

---

30. Fontes, "10 Risks of Domestic Abusers as Parents," para. 6.
31. Fontes, "10 Risks of Domestic Abusers as Parents," para. 8.

be depressed, or exhibit PTSD symptoms. She may look angry, fearful, sad, anxious, or distracted. Imagine the difficulty a woman has in speaking to the judge or taking the stand and facing her abuser in court. Imagine the stress of appearing in court when she realizes that the court regularly makes wrong decisions in domestic violence cases. The court's lack of understanding of the psychology of abused women can lead to a complete misinterpretation of the indicators she presents while in court or during an investigation by a custody evaluator or Social Services. This places her at a disadvantage. If others are suspicious of her assertions about the abuse, the so-called friendly parent statutes work against her:

> Friendly parent principle is a principle of family law that if one parent is more likely to support the child's relationship with the other parent after a divorce is granted, then that more supportive parent should be awarded custody. However, this theory is subject to much criticisms [sic] as the theory's simplicity discourages a parent from revealing anything negative about the other parent to the child, even if relevant to the child's safety, for fear of being viewed as too hostile. Further, the court may not consider the legitimate fears and concerns that motivate a parent's unfriendly behavior.[32]

From the beginning of the court experience, a woman has the disadvantage of having to face her abuser. Court professionals too often seem oblivious to what this direct contact means for an abused woman.

## The Batterer's Advantage in Court

The batterer has advantages in court in addition to those already noted. Family law "is frequently inadequate to address domestic violence."[33] In child custody cases, family law concerns itself with the qualifications a person has to parent and the process of making that determination.[34] A batterer can be skilled at appearing to be winsome and capable and a warm, qualified parent when an assessor is watching. Children may long for the opportunity to experience good attention from their father, and so they seem attentive and caring as well.

Prior to the 1970s, women may have had an advantage in efforts to secure custody of the children because of the "tender years doctrine," which

32. US Legal, "Friendly-Parent Principle Law and Legal Definition," para. 1.
33. Farney and Valente, "Creating Justice Through Balance," 35.
34. Farney and Valente, "Creating Justice Through Balance," 36.

held that mothers should care for younger children. Since then, fathers have had a specific advantage in custody cases:

> A call for gender-neutrality grounded in equal-rights philosophy, fathers' rights activism, and research on children of divorce all contributed to the 1970s "best interests of the child" standard for custody decisions. The key aspect to "best interests" became the underlying assumption that the court be gender-blind in its choice between two "fit" parents so as to provide the "least detrimental alternative."[35]

The court cannot and should not treat a domestic violence divorce like any other divorce, even a "contentious divorce." The court too often does not consider domestic violence when determining custody, putting the children at risk of harm.

Abusers persist in their mistreatment of the mother and oftentimes will use the court system as an instrument. An abuser will continue to undermine the mother's parenting and authority, and will attempt to damage her relationship with her children. The abuser will even attempt to ruin the children's relationships with their therapist, as Damon did more than once.

Another important consideration is that fathers generally have more money to spend on lawyers than their victims do.[36] Victims are often pushed into the position of settling rather than spending more money on lawyers.

## Children Harmed by the Courts

Judges regularly award abusive fathers shared or full custody of the children, creating a pathway for additional abuse. Sometimes good, protective mothers lose all ability to spend time with their children. "In child custody cases, courts overwhelmingly side with the manipulative, abusive fathers."[37] This leads to continued adverse childhood experiences and may even end in the death of the mother and/or the children.

A 2011 report published by the US Department of Justice states:

> High rates of domestic violence exist in families referred for child custody evaluations. These evaluations can produce potentially harmful outcomes, including the custody of children being

---

35. Farney and Valente, "Creating Justice Through Balance," 37 n. 18.
36. Custody X Change. "Family Court Bias Against Mothers: Real or Not?," para. 11.
37. Goldstein, "California Courts Harm Kids by Ignoring the Science," para. 1.

awarded to a violent parent, unsupervised or poorly supervised visitation between violent parents and their children, and mediation sessions that increase danger to domestic violence victims. Past research shows that domestic violence is frequently undetected in custody cases or ignored as a significant factor in custody-visitation determinations. Previous research also indicates that violence—and its harmful effects on victims and children—often continues or increases after separation.[38]

Children who have adverse childhood experiences (ACEs), or "potentially traumatic events that occur in childhood (0–17 years) such as experiencing violence, abuse, or neglect; witnessing violence in the home; and having a family member attempt or die by suicide . . . can have effects that persist for years."[39] A poor court decision puts children at continued risk not only during childhood, but also into adulthood. Negative consequences impact their long term "health, wellbeing, and opportunity."[40] ACE research by the Centers for Disease Control shows:

> These exposures [to traumatic events] can disrupt healthy brain development, affect social development, compromise immune systems, and can lead to substance misuse and other unhealthy coping behaviors. The evidence confirms that these exposures increase the risks of injury, sexually transmitted infections, including HIV, mental health problems, maternal and child health problems, teen pregnancy, involvement in sex trafficking, a wide range of chronic diseases and the leading causes of death such as cancer, diabetes, heart disease, and suicide. ACE's can also negatively impact education, employment, and earnings potential. The total economic and social costs to families, communities, and society is in the hundreds of billions of dollars each year.[41]

When courts make harmful decisions concerning children in domestic violence families, the consequences, for the children, last a lifetime.

---

38. Saunders et al., "Child Custody Evaluators' Beliefs," 4.

39. Centers for Disease Control, "Preventing Adverse Childhood Experiences," 7 n. 1, 2. Felitti et al., National Child Traumatic Stress Network.

40. Centers for Disease Control, "Preventing Adverse Childhood Experiences," 7.

41. Centers for Disease Control, "Preventing Adverse Childhood Experiences," 7 n. 1, 4, 9, 10, 16, 17, 18, 21. Felitti et al., Hillis et al., Leeb et al., Dube et al., Metzler et al., Peterson et al., Peterson et al.

## Court Appearance Recommendations

The information provided here does not constitute legal advice, but helpful suggestions for a victim during the court process. Usually, a victim has a lawyer whom she relies on for legal advice. She may also have an advocate who can provide help in understanding the court process, provide encouragement, and identify resources.

### Finding a Lawyer

Finding the right lawyer, one who is well informed about domestic violence issues, can be a daunting task. A good attorney will be honest about what the court will likely do or decide. Barry Goldstein, a former attorney who now advocates for protective mothers, gives some suggestions in trying to find the right lawyer:

> Attorneys have distinct roles to provide advice that might be hard to hear and to advocate for you once a strategy is decided. The attorney needs to understand that the mother is the expert on what the father might do; the research has the expertise on what is best for the children and the attorney is the expert in what the judge is likely to do. The attorney must be willing to understand and learn about the reality in order to have an informed discussion.[42]

Goldstein also emphasizes the importance of enlisting help from an attorney who will "present the research and other evidence" to the court.[43] Some judges have beliefs that run contrary to the evidence and research. Thus, the attorney must warn the client if the judge handling her case harbors those beliefs, while still understanding that the client has the last word concerning whether the evidence of abuse will be presented or not.[44]

As mentioned before, a high-conflict or contentious divorce is not the same as a domestic violence divorce. An attorney must understand the differences and prepare for a trial, whether the case ultimately has one or not.[45] An attorney for a protective mother also needs to ask the court to consider research that refutes the belief that children can be safe in the

---

42. Goldstein, "How Can Protective Mothers Find a Good Attorney?," para. 7.
43. Goldstein, "How Can Protective Mothers Find a Good Attorney?," para. 8.
44. Goldstein, "How Can Protective Mothers Find a Good Attorney?," para. 8.
45. Goldstein, "How Can Protective Mothers Find a Good Attorney?," para. 10.

custody of an abusive father, and must encourage the mother to advocate for her children.[46]

## PRESENTATION IN COURT

Try to visit the courthouse ahead of time to familiarize yourself with its appearance and layout. Knowing the location of parking, the clerk's office, courtrooms, and restrooms ahead of time removes some of the anxiety and will produce more confidence.

Preparing the evening before makes it easier and less stressful to arrive at court on time, which means arriving at least fifteen minutes early. Decide on clothing the evening before and plan what to eat for breakfast. Be neat and clean, which communicates to the judge that you respect the court and take it seriously. Have any needed paperwork and documents ready the night before.

Taking the court seriously also means waiting until after leaving court to tell jokes, laugh, or giggle. Those attending court with the victim to provide moral support must understand the need for seriousness. Simply sit quietly while waiting. Additionally, "do not chew gum, eat, drink, read a newspaper, sleep, wear a hat, listen to earphones, use a cell phone, camera, or camera phone, or carry a weapon."[47] Today, courts will generally screen for weapons, cell phones, and food.

Try to remain calm and in control of any emotions during court proceedings. If a short break is needed, simply ask for one. Keep hands away from the mouth and speak clearly so the judge and, in the case of a trial, all jury members can hear what is being said. If the proceeding is a trial, then look at the jury when speaking and speak loudly enough for each of them to hear. Otherwise, look at the judge when speaking and address her or him as "Your Honor." Do not interrupt others when they are speaking, even if they are interruptive. And above all, tell the truth.

If a question is not clear or understandable, or if the opposing lawyer is asking a leading question, ask that the question be rephrased. Try not to be intimidated by an aggressive lawyer; a defense attorney will try to make a plaintiff's testimony appear untrustworthy. That is their job.

Finally, refrain from talking about the case in the hallways or restrooms, because someone else involved in the case may hear. One mother of

---

46. Goldstein, "How Can Protective Mothers Find a Good Attorney?," para. 11.

47. Northwest Justice Project, "Getting Ready for a Court Trial or Hearing," 6.

a victim, as she made copies of a document in the clerk's office, overheard a witness for the opposing side speaking with the opposing lawyer about the case. The mother of the victim gave the information to her daughter's lawyer, which proved helpful. In this case, the information benefitted the victim, but it could easily have been the opposite.

## FACING THE ABUSER

Facing the abuser in court can be daunting but also empowering as the victim has an opportunity to speak her truth. She will have to appear in court with the abuser present during divorce proceedings or if she is defending her request to extend an order of protection (restraining order). The victim will also have to face her abuser when she appears in court to protect her children in custody cases. Likewise, she will face him if there is an accusation of abuse of the children.

When a court date approaches, victims can take action to diminish feelings of anxiety. The National Center on Domestic Violence suggests that lawyers and clients strategize to avoid potential triggers in court:

> A good course of practice in your work with survivors of domestic violence is to anticipate some of the ways trauma can manifest itself. Start by creating a partnership, proactively providing information about trauma and how it can come up in court, and asking survivors if they would like to strategize with you around ways that the legal process might be triggering or retraumatizing. In general, work with survivors of domestic violence in ways that help them to identify and prepare for trauma triggers in every step of their legal case.[48]

Of course, not every victim will attend court with a lawyer or have the help of a victim's advocate (ask if one is available). A supportive parent, friend, or therapist can help to reduce anxiety.

Ask a friend or family member to attend court with you and ask them to stay with you as you move through the courthouse and to and from the parking lot or public transit. Remember to not discuss your case with the supportive person in the courthouse, including its restrooms.

Arrive early in an effort to avoid your abuser in the lobby or parking lot and to avoid traffic or lines entering the courthouse. Leave the children at home with a caretaker, as the court experience and seeing their father

48. National Center on Domestic Violence, "Preparing for Court Proceedings," 2.

could be difficult. When you arrive, let the bailiff or courthouse security officer know if you have a restraining order; regardless, they can keep him away from you. Do not initiate or receive conversation with the abuser or anyone who might attend court with him to support him.

If the victim leaves court after the abuser leaves, he cannot follow her. Someone (your friend or family member, lawyer, advocate, or a member of law enforcement in the court house) should accompany her to the car or bus stop for added assurance of safety. If the protective mother wants to leave first, the abuser can be restrained by law enforcement or his attorney long enough for her to leave. If the victim has an advocate or lawyer, one of them can ask the opposing lawyer to hold him back.

## CUSTODY DETERMINATIONS

### *Journaling.*

A journal will help a protective mother, especially when she endeavors to counter the abuser's false assertions. The journal will ensure that she will have recorded evidence providing dates and times for certain occurrences. The mother must remember to describe the situation accurately. Keeping a journal may also help dispel the notion that the protective mother exaggerates or skews her concerns about the father. Journaling can help the victim's lawyer and custody evaluators. Store the journal in a secure place where the abuser cannot find it.

### *Custody Evaluators.*

Custody evaluators, also known as guardians ad litem in some states, have the responsibility for conducting a complete investigation of the family with regard to those issues assigned to them by the court. After the custody evaluator has completed inquiries of the parents' collaterals and observations of the children and parents, his/her recommendations are used by the court to make final decisions about custody and other matters.

Very few courts require that custody evaluators have specialized domestic violence training.[49] Consequently, evaluators often make judgments and recommendations they do not have qualifications to make.

49. Pence, "Mind the Gap," 32.

The victim can help the evaluator best by presenting as much useful information as possible, including a list of those people she wants the evaluator to interview. This may include family, friends, medical clinicians (for both her and the children), teachers, and other witnesses who may have helpful information, such as former partner(s) of the abuser. She can also provide criminal records and police reports, child protective services documentation, and other documents and recordings.

Being interviewed by someone who will make custody recommendations to the court may cause a high level of stress and anxiety, but remaining as calm as possible during the interview will help. When the evaluator views the mother and children together, staying calm not only benefits the mother, but the children as well. Children sense their mother's angst, which makes the situation more difficult for them.

Always provide the evaluator with the truth.

*Parental Alienation Syndrome.*

Parental Alienation Syndrome, a theory developed by psychiatrist Richard Gardner in 1987,[50] has not been found to be scientifically sound and is not found in the *Diagnostic and Statistical Manual of Mental Health Diseases.* Abusers will often attempt to use PAS in court as a reason to gain favor and to further abuse the victim. This often happens when the children do not want to spend time with their father.

Courts often hear one or both parties complain about parent alienation, which can and does often sway the court in their decisions. Even though Parent Alienation Syndrome is not a recognized syndrome, one parent can still make an effort to alienate the children from the other parent. Abusers regularly try to alienate the children from their mother, even after separation and divorce. If a mother suspects that the father is doing this, her best course of action is to consult with her lawyer.

Children are adversely affected when one parent speaks poorly of or is rude to the other. For protective mothers, not speaking poorly about the father is a part of protecting the children. This entails being careful how they speak about the children's father and what they say when the children are present. One client stated that she made a rule that no one was to speak of the father during visits. If they did, they must talk respectfully and say only benign or positive things.

50. Bancroft and Silverman, *The Batterer as Parent,* 135.

*Child Protective Services.*

For a protective mother, CPS involvement often produces angst and fear, especially if false claims have been made by the abuser, but working with them will help if there is a possibility that they might influence custody proceedings.

## Scriptural Encouragement

The controlling influence of an abusive husband and father can include physical, emotional, spiritual, sexual, and financial abuses. The house in which the protective mother resides is one of tension, anxiety, and fear. She and the children do not experience peace or feelings of safety.

Victims of abuse who are women of faith can find peace in the words of Psalm 27:4: "One thing I asked of the Lord, that I will seek after: to live in the house of the Lord all the days of my life, to behold the beauty of the Lord, and to inquire in his temple." A look at the culture of the day in which the psalmist lived can give us a deeper appreciation of its meaning.

The house referred to here is not a physical house. Only the high priest entered the "secret place of the Most High" one time each year.[51] But the psalmist requests that he "live in the house of the Lord all the days" of his life. Alexander MacLaren tells us that the fulfillment of this Scripture "depends not on where we are, but on what we think and feel; for every place is God's house, and what the Psalmist desires is that he [or she] should be able to keep up unbroken consciousness of being in God's presence and should be always in touch with Him."[52]

Dwelling in God's house means we find ourselves in his presence, not just during devotions and prayer in the morning, but in the kitchen, the grocery store, the doctor's office, the children's school, the courthouse, everywhere, all the time. According to MacLaren, to dwell in the house of the Lord

> is an allusion, not only, as I think, to the Temple, but also to the Oriental habit of giving a man who took refuge in the tent of the sheikh, guest-rites of protection and provision and friendship. The habit exists to this day, and travellers among the Bedouins tell us lovely stories of how even an enemy with the blood of the closest

51. MacLaren, "Psalm 27," para. 3.
52. MacLaren, "Psalm 27," para. 5.

relative of the owner of the tent on his hands, if he can once get in there and partake of the salt of the host, is safe, and the first obligation of the owner of the tent is to watch over the life of the fugitive as over his own. So the Psalmist says, 'I desire to have guest-rites in Thy tent; to lift up its fold, and shelter there from the heat of the desert. And although I be dark and stained with many evils and transgressions against Thee, yet I come to claim the hospitality and provision and protection and friendship which the laws of the house do bestow upon a guest.' Carrying out substantially the same idea, Paul tells the Ephesians, as if it were the very highest privilege that the Gospel brought to the Gentiles: 'Ye are no more strangers, but fellow-citizens with the saints, and of the household of God'; incorporated into His family, and dwelling safely in His pavilion as their home.[53]

Thus, regardless of what we undergo in this world full of difficulties, regardless of where we are physically or geographically, we can experience his presence.

His presence goes with the victim into a courtroom where she not only faces the abuser, but also strangers who will make recommendations and, ultimately, decisions concerning her and the children. One stranger, the abuser's lawyer, will likely make statements about the victim that are untrue and skewed, will make recommendations in the form of motions to the court that do not favor the victim, and will advocate for his or her client, sometimes making him look like the victim, but always worthy of receiving more in a settlement than he should have. Regardless of her best efforts to advocate for herself and the best efforts by her lawyer, the victim does not have control of her situation. She does not have to enter the courtroom powerless, however.

Many suggestions have been offered concerning how to prepare for court, but there is one type of preparation left to address. We may often hear encouragement to put on the armor of God every day. As described in Ephesians 6:14–17, the armor consists of the "belt of truth," the "breastplate of righteousness," the "shield of faith," the "helmet of salvation," the "sword of the spirit," and as "shoes for your feet, put on whatever will make you ready to proclaim the gospel of peace." Ephesians 6 also tells us in verse 18a to pray at all times.

What is the sword of the Spirit? Ephesians 6:17 defines it as the word of God. Having the encouragement of God's word with us provides strength,

53. MacLaren, "Psalm 27," para. 11.

comfort, peace, and the surety that his presence stays with us wherever we go. Second Corinthians 12:9–10 has been taped to the computer used while writing this book and has provided incalculable hours of support over many months:

> But he said to me, "My grace is sufficient for you, for power is made perfect in weakness." So, I will boast all the more gladly of my weaknesses, so that the power of Christ may dwell in me. Therefore I am content with weaknesses, insults, hardships, persecutions, and calamities for the sake of Christ; for whenever I am weak, then I am strong.

No matter how daunting a task may be, he is present to provide whatever we need to move through difficult situations with his grace. Hebrews 13:5 tells us that he "will never leave you or forsake you."

While there are countless helpful parts of the "sword" we may reflect on, consider Isaiah 41:10: "Do not fear, for I am with you, do not be afraid, for I am your God; I will strengthen you, I will help you, I will uphold you with my victorious right hand." Here again, God assures us that he will strengthen us during hard times. Joshua 1:9 reminds us to be "strong and courageous; do not be frightened or dismayed, for the Lord your God is with you wherever you go."

Paul, after describing the armor of God in Ephesians 6:18, tells us to pray; he tells us again in Philippians 4:5–7 to pray unceasingly:

> Let your gentleness be known to everyone. The Lord is near. Do not worry about anything, but in everything by prayer and supplication with thanksgiving let your requests be made known to God. And the peace of God, which surpasses all understanding, will guard your hearts and your minds in Christ Jesus.

Through these Scriptures, we see that God gives us strength, comfort, peace, and his presence, regardless of our situation and regardless of the outcome. He accepts us as we are with all our frailties. Prayer and the assurance of God's presence are essential parts of our preparation for stressful, difficult situations, including facing our abuser, revealing troubles to strangers in court, and having other strangers investigate our family.

# 8

# Children's Experiences

## Case Study

D EBORAH ALWAYS READ STORIES to the girls as they fell asleep in their king-sized bed. On the evenings when Lori had class, Deborah took care of Poppy and Rayne and stayed overnight so she would not have to drive the hour it took to get home late at night. Deborah would snuggle down between the girls on top of the blankets that covered them up to their necks, which made Deborah's exit easy once they both fell asleep.

One evening during bedtime reading, Poppy, who was seven, interrupted Deborah in the middle of a sentence, asking, "Do we have to go to our father's tomorrow after school?" Deborah responded by telling the girls that their dad's weekend with them started after school the next day when he would pick them up, as indicated on the calendar Lori made for them, and as she had already reminded them before leaving for class.

Poppy's appearance fell into a sadness that covered her entire face, from her deeply furrowed brow to her quivering chin. She turned her back on Deborah and told her she would not listen to the story anymore. Deborah tried active feedback, a tool to help children understand that you know what they are feeling, saying, "You don't want to go to your dad's tomorrow." Poppy responded by telling Deborah she would not go to her father's and she wanted to go to sleep. Rayne agreed. Deborah made sure both girls were tucked in, under the covers, with a kiss, and left the room. She checked on them several times before they both fell asleep. When Lori arrived home, Deborah gave her a full report.

In the morning, the girls got ready, but when they sat at the table for breakfast, they both said they did not want to go to their father's house after school. Crying and yelling in protest, both girls hid under the table.

Lori could not console them. After a few minutes passed, Poppy emerged and asked her mother where she kept her special, very sharp knife. Lori reported that it needed to be kept in a very high place because it is too sharp for children. Poppy pleaded with her mother to give her the knife because she wanted to kill herself and her sister so they could go to heaven, a safe place, away from their father, and that she wanted her mother, Deborah, and Bob to be there, too. Then she said that she would have to kill them before she could kill herself to keep everyone safe.

A look of horror suddenly passed over her face. "Oh, no, no, no! Will Daddy ever get to heaven? If he does, we can't go there!" Lori told Poppy and Rayne that everyone is very safe in heaven, and that no matter who goes there, everyone is safe. Then Poppy asked if people could go to heaven if they kill themselves. Lori, because the girls attended a Christian school, said that maybe she could talk to her teacher about that when they get to school. Poppy said that she would talk to Rayne's teacher instead, a teacher Poppy already had two years earlier. During the ride to school, the girls continued to protest going to their father's, and Lori told them that she would call their therapist and tell her how they felt.

Finally, after arriving at the school parking lot, Poppy helped Rayne out of the car, told her to stop her crying, and that they needed to talk with her teacher about heaven. Later, the teacher made a call to Lori and described the conversation the girls had with her. Lori immediately returned to school to pick up Poppy and take her to her therapist, whom she had already called. The therapist decided Poppy was not a danger to herself or to others.

During her time with the therapist, Poppy explained that on several occasions her father took a blank journal and tried to coerce her to write terrible things about her mother, saying if she did not, she would never be able to see her father or paternal grandparents again. Damon further said that she and her sister would be taken far away. He then tried to make her say bad things into a tape recorder about her mother and her maternal grandparents, telling her what to say about them. Poppy's resolve prevented her from doing so, which made her father very angry. Then Poppy reported that he had said, "I wish your mother would die!"

Upon hearing what Poppy had to say, both her therapist and Lori told Poppy that she was very brave to let them know what happened and that she did the right thing by telling them. Lori further let Poppy know that she could tell her or her therapist anything she wanted and anything that happened, and that she will never have to keep secrets about what has happened to either her or Rayne.

The therapist suggested to Lori that she obtain a restraining order against Damon on behalf of the girls, which she did, after calling Deborah to double back from her trip home to take care of Poppy while she did so. Both Lori and the therapist assured Poppy that she and Rayne would not be going to their father's that weekend.

Deborah got Poppy's favorite sandwich and juice at the local lunch café and they took their purchase to the park. Poppy smiled and sang while she chewed, and carried her sandwich in her hands while she danced around the trees and flowers, exclaiming how the park bushes were more beautiful than ever.

During the long court process that followed, the guardian ad litem assigned to the case asked that Poppy's therapist recommend another therapist to do restorative therapy to repair the relationship between Damon and the girls. Poppy and Rayne did not want to participate. Lori assured them that she would be in the waiting room the whole time and that the therapist would not leave them while their father spent time with them in her office. Lori confirmed with the therapist that this would be the case.

In the therapist's office, in the first appointment, Damon apologized to the girls. He told them he should not have tried to force Poppy to write in the journal and that he did not mean what he said about them being taken away. Very gradually, over the course of months, the girls resumed the regular parenting schedule with Damon. However, after the guardian ad litem formed her recommendations for the court, Damon told the therapist in a final session that he did not regret what he had done. He said that he believed what he did was right and he was not sorry for telling Poppy what he told her. At this juncture, since a new court order had been signed by the judge, the time had passed for Damon's statements to affect his parenting time.

## Background

Children in domestic violence families are impacted not only by the many different forms of abuse they experience directly, but also from observing the abuse of their mother. "Even when they are not physically attacked, children witness 68% to 80% of domestic assaults."[1] "Exposure to vio-

---

1. Edwards, "Alarming Effects," para. 2.

lence, whether directly or as a bystander, can have far-reaching, negative consequences for children."[2]

A 1985 survey showed that approximately 10 million children witnessed physical violence between parents.[3] This is an increase of 6.5 million from the 3.3 million children exposed in the 1970s.[4] In a 2006 report, researchers estimate that approximately 15.5 million children in the United States live in homes where IPV has taken place at least once.[5] "As many as 275 million children worldwide are exposed to IPV every year."[6] When Dad abuses Mom, whether through physical or nonphysical means, the children also experience abuse because their father has harmed their mother, even if he does not touch, speak to, or look at the children. They experience abuse even if he ignores the children.

When the mother is abused, the children are harmed in many ways:

> Exposure to violence can harm a child's emotional, psychological and even physical development. Children exposed to violence are more likely to have difficulty in school, abuse drugs or alcohol, act aggressively, suffer from depression or other mental health problems and engage in criminal behavior as adults.[7]

When they see or hear Dad harm Mom, they feel pain, fear, and guilt; guilt comes from not rescuing their mother and sometimes in thinking they are to blame for their father's behavior.[8] Even when "children don't see or hear the abusive man's mistreatment of their mother, they feel the aftershocks. They see her pain, they feel her withdrawal, they hear whisperings among their older siblings about what happened."[9] Children who witness violence are not just bystanders; they are victims of the abuse they witness.

When the children are afraid to talk about what happens in their home, they become secretive. Perhaps they fear their father, who may have warned and threatened them, or maybe they fear consequences from their father without such warnings or threats. They may think that revealing what happens will upset their mother. Mom may not be ready to speak out and

2. National Institute of Justice, "Children Exposed to Violence," para. 1.
3. Brown and Bzostek, "Violence in the Lives of Children," 4 n. 25.
4. Brown and Bzostek, "Violence in the Lives of Children," 4 n. 24.
5. McDonald et al., "Estimating the Number," para. 1.
6. Cameranesi and Pitrowski, "Self-Esteem in Children," para. 2 n. 74.
7. National Institute of Justice, "Children Exposed to Violence," para. 4.
8. Bancroft, *When Dad Hurts Mom*, 13, 66.
9. Bancroft, *When Dad Hurts Mom*, 14.

may fear the involvement of Social Services. The expectation that children must keep their trauma quiet will have lasting repercussions. Lori and the girls' therapist were very wise to tell Poppy that there are no secrets about what she experiences, that she can tell them anything, and they will listen.

## Brain Development: Emotions, Cognition, and Behaviors

Children, including infants, experience harmful effects related to brain development when they witness violence. One of the predominant things parents hear when nurturing infants is the importance of stimulating the child. Both positive and negative stimuli affect infants, specifically in the realm of neurological development. "The infant's brain and stress-related systems are especially susceptible to environment stimuli."[10]

Some researchers have discovered that adverse neurological effects occur even before birth. Currently, research does not adequately address the negative effects of exposure to intimate partner violence (IPV) during the perinatal phase and infancy, but the "assumed harm" exists.[11] The perinatal phase includes the period of time between about the twentieth to the twenty-eighth week of pregnancy to any time one to four weeks after birth.[12] Because of what research does reveal about the extent of detriment to infants, the World Health Organization recommends standardized screening for IPV during pregnancy, and they also want to see an increase in research related to prevention of IPV's adverse effects.[13]

IPV can "affect the fetus and its neurohormonal chemistry" because of the high stress levels the mother experiences during the pregnancy. These experiences also belong to the developing infant because the womb is a "shared environment."[14]

"Exposure to intimate partner violence . . . can have long-lasting effects on a child's socio-emotional and neurological development."[15] The areas of the brain affected by IPV include the "midbrain, cerebral cortex, limbic system, corpus callosum, cerebellum, and the hypothalamic, pituitary, and

10. Edwards, "Alarming Effects," para. 3 n. Siegel and Hartzell.
11. Mueller and Tronick, "Early Life Exposure to Violence," para. 2.
12. MedicineNet, "Medical Definition of Perinatal," para. 1.
13. World Health Organization, "Intimate Partner Violence during Pregnancy," 3.
14. Mueller and Tronick, "Early Life Exposure to Violence," para. 7.
15. Mueller and Tronick, "Early Life Exposure to Violence," para. 3 n. Perry, Fox et al., Bick and Nelson.

adrenal axis" (HPA), which are related to posttraumatic stress disorder.[16] The midbrain is the "'relay point' for visual and auditory messages," and children who witness IPV can also experience distraction, an inability to pay attention, attachment disorders, and attention deficit hyperactivity disorder.[17] "The limbic system (amygdala, hippocampus, and hypothalamus) houses the primitive centers for emotion, survival, fear, anger, and pleasure, including sex. It is also important for memory information and storage, as well as gauging the magnitude of a response."[18] The cortex houses executive function abilities, or cognitive skills that include the ability "to plan, organise, initiate, self-monitor and control one's responses in order to achieve a goal," and to know what consequences are attached to different actions.[19] Controlling one's responses includes control over one's emotions. The prefrontal cortex relates to "mature adult behavior, including attention, inhibition, memory, motor control, motivation, emotion, expression of personality, and moderation of learned social behavior."[20]

The frontal lobes control emotions and behaviors and are where our personality resides. These lobes undergo rapid development in the first twelve months of life.[21] Studies reveal that "early adverse environments" harm the prefrontal cortex.[22] The cerebellum deals with emotion and cognitive development and connects to the frontal lobes where behavior is regulated and can negatively affect behaviors in children who experience harm.[23] The corpus callosum connects both hemispheres of the brain and helps them communicate regarding auditory, visual, and cognitive stimuli. This communication decreases in the presence of abuse or witnessing IPV.[24]

Exposure to trauma also involves the sympathetic nervous system and the HPA axis, which activate when someone experiences a stressor. The sympathetic nervous system engages first, and then the HPA axis kicks in. Shortly after a stressor occurs, the adrenal glands become stimulated and secrete adrenalin and noradrenalin. The rush of adrenalin helps the body

16. Tsavoussis et al., "Child-Witnessed Domestic Violence," para. 1.

17. Tsavoussis et al., "Child-Witnessed Domestic Violence," para. 12.

18. Tsavoussis et al., "Child-Witnessed Domestic Violence," para. 12.

19. Queensland Health, "Brain Map Frontal Lobes," para. 1.

20. Tsavoussis et al., "Child-Witnessed Domestic Violence," para. 12.

21. Hodel, "Rapid Infant Prefrontal Cortex Development," para. 1.

22. Hodel, "Rapid Infant Prefrontal Cortex Development," para. 1.

23. Tsavoussis et al., "Child-Witnessed Domestic Violence," para. 12.

24. Tsavoussis et al., "Child-Witnessed Domestic Violence," para. 12.

prepare for the response to the stressor—sometimes thought of as a fight, flight, or freeze response. The physiological response includes an "increase in pulse, breathing and cardio-vascular efficiency, [and] dilates the bronchioles and pupils."[25] Other hormones, including cortisol, are excreted, and negatively influence the immunological system; however, short-term stress does not reduce immunity.[26] Continued and long-term stress does reduce immunity. When children who have been exposed to violence become adults, they have high levels of corticotropin releasing hormone (CRH), and "this chronic elevation leads to arousal, anxiety, aggression, hypervigilance, general sympathetic nervous system stimulation, depression, and problems with eating and sex, i.e., symptoms of PTSD and depression."[27]

There are . . .

> known effects to witnessing violence during the perinatal period on socio-emotional development and the possible pathways by which IPV affects brain and stress regulating systems. Exposure to IPV during infancy disrupts the infant's emotional and cognitive development, the development of the Hypothalamus-Pituitary-Adrenal axis and brain structures related to witnessing itself (auditory and visual cortex).[28]

The HPA axis is a responder to stress: "Stress activates a complex network of hormones known as the Hypothalamus-Pituitary-Adrenal (HPA) axis. The HPA axis is dysregulated [not controlled in the way that is normal] in chronic stress and psychiatric disorders."[29] This leads to abnormal behavioral coping strategies.

Research is lacking for infants and younger children, but evidence shows that exposure to IPV over the first five years of life can strongly and adversely affect brain development.[30] Children who witness IPV have altered neurological anatomy and cognitive functions "including changes in structure, physiology, and signaling pathways" as the result of acts of commission (intentional harm) and omission (neglect), including direct

25. Maja, "The Biology of Stress," para. 2.

26. Maja, "The Biology of Stress," para. 5.

27. Tsavoussis et al., "Child-Witnessed Domestic Violence," 14 n. 49.

28. Mueller and Tronick, "Early Life Exposure to Violence," para. 1.

29. Karin et al., "A New Model for the HPA Axis," para. 1.

30. Mueller and Tronick, "Early Life Exposure to Violence," para. 3, n. Perry, Fox et al., Bick and Nelson.

and indirect abuse, and witnessing abuse, as well as experiencing direct physical, verbal, and emotional abuse.[31]

The extent to which an abused caregiver can attend to a child's emotional needs can be limited: "The circumstances of DV leave caregivers—emotionally and otherwise—unavailable and unresponsive, and activate in kids a primal fear and a host of other raw, complex, and unresolved emotions."[32] Both parents, for different reasons, are less aware of their children's emotions. The perpetrator of violence generally exhibits more selfish "parenting" and less involvement; the victim is preoccupied with the safety and wellbeing of her children, along with dealing with her own emotions and the need to navigate the abuser. Abusive fathers will often prevent a mother from offering nurturing care to the children. As children and infants experience the environment around them, "the mind develops as the brain responds."[33]

A secure attachment to a child's caregiver is necessary for proper development; an attentive and nurturing caregiver helps to buffer a child's "hormonal stress responses" and then "protects the developing brain from harmful effects of stress hormones."[34] Reactive attachment disorder occurs in 1 to 2 percent of children, "and is a rare condition where children don't form an emotional bond with their caretakers" because of abuse or emotional neglect at an early age.[35] These children understand what happens in their environment, but do not provide emotional responses: they may not display or look for affection and often want to be alone.[36]

Bancroft explains that oppositional behaviors and violence are sometimes an imitation of Dad's behavior and will be directed toward Mom and siblings. Behavior toward others may include bullying and aggressiveness.[37]

> A growing body of literature has revealed that children who have been exposed to DV are more likely than their peers to experience a wide range of difficulties, from anger and oppositional behavior, to fear, low self-worth and withdrawal, to poor sibling, peer, and

31. Tsavoussis et al., "Child-Witnessed Domestic Violence," 10 n. 22, 28, 34–37.

32. Edwards, "Alarming Effects," para. 3.

33. Edwards, "Alarming Effects," para. 3 n. Siegel and Hartzell.

34. Karin et al., A New Model for the HPA Axis," para. 3 n. Gunnar and Donzella, Tronick.

35. Cleveland Clinic, "Reactive Attachment Disorder," para. 1–2, 5.

36. Cleveland Clinic, "Reactive Attachment Disorder," para. 8.

37. Bancroft, *When Dad Hurts Mom*, 72–73.

social relationships. Studies have found evidence of much higher rates of pro-violence attitudes, rigid stereotypical gender beliefs involving male privilege, animal abuse, bullying, assault, property destruction, and substance abuse.[38]

Domestic violence is not an event, but rather, IPV subjects the victims to an ongoing traumatic experience. Paradigm Treatment Center provides a list of risks for adolescents who experience ongoing domestic violence:

> Post-traumatic stress disorder; anxiety; high degree of stress; depression; substance use and addiction; truancy and delinquency; self-blame and low self-esteem; displays of aggression; eating disorders; trouble with sleeping regularly; somatic complaints (headaches, stomachaches, etc.); hyperactivity; hyper-vigilance; regression; numbing; self-harm.[39]

Both young children and teens may deal with their negative emotions by either talking about their experiences or by acting out behaviorally. Often, they draw back socially and choose to be alone, and may also exhibit defiance or rebellion.[40] Other signs include: "irritability; frequent fighting or aggression at school or between siblings; lashing out at objects; treating pets with cruelty; using aggression as a means to gain attention."[41] Additionally, when dating, teens may exhibit verbal abuse or violence, including sexual assault, or may be victimized by the same abuses.[42]

## Physical Welfare

In previous chapters, we have seen some of the physical difficulties children experience in domestic violence families, including sexual abuse. Much of what the mother experiences physically the child may also face, including injury from trying to protect the mother from harm. Infants may also be injured in the crossfire. Infants, children, and teens, as well as their mothers, can be killed by the abuser.

38. Edwards, "Alarming Effects," para. 9.

39. Paradigm Treatment, "What are the Effects of Domestic Violence on Teens?," para. 10.

40. Paradigm Treatment, "What are the Effects of Domestic Violence on Teens?," para. 11.

41. Paradigm Treatment, "What are the Effects of Domestic Violence on Teens?," para. 11.

42. Bancroft, *When Dad Hurts Mom*, 72–73.

"The Centers for Disease Control and Prevention have reported that in homes where violence between partners occurs, there is a 45% to 60% chance of co-occurring child abuse, a rate 15 times higher than the average."[43] Other research shows that children exposed to domestic violence are 15 percent more likely to experience physical abuse and neglect than other children.[44] Children of batterers are 6.5 to 19 times more likely to experience sexual abuse by the batterer compared with non-battering parents.[45]

We have already shown how witnessing IPV affects the brains of both prenatal and postnatal infants, children, and teens. Many physical problems result from neurological and hormonal responses to witnessing abuse: altered brain physiology; headaches, stomachaches, etc. In addition, as research shows, abusers often direct physical abuse toward the children. Worth mentioning here are other risks to infants during the perinatal period when the mother experiences IPV: antepartum hemorrhage (sometimes fatal for the unborn);[46] low birth weight;[47] intrauterine growth restriction;[48] and preterm delivery.[49]

"Infants and toddlers who are exposed to domestic violence may experience increased listlessness, failure to thrive, and problems with trust."[50] Children exposed to IPV often experience bedwetting and insomnia, which affects physical health.[51] They can also have nightmares,[52] which interrupt sleep.

43. Edwards, "Alarming Effects," para. 2.

44. Holt et al., "The Impact of Exposure to Domestic Violence," 800 n. Osofsky.

45. Child Abuse Solutions, Inc., "Fact Sheet: Child Sexual Abuse in Custody Disputes," 3.

46. Mueller and Tronick, "Early Life Exposure to Violence," para. 6 n. Janssen et al., Han et al.

47. Mueller and Tronick, "Early Life Exposure to Violence," para. 6 n. Lipsky et al., Silverman et al., Rosen et al.

48. Mueller and Tronick, "Early Life Exposure to Violence," para. 6 n. Janssen et al.

49. Mueller and Tronick, "Early Life Exposure to Violence," para. 6 n. Lipsky, Donovan et al.

50. Brown and Bzostek, "Violence in the Lives of Children," 4 n. 44.

51. Brown and Bzostek, "Violence in the Lives of Children," 4 n. 26.

52. Bancroft, *When Dad Hurts Mom*, 72.

## Mental Health Welfare

Injuring oneself in an attempt to end one's own life in a suicide attempt can be considered both a physical and a mental health issue. Children in domestic violence families may experience many of the same mental health problems that women victims do: attention deficit hyperactivity disorder, low self-esteem, depression, anxiety, posttraumatic stress disorder, bipolar disorder, dissociation and dissociative disorders, trauma bonding, substance abuse, and disenfranchised grief.

Children do not escape the stigma of mental illness. A grandmother recently told a story about her eight-year-old granddaughter, who had a perfect response to a boy in her class who bullied her, just once, because of her dyslexia. Molly responded to the bully by saying: "Yes, I have dyslexia and it's all mine and you can't have it. Everyone has a challenge. This is mine. What's yours?" This granddaughter's mom and dad, with much help from her grandmother and granddad, taught Molly that everyone has challenges that we can, with hard work and bravery, move through toward success.

> But the people who love me
> They wrap me up tight
> To calm these big feelings
> And hold me just right[53]

This little girl knows what support and healing in community means; her loving community knows how to respond to her and reinforce their care and support.

Graeme Hanson, MD, tells us that "children who witness domestic violence may have twice the rate of psychiatric disorders as those who do not witness violence in the home."[54] These disorders may include "aggression, phobias, insomnia, poor self-esteem, poor academic performance, and decreased problem-solving skills" as well as posttraumatic stress disorder.[55] At the University of California, San Francisco, Dr. Hanson has clinical professorial responsibilities in psychiatry and pediatrics and is the director of residency training in child and adolescent psychiatry.[56]

---

53. Bacon-Davis, *This Thing Has a Name*, 9.
54. Bender, "PTSD, Other Disorders Evident," para. 3.
55. Bender, "PTSD, Other Disorders Evident," para. 4–5.
56. Bender, "PTSD, Other Disorders Evident," para. 1.

The psychological aftermath of exposure to DV can include fear of harm or abandonment, excessive worry or sadness, guilt, inability to experience empathy or guilt, habitual lying, low frustration tolerance, emotional distancing, poor judgment, shame, and fear about the future.[57]

From prenatal development forward, stress has a negative effect on a child's progress. The body's immune system and response to stress may not develop normally. Growing up under constant stress results in a heightened response, or one may completely shut down when facing normal stresses.[58]

## Attention Deficit/Hyperactivity Disorder

Nationally, the "estimates of ADHD in children range from 9% to 19%" and boys are diagnosed in higher numbers than girls.[59] A study done by Lewis et al., defines exposure to violence as witnessing violence, victimization, or both. It concludes that a child who is "both victim of and witness to violence is significantly associated with ADHD symptoms particularly among girls."[60] Girls usually present with more subdued symptoms and may be underdiagnosed.[61] A significant, positive correlation exists between both witnessing and directly experiencing violence and ADHD symptoms.[62] At the same time, children who have ADHD become more at risk for being victims of abuse and neglect.[63] The midbrain is associated with the development of ADHD and can be affected when witnessing or directly experiencing violence.

## Low Self-Esteem

Self-esteem, in a nutshell, is the view we have of ourselves, positive or negative, and is based on how we see ourselves and how we think others see us. The American Psychological Association defines self-esteem as follows:

57. Edwards, "Alarming Effects," para. 4.
58. The National Child Traumatic Stress Network, "Effects," para. 5.
59. Lewis et al., "Association," para. 3 n. 8.
60. Lewis et al., "Association," para. 1.
61. Lewis et al., "Association," para. 6 n. 45.
62. Lewis et al., "Association," para. 19.
63. Hadianfard, "Child Abuse in Group of Children," para. 4.

The degree to which the qualities and characteristics contained in one's self-concept are perceived to be positive. It reflects a person's physical self-image, view of his or her accomplishments and capabilities, and values and perceived success in living up to them, as well as the ways in which others view and respond to that person. The more positive the cumulative perception of these qualities and characteristics, the higher one's self-esteem. A reasonably high degree of self-esteem is considered an important ingredient of mental health, whereas low self-esteem and feelings of worthlessness are common depressive symptoms.[64]

Abuse in any form can lead to lower self-esteem or self-worth in the recipient. Parents play a significant role in the development of self-esteem in their children.[65] Welcoming and engaging responses from parents coupled with a positive family atmosphere shape positive self-esteem in children and adolescents.[66] A parent's negativity or lack of positive emotional engagement does the opposite.[67] Consistent social support through family, friends, and others has been found to help boost a child's self-esteem.[68]

## Depression, Anxiety, and Posttraumatic Stress Disorder (PTSD)

In general, children who witness IPV are more likely to have depression and anxiety.[69] Children and adolescents who are abused (physically, sexually, emotionally, or through neglect) tend toward more severe depression, increased and prolonged episodes of depression, increased propensity for anxiety, PTSD, substance abuse, and increased risk for suicide attempts with first attempts at an earlier age.[70] In a 2019 study, researchers found that 46 percent of those with depression had experienced childhood abuse.[71]

IPV and childhood trauma lead to adults with higher rates of mental health disorders, including anxiety disorders:

---

64. *APA Dictionary of Psychology*, s.v. "Self-Esteem."

65. Xiang et al., "Relationship," 5 n. Harter; Shaffer and Kipp.

66. Xiang et al., "Relationship," 5 n. Shaffer and Kipp.

67. Xiang et al., "Relationship," 5.

68. Xiang et al., "Relationship," 7.

69. Brown and Bzostek, "Violence in the Lives of Children," 4 n. 27.

70. Camber Children's Mental Health, "What's the Connection?," para. 8.

71. Camber Children's Mental Health, "What's the Connection?," para. 7.

(1) Generalized anxiety disorder: a chronic, profound worry about seemingly everything; (2) panic disorder: a recurrent panic attacks; an intense, overwhelming surge of anxiety with physical, emotional, and cognitive symptoms; (3) agoraphobia: intense fear, worry, or panic that arises in public or crowded places that are difficult to leave; (4) social anxiety disorder: intense fear of being judged, criticized, or rejected in social situations or when performing in front of others.[72]

A child's brain focuses on self-protection, and children view their environment as unsafe when they experience trauma, fear, or a feeling of helplessness. These children withdraw to protect themselves and do not connect well with others. When a child sees the environment as unsafe, the brain responds to harm even when there is no risk of harm present. "This anticipation of future trauma turns into anxiety that can continue into their adult life."[73]

Posttraumatic stress disorder occurs in many children exposed to domestic violence, whether they witness IPV or the abuser hurts them directly. In children six years of age and older, symptoms encompass the following:

(1) exposure to actual or threatened death, serious injury, or sexual violence, (2) the presence of intrusion symptoms associated with the traumatic event(s) (repetitive play themes, distressing dreams, flashbacks, physiological reactions, marked psychological distress), (3) persistent avoidance of stimuli associated with the traumatic event(s), (4) negative alterations in cognition and mood associated with the event, and (5) marked alterations in arousal associated with the event(s) (irritability, anger, recklessness, hypervigilance, exaggerated startle response, problems with concentration, and sleep disturbances).[74]

In children younger than six years old, a child may experience PTSD whether the trauma is directly experienced, they have witnessed the violence, or they merely learn that a parent or primary caregiver was harmed.[75] A child "may present as disorganized or agitated" behaviorally, and may be re-experiencing events; this works

72. Dibdin, "Why Childhood Trauma Could be Causing Your Anxiety," para. 12.
73. Tschampa, "Can Childhood Trauma Cause Anxiety?," para. 17.
74. Tsavoussis et al., Child-Witnessed Domestic Violence," para. 7 n. 15.
75. Tsavoussis et al., Child-Witnessed Domestic Violence," para. 7 n. 15.

as an "instant replay" in the following ways by a child's psyche: (a) they may engage in play where certain themes or aspects of the trauma are expressed; (b) it may be manifested as the appearance of frightening dreams without discernable content; and (c) the child may reenact specific aspects of the traumatic event.[76]

## BIPOLAR DISORDER

Children who experience abuse are at higher risk for bipolar disorder. The University of Manchester (England) did a study involving more than thirty years of research into bipolar disorder and discovered that people with BD are "2.63 times more likely to have suffered emotional, physical or sexual abuse as children than the general population."[77] Because of the body's response to childhood trauma, these experiences will potentially decrease the age for the onset of BD or will increase the risk of suicide.[78]

## DISSOCIATION AND DISSOCIATIVE DISORDERS

Children who develop a dissociative disorder to help cope with abuse and neglect will carry the disorder into adulthood if no intervention occurs, and will become particularly vulnerable and susceptible to forming relationships with an abusive partner.[79] Approximately 90 percent of those who have dissociative identity disorder experienced abuse or neglect as children.[80] These disorders usually develop before the age of 20.[81]

> Severe dissociative symptoms that continue beyond their adaptive capacity may lead to dissociative identity disorder (DID), which involves a compartmentalization of the individual's identity into self-states (distinct and alternate personality states and identities), accompanied by amnesia.[82]

76. Tsavoussis et al., Child-Witnessed Domestic Violence," para. 7 n. 15, 16.

77. Science Daily, "People with Bipolar Disorder," para. 1, 3.

78. Aas et al., "The Role of Childhood Trauma in Bipolar Disorders," para. 1.

79. Snyder, "Women with Dissociative Identity Disorder," para. 1.

80. Dissociative Identity Disorder Research, "Types of Trauma," para. 1.

81. The Recovery Village, "Dissociative Disorders Statistics," para. 4.

82. Webermann et al., "Childhood Maltreatment and Intimate Partner Violence," para. 10 n. American Psychiatric Association.

## Schizophrenia

The American Psychiatric Association offers the following description:

> Schizophrenia is a chronic brain disorder that affects less than one percent of the U.S. population. When schizophrenia is active, symptoms can include delusions, hallucinations, disorganized speech, trouble with thinking and lack of motivation. However, with treatment, most symptoms of schizophrenia will greatly improve and the likelihood of a recurrence can be diminished. . . . The complexity of schizophrenia may help explain why there are misconceptions about the disease. Schizophrenia does not mean split personality or multiple personality. Most people with schizophrenia are not any more dangerous or violent than people in the general population.[83]

A person does not have to experience childhood trauma to be diagnosed with schizophrenia, but a connection does exist. If someone has a genetic link to schizophrenia, trauma may trigger this disorder. Both genetic and environmental factors (e.g., poverty, dangerous surroundings) can give rise to this mental health condition by creating "abnormal development in the brain."[84] Experiencing trauma at a young age affects normal neurodevelopment. Normally, symptoms occur in adulthood; children under twelve years of age do not commonly exhibit symptoms.[85]

## Trauma Bonding

We have already shown that a child who is abused or neglected equates that bad attention with love. The brain becomes wired to equate abuse with love because eventually the abuser will "rescue" the victim and bring relief.[86] The eventual relief causes the brain to release dopamine and oxytocin, making the child feel good.[87] Consequently, trauma bonding develops.

Parents provide the first relationship children experience, so children want to become attached, even to abusive parents. Understanding how healthy relationships work escapes abused children. A protective mother

---

83. American Psychiatric Association, "What is Schizophrenia?," para. 1, 3.

84. Sissons, "What is the Link between Trauma and Schizophrenia?," para. 2, 7.

85. Sissons, "What is the Link between Trauma and Schizophrenia?," para. 11.

86. Clayton, "What is Trauma-Bonding?," para. 6.

87. Raypole, "How to Recognize and Break Traumatic Bonds," para. 28, 37.

cannot always counteract the development of trauma bonding with the abusive parent. We do not fault women who trauma bond to an abusive partner; neither do we fault children for trauma bonding to an abusive parent.

## Substance Abuse

Study after study has shown the association between trauma experiences and substance abuse in adolescents. Substance abuse provides an unhealthy coping strategy when healthy ways to cope are not available. A vicious circle of trauma can result through substance abuse: when trauma causes children or adolescents to use substances, this can lead to risky behaviors that result in further trauma, leading to further "victimization and injury."[88] One problem compounds the other.

Often when teens present with mental illness and substance abuse problems, professionals involved treat either one problem or the other, but not both. Sadly, few facilities engage in integrating services so both problems can be addressed.[89] More professionals need both training and experience in both fields to better identify the problems and to give these teens a better opportunity to experience healing.

"More than 13% of 17-year-olds—one in eight—have experienced posttraumatic stress disorder at some point in their lives."[90] More than half of young people with PTSD symptoms use drugs, alcohol, or both to lessen their distress.[91] By the time adolescents complete eighth grade, an estimated 29 percent have tried illegal drugs and 41 percent have consumed alcohol. In the United States, approximately one in five of those between the ages of 12 and 17 are dependent on or abuse illegal drugs or alcohol.[92] "Teens who had experienced physical or sexual abuse/assault were three times more likely to report past or current substance abuse than those without a history of trauma,"[93] and "more than 70% of patients have a history of trauma exposure."[94]

88. National Child Traumatic Stress Network, "Helping Your Teen Cope," 7 n. 12–13.
89. National Child Traumatic Stress Network, "Making the Connection," 4.
90. National Child Traumatic Stress Network, "Making the Connection," 1.
91. National Child Traumatic Stress Network, "Helping Your Teen Cope," 7 n. 8–11.
92. National Child Traumatic Stress Network, "Making the Connection," 1 n. 4–6.
93. National Child Traumatic Stress Network, "Making the Connection," 1 n. 3.
94. National Child Traumatic Stress Network, "Making the Connection," 1 n. 7–8.

## Disenfranchised Grief

Children and teens who experience domestic violence do not fit the mold for experiencing grief as we generally understand it. Others do not recognize and consequently do not validate their grief, so they experience disenfranchised grief. With IPV, there are many secrets; children are often told not to reveal what happens inside their house. Often, they keep their feelings to themselves as well.

But these children and teens experience many losses and continual stressors and need a safe person to talk with about their experiences and emotions. They need to express their sadness, anger, and other emotions caused by what they have experienced and witness. Protective mothers and other supportive adults can let them know that their feelings of loss, worry, fear, sadness, and anger are okay. Those feelings need validation and understanding. Supportive adults should emphasize that they are there to help. Children and teens should not be denied the ability to feel and express their loss or to ask for help.

But how can children feel a sense of loss when their traumatic experiences at home are all they know about relationships? As a friend who serves as a grief guide says, "Children are heat-seeking missiles, wanting to gravitate toward safety. When they sense the heat of safety, they simply gravitate toward it." When children are old enough to venture outside their house and meet other children and adults, they experience other environments where they feel safe. They may find safety with a teacher, neighbor, pastor, or someone else. Now they have a comparison because their safe place provides consistent listening, kindness, and structure.

## Desensitization

When children are regularly exposed to violence, they can become desensitized. Desensitization damages one's view of what relationships should look like and paints a distorted picture.[95] Witnessing multiple incidences of violence increases the possibility that children will come to view such behaviors as normal and readily imitate those behaviors.

---

95. Al-Zubi, "Reversing Real-Life Violence Desensitization in Children," para.1.

## SUICIDE

A link definitely exists between childhood trauma and suicidal ideation. Research has shed light on what types of maltreatment are more likely to cause suicidal ideation and what factors connect trauma and suicidal thoughts.[96] A study done by Bahk et al., with 211 participants, showed that "childhood sexual abuse directly predicted suicidal ideation"; both physical and emotional abuses indirectly predicted suicidal ideation coupled with anxiety; and neglect also predicted suicidal ideation, but was influenced by perceived social support.[97] Interventions should include a focus on anxiety symptoms and involve an increase in social support for trauma survivors.[98] Suicidal ideation and follow-through can be a lifelong risk.[99]

Another study by Angelakis et al., examined 79 different studies and found that there were "core types of childhood maltreatment and suicide behaviors in children and young adults."[100] "Younger individuals with experiences of sexual abuse who were not under the care of clinicians had higher rates of suicide attempt, and young age was also associated more strongly with suicide ideation."[101]

Because children of batterers are 6.5 to 19 times more likely to experience sexual abuse by the batterer compared with non-battering parents,[102] courts need to take accusations of sexual abuse far more seriously and not automatically discount the accusation as hostility on the part of protective mothers. Proper intervention can protect and bring healing to the child and can reduce the risk of suicidal ideation.

96. Bahk et al., "The Relationship between Childhood Trauma and Suicidal Ideation," para. 1.

97. Bahk et al., "The Relationship between Childhood Trauma and Suicidal Ideation," para. 3.

98. Bahk et al., "The Relationship between Childhood Trauma and Suicidal Ideation," para. 4.

99. Bahk et al., "The Relationship between Childhood Trauma and Suicidal Ideation," para. 5.

100. Angelakis et al., "Association of Childhood Maltreatment," para. 2.

101. Angelakis et al., "Association of Childhood Maltreatment," para. 2.

102. Child Abuse Solutions, Inc., "Fact Sheet," 3.

## Trauma-Induced Dyslexia

People with dyslexia have a learning disorder that alters their ability to read, spell, write, or speak. They are no less intelligent than their peers, but simply "have trouble connecting the letters they see to the sounds those letters make."[103] One does not outgrow dyslexia, but if it is diagnosed early with proper intervention and support, the struggles in navigating this learning disability may be lessened.

Dyslexia comes from either a developmental source (genetic) or acquired (from traumatic brain injury or disease).[104] Trauma dyslexia can result from a stroke or an injury to the head, such as a fall or an accident. Emotional trauma can also cause trauma dyslexia: "Although there is little research behind this type of dyslexia, it is cited that early exposure to stressful circumstances such as emotional abuse, neglect, environmental disaster, bullying, witnessing disaster or death, etc. [sic] may result in dyslexia and other learning disorders."[105] In a study involving 13,054 respondents, "one third (34.8%) of respondents who reported they had been physically abused during their childhood or adolescence also reported being diagnosed with dyslexia in comparison with 7.2% of those who did not report being physically abused."[106]

## Financial Welfare

Financial abuse hurts children as the mother's ability to pay for food, medical bills, school trips, clothes, dance lessons, etc., may be diminished, stop, or become less predictable. Consequently, a child's physical and social welfare may be harmed.

## Spiritual Welfare

Trauma has the power to produce both positive and negative responses to spiritual thoughts, perceptions, and beliefs. Some may view life and their faith as more significant and then draw closer to God in spite of their difficult experiences. For others, trauma can produce a loss of faith and

103. WebMD, "What is Dyslexia?," para. 1.
104. Neuro Health, "Types of Dyslexia," para. 1.
105. Neuro Health, "Types of Dyslexia," para. 18, 20.
106. Fuller-Thomson and Hooper, "Association," para. 1.

feelings that God has abandoned or is punishing them. Negative responses can move in a more positive direction as a person moves through trauma recovery.[107]

Children who experience trauma very often will move away from their spiritual upbringing.[108] Coupling a child's spirituality with traditional psychological methods is particularly effective for healing.[109] Religious communities can provide "healthy forms of relationship building and community attentiveness, while providing a safe environment for coping."[110]

For those with good spiritual health, mental health obstacles create comparatively "lower levels of symptoms and clinical problems."[111] Those within a faith community have experiences within that community that allow for a more positive result in working through the trauma: "reduction of behavioral risks through healthy religious lifestyles . . . ; social support . . . ; enhancement of coping skills . . . ; the 'relaxation response' through prayer or meditation."[112]

## Educational Welfare

Both lower-level cognitive skills and behavioral problems impede the educational process for children in homes with IPV. These children have lower scores on "assessments of verbal, motor, and cognitive skills" as well as slower cognitive development.[113] In addition, Tsavoussis et al., found "lower intelligence quotients, as well as poor language skills, deficient memory, lack of inhibition, and inattention."[114]

The National Child Traumatic Stress Network encapsulates the cognitive and educational challenges for children exposed to trauma:

> Children with complex trauma histories may have problems thinking clearly, reasoning, or problem solving. They may be unable to plan ahead, anticipate the future, and act accordingly. When children grow up under conditions of constant threat, all

107. US Department of Veterans Affairs, "Spirituality and Trauma," para. 4.

108. Westerfield and Doolittle, "Spirituality of the Traumatized Child," para. 1.

109. Westerfield and Doolittle, "Spirituality of the Traumatized Child," para. 1.

110. Westerfield and Doolittle, "Spirituality of the Traumatized Child," para. 1.

111. US Department of Veterans Affairs, "Spirituality and Trauma," para. 5.

112. US Department of Veterans Affairs, "Spirituality and Trauma," para. 6 n. 6.

113. Brown and Bzostek, "Violence in the Lives of Children," 4 n. 26, 27.

114. Tsavoussis et al., "Child-Witnessed Domestic Violence," para. 7 n. 21.

their internal resources go toward survival. When their bodies and minds have learned to be in chronic stress response mode, they may have trouble thinking a problem through calmly and considering multiple alternatives. They may find it hard to acquire new skills or take in new information. They may struggle with sustaining attention or curiosity or be distracted by reactions to trauma reminders. They may show deficits in language development and abstract reasoning skills. Many children who have experienced complex trauma have learning difficulties that may require support in the academic environment.[115]

In infancy and early childhood, the brain has the most adaptability. Neuroplasticity is when the brain adjusts its connections, or rewires itself, allowing for development from infancy into adulthood, and also in recovery from brain injury.[116] By age 5, the brain is 90 percent the size of an adult brain.[117] When trauma continues into school-age years from early childhood, the "impact is greater on overall functioning" compared to children whose trauma begins during school years.[118] During adolescence, brain development speeds up again. During this time, the brain prunes unused pathways, as it did in childhood, which "supports attention, concentration, reasoning, and advanced thinking."[119] During adolescence, trauma "disrupts both the development of this part of the brain and the strengthening of the systems that allow this part of the brain to effectively communicate with other systems."[120] Interventions to help traumatized infants, children, and teens never come too early or too late.

Trauma sensitive schools help "students feel safe, welcomed, and supported," in an environment "where addressing trauma's impact on learning on a school-wide basis is at the center of its educational mission."[121] Schools that are trauma sensitive require a whole-school approach, from the

115. National Child Traumatic Stress Network, "Effects," para. 13.

116. Banks, "What is Brain Plasticity and Why Is It So Important?," para. 1.

117. Children's Services Practice Notes, "How Trauma Affects Child Brain Development," para. 7.

118. Children's Services Practice Notes, "How Trauma Affects Child Brain Development," para. 9.

119. Children's Services Practice Notes, "How Trauma Affects Child Brain Development," para. 10.

120. Children's Services Practice Notes, "How Trauma Affects Child Brain Development," para. 10.

121. Trauma and Learning Policy Initiative, "Helping Traumatized Children Learn," para. 1, 5.

principal to teachers to administration. Adults who work in this environment do not always know who has or who has not experienced trauma, but their philosophy includes making all students feel safe and supported.

## Risk of Criminal Behaviors

When children witness violence, "the impact on the community at large is of importance and concern; the effects on child witnesses of DV extend beyond the families and children. These children often have impaired learning skills, poor school performance, poor life development skills, and lose their ability to self-regulate."[122] Identifying those children who need help is essential, not only for their sakes, but ultimately for the health of the greater community. Think of how many times children who live in IPV homes witness and experience violence. Consider these statistics from the US Department of Justice:

- Within the past year, "almost 1 in 10 American children saw one family member assault another family member, and more than 25 per cent had been exposed to family violence in their life."[123]

- "Being the victim of physical assault increases the likelihood of violent juvenile offending by 3.3 times."[124]

- Regarding compound victimization, "A number of studies have found that exposure to multiple kinds of violence predicts negative outcomes beyond the effects of any specific type of exposure."[125]

Some children witness sexual assault on the adults in their home.[126] The most common perpetrator is the one who violates an intimate partner, and not "strangers or casual dates."[127]

Children exposed to sexual abuse have a greater risk of experiencing mental health issues such as PTSD, and are at risk for developing more severe

---

122. Tsavoussis et al., Child-Witnessed Domestic Violence," para. 15 n. 4, 23, 54–56.

123. US Department of Justice, "Children Exposed to Violence," para. 1 n. Finkelhor et al.

124. US Department of Justice, "Children Exposed to Violence," para. 9 n. Nofzinger and Kurtz.

125. US Department of Justice, "Children Exposed to Violence," para. 10.

126. Ford, "Children's Exposure to Intimate Partner Sexual Assault," 141.

127. Ford, "Children's Exposure to Intimate Partner Sexual Assault," 142.

mental health symptoms than others.[128] They also have a decided risk of developing wrong attitudes toward sex and gender roles, as Ford describes:

- Sexuality and violence occurring together is normal.
- Women are obliged to provide sex anytime a man wants or demands it.
- Asserting oneself sexually, even aggressively, is justified.
- What a partner wants is of no consequence, so just comply.[129]

Physical abuse, including sexual abuse, puts children at greater risk of exhibiting criminal behaviors, which puts those around them at risk. Those who were victims of abuse and neglect as children victimize others. Children exposed to violence have approximately double the probability of eventually engaging in crimes, and multiple experiences of abuse raises that probability. Sexual abuse has the "largest negative effects."[130]

The National Institute of Justice provides information developed from the Lehigh Longitudinal Study, one of the longest of its kind examining the long-term effects of child abuse and neglect.

> Beginning in the 1970s, the study has tracked approximately 450 children from preschool to adulthood. Reports of child abuse from Child Protective Services records and parental reports of abusive parenting were collected when the children were 18 months to 6 years of age and linked to self-reported criminal involvement three decades later. Antisocial behavior also was measured in the intervening years during middle childhood and adolescence.[131]

The study showed not only that abuse in childhood increased the risk of adult crime, but also that the promotion of "antisocial behavior during childhood and adolescence" and the "formation of relationships with antisocial romantic partners and peers in adulthood" encouraged criminal behaviors.[132]

"Recent research indicates that males exposed to domestic violence as children are more likely to engage in domestic violence as adults, and females are more likely to be victims as adults."[133] Those with a substanti-

128. Ford, "Children's Exposure to Intimate Partner Sexual Assault," 144.
129. Ford, "Children's Exposure to Intimate Partner Sexual Assault," 144.
130. Currie et al., "Does Child Abuse Cause Crime?," 3.
131. National Institute of Justice, "Pathways," para. 1.
132. National Institute of Justice, "Pathways," para. 2.
133. Brown and Bzostek, "Violence in the Lives of Children," 4 n. 28.

ated history of maltreatment in childhood were at high risk of sexual and physical intimate partner violence as adults compared with those who were not mistreated as children.[134]

Female victims of childhood maltreatment were more likely than male victims to internalize "depression, social withdrawal, and anxiety during middle childhood, which in turn increased the risk of adult crime."[135] Males were more likely to externalize behaviors, "such as aggression, hostility, and delinquency during middle childhood, which subsequently led to adult criminal behavior."[136]

Children who witness and/or experience IPV, neglect, or sexual abuse suffer incalculable personal consequences. At the same time, the damage done flows into the community. The children's spiritual, physical, and mental health difficulties put the greater community at risk economically through medical costs and the costs related to law enforcement. The children's educational abilities are not what they could have been had they avoided the damage done to their brain development, and the same is true of their behavioral challenges. Their circle of friends may create the risk of continuing the experiences they had as children and adolescents, and their future families are at higher risk for the abuses these children faced growing up. Babies, children, and adolescents in these situations must be identified in order to break the cycle and become empowered, understand boundaries, and heal.

## Empowerment, Boundaries, and Healing

### EMPOWERING CHILDREN

Giving children a sense of empowerment helps them feel stronger, more valued, and more confident in how they manage the world around them. Confidence and self-esteem lead to resilience. Empowerment helps children realize that they have some control over their environment and their lives. Self-respect also develops from a feeling of empowerment and is important for good decision making. A therapist once said, "You can only respect others inasmuch as you respect yourself."

---

134. Herrenkohl et al., "Effects of Child Maltreatment," 15.
135. National Institute of Justice, "Pathways," para. 6.
136. National Institute of Justice, "Pathways," para. 6.

For children who have experienced trauma—and if they live in a home that includes domestic violence, they have experienced trauma—"the first principle of recovery is the empowerment of the survivor."[137] The importance of restoring control to a child who has experienced trauma is essential for treatment and healing.

A protective mother or other trusted adult will be able to teach a child the importance of following rules, laws, and the authority figures in their lives, including teachers and parents. Empowering children to help them experience some control in their lives does not mean that they have the ability to do whatever they want. We all operate within guidelines, regardless of age.

Empowering a child includes giving them responsibilities, providing encouragement and recognition in their successes, involving them in decision making, leading by example, and being present to show support and guidance.[138] Being present includes talking with children about their choices and about the consequences of a decision. Help them learn how to think logically and critically.

For children who reside in a home that includes domestic violence, talk with them about what they might do to be more safe when Dad becomes scary or violent. If Dad no longer resides with the children but has them for unsupervised parenting time, discuss what they might do when with him. Assure them that they do not bear the responsibility if they forget the plan, if the plan fails, or if someone gets hurt.[139] Adults are responsible for keeping themselves and children safe, but children can help if they want to.[140]

## PROTECTING CHILDREN'S BOUNDARIES

There are many different types of boundaries: physical, sexual, emotional or mental, spiritual or religious, financial and material, time, and nonnegotiable boundaries (usually physical and emotional safety issues).[141] Most of these boundaries are crossed for the children in families that experience domestic violence.

137. Herman, *Trauma and Recovery*, 133.
138. Early Learning Childhood Education, "5 Reasons to Empower Children," para. 12.
139. Bancroft, *When Dad Hurts Mom*, 304.
140. Bancroft, *When Dad Hurts Mom*, 304.
141. Martin, "What Kind of Boundaries Do You Need to Set?," para. 3–9.

Talk to children about the definition of boundaries and provide examples. Explain that there is good touch and bad touch, and that bad touch crosses a boundary. Bad touches make us uncomfortable. Let them know that no one, including family members, friends, teachers, anyone who is an authority figure, any stranger—no one—has the right to touch them in a way that makes them uncomfortable. At the same time, they must not touch others in a way that would make them feel uncomfortable and must stop if someone tells them to stop. Touching refers to not only sexual abuse, but also any physical "touch," which includes hitting, spitting, tripping, etc.

Further explain that others cross boundaries when they say things that are hurtful. Name calling, making fun of someone, putting them down for whatever reason (how they dress, their accent, what they believe, etc.) are some examples.

Then, be an example of someone who does not want to cross boundaries with others. When a parent models good and moral behaviors and shows their children love and affection, children feel safer and can then be more encouraged to talk to that parent and perhaps disclose how others treat them in unsafe, unkind ways. When a child does disclose anything that has happened to them, show them support and calmness. Disclosing may not be easy for a child whose boundaries have been overstepped. They feel unsafe, dirty, confused (Was that okay or not okay? Was I pressured or not?), abandoned and misunderstood, untrusting, angry, or defiant.[142]

## HELPING CHILDREN HEAL

Healing for children becomes more challenging when they continue to see the abuser without supervision after separation or divorce. They continue to see their father undermine their mother. If the abuser harmed the children physically, sexually, or emotionally when he lived with them before separation, he will continue after separation.

The one person who can make a significant impact on the children's healing is the protective mother; other caring adults can also make a substantial impact. Mom's ability to show and express love for the children both physically and emotionally is essential. Children need reassurance from supportive adults to help them understand that no one faults them for the violence they see and hear and experience directly. A caring adult assuring children and teens that they have the full ability to talk about their

142. Bancroft, *When Dad Hurts Mom*, 94–95.

feelings, fears, and what happens in the home means they will know they do not have to remain silent. They may even ask for help. Helping them feel safe and having conversations about healthy relationships reinforces the support and love caring adults have for them.

Resilience in children depends on the strength of the mother-child relationship, mother's protectiveness, strength of sibling relationships, other healthy relatives, and the strength of peer relationships.[143] Children should observe and learn how the people supporting them, including their siblings, support one another: Mom supports the children, the children support Mom, and siblings support one another. The children and the protective mother do not ever give up on one another.[144] Paternal grandparent involvement does not work well when they support the abusive father, because they further poison the relationship the children have with their mother.[145]

Finding others who can support the children, including professional help, will benefit not only the children, but also the protective mother. The challenge is to find someone who understands domestic violence issues thoroughly and does not simply know "about" domestic violence. For some children, "there are protective factors that can mitigate the worst impacts, including a child's literacy and overall intelligence, the extent to which the child is outgoing and socially competent, and whether the child has safe and supportive relationships with at least one influential adult."[146]

Resilience also depends on positive school exposure and school relationships (especially teachers); positive activities such as sports, music, clubs, arts, etc.; the ability to express oneself (e.g., through the arts); having safe places to go or even safe things (e.g., animals) they can feel good about; and not feeling guilty or blaming Mom.[147] When children have positive experiences they develop a healthy sense of empowerment, that does not mimic the unhealthy and damaging power and control their father exhibits.

Crying and tantrums are a way for children to relieve stress. As long as they are safe, others around them are safe, and the environment around them is safe, they must be allowed to cry and throw a tantrum. Exhibiting their emotions in this way leads to healing. In the case study above,

---

143. Bancroft, "Healing and Recovery in Children Exposed to Domestic Violence."

144. Bancroft, "Healing and Recovery in Children Exposed to Domestic Violence."

145. Bancroft, "Healing and Recovery in Children Exposed to Domestic Violence."

146. Edwards, "Alarming Effects," para. 15 n. Carlson, Edleson, Hughes.

147. Bancroft, "Healing and Recovery in Children Exposed to Domestic Violence."

neither Lori nor Deborah tried to stop Poppy or Rayne from their crying and upset. Just make sure everyone is safe and let the children express their emotions. Displays of emotional upset are common when children return from spending time with the abusive parent. They are wound up so tightly from having to be good with their father, managing their emotions, and "reading" him so they can adjust their own behaviors to keep peace, that they release all that tension where they feel safe: at home with Mom.

Any form of abuse on an infant, child, or adolescent is serious, but healing is possible if the child's difficult experiences are identified and love, support, and the right resources are put into place.

## Scriptural Encouragement

Domestic violence is an issue in the larger community and is also an issue in the church. The conservative, pro-family, pro-church Family Studies Institute conducted a study showing that one in four highly religious marriages in the United States include IPV.[148] Theoretically, one can sit in the pew of a church, look at those families seated in the sanctuary, and realize that 25 percent of them have experienced IPV. Too many churches are not equipped to address domestic violence. Those in the domestic violence field find themselves grateful for all those churches that have pastors, priests, ministry leaders, and laypeople who can identify and properly minister to those caught in an abusive family. Helping victims of domestic violence requires helping both the woman and any children in the home. While help for the abuser is also necessary, it is most urgent to assist women and children and to help them find safety.

Research shows that faith makes a significant difference in adults and children who are experiencing difficult circumstances, healing from trauma, and coping with physical and mental illness. Given the prevalence of IPV, our churches have a ministerial emergency. Over time, these children face a higher and higher risk of physical and mental illnesses, of engaging in familial and other serious social problems, and of repeating what they learned growing up.

If those in the church, particularly pastors and priests, had the ability to identify domestic violence families and address their situations properly, they would be taking the first step toward helping women and children in these families find healing and safety. Help cannot be provided when the

148. Wilcox et al., "The Ties that Bind," 36–37.

problem has not been identified. The next steps include knowing what to do and say (and what not to do and say), having resources at hand (e.g., legal aid, safe housing), and knowing when to refer family members to another professional who has the expertise to help.

The church is responsible for helping people and communities address the difficulties they face. God has freely shown the world how much he loves those in the world by giving us his only Son as a sacrifice so that those who believe can experience redemption (John 3:16). The church should be the primary source and innovator for helping those in the community who need help. The resources in our communities that provide safety and healing must start with the church.

The church needs to engage in biblical justice, where everyone is united and uplifted, there are no divisions among people groups, and all are united in Christ and encouraged to view the beauty and worth in each individual. The church does not need to surrender to the government to solve problems. Reliance on the government for answers and direction is idolatry and, sooner or later, will fail those who depend on it. While we need laws in place for safer communities, government will not solve the scourge of domestic violence in the United States or anywhere in the world.

On the other hand, God is all-loving and all-powerful, and will not fail us as we depend on him to provide answers and direction. The church must recognize that the motivation for reaching out to the lost and hurt springs from God's love and power to heal the hurting. God wants his church to help those in difficult situations move through their painful circumstances, providing counsel and being available to help as needed. God's truth, love, strength, power, and understanding infuse and overarch all he does. Isaiah 40:28–31 says:

> Have you not known? Have you not heard? The Lord is the everlasting God, the Creator of the ends of the earth. He does not faint or grow weary; his understanding is unsearchable. He gives power to the faint, and strengthens the powerless. Even youths will faint and be weary, and the young will fall exhausted; but those who wait for the Lord shall renew their strength, they shall mount up with wings like eagles.

In a healthy church community, where congregants form relationships and individuals know one another well, sin cannot be hidden easily. Individuals know one another well enough to admonish and encourage each other. First Thessalonians 5:14–17 persuades us to be so connected with one another: "And we urge you, beloved, to admonish the idlers, encourage the fainthearted, help the weak, be patient with all of them. See that none of you repays evil for evil, but always seek to do good to one another and to all. Rejoice always, pray without ceasing. . . ."

Children need to belong to a church community that can offer them teaching, healing, assurance of love, and encouragement. In many churches, during the baptism of an infant or child, the priest or pastor asks the congregation to help nourish the young person's faith. As a community of believers, we must take this request for support seriously. Whatever needs, questions, or complexities children present must be addressed by not only loving families, but also their loving and safe community of believers. Galatians 6:2 tells us, "Bear one another's burdens, and in this way you will fulfill the law of Christ." Children caught in domestic violence homes have many burdens and desperately need our love and assurance, as do their mothers.

Remember: Healing happens in community. A greater opportunity for healing for adults and children is present in a wise, healthy, Christ-centered church community.

# 9

# The Woman's Parents

ONE MAY WONDER WHY a book about domestic violence would include a chapter on the victim's parents. When women caught in the perils of domestic violence are asked who they have as a part of their support system, more often than not, they mention their parents. However, very little research on this topic has been done. Because of the lack of research and studies, this chapter includes many hypotheses based on conversations with parents and grandparents who have, sadly, been the connected parents of an abuse victim. For simplicity, we will refer to the victim's parents as the grandparents. After all, any parent who endeavors to help their abused daughter, whether she has children or not, is a "grand" parent.

The case study below, like all others in this volume, is an amalgamation of different stories told by parents of abuse victims, with all the names changed. It focuses on the experiences, viewpoints, health, and emotions of the abused woman's parents rather than those of the victim.

## Case Study

Emma and John got word from a friend of their daughter's that Hal, her husband, had been abusing her. Dee, their daughter, confirmed that he had been hurting her, and not just physically. Over the next few weeks, Dee gradually described more of Hal's efforts to control her. At one point, after Hal realized that Emma and John knew about his actions against his wife, John had to stand in between him and Dee to protect her from his aggressive behavior.

Hal, because he feared that Dee would leave him, said that once she had delivered their last baby, he would take all their children away and she would never see them again. A few days before the baby's birth, Dee's labor began. But when Hal yelled and screamed at her, berating and threatening her, labor stopped. Dee was focused on making Hal's ability to leave with their children more difficult. Emma and John had already been told about Hal's treatment of their daughter, so Dee asked them if they could come to the birth of the baby. They agreed, and John arranged to take time off from work when Dee went into labor. After her parents arrived, Dee told Hal he could not attend the birth. The midwife had already arrived for the home birth, so they presented a united front in assuring Hal someone would call him when the baby arrived. Either Emma or John, or both of them, stayed with Dee and the children twenty-four hours a day and all seven days the first week after the delivery of the baby to protect their daughter and the children.

Emma and John struggled to come to terms with their thoughts and emotions. The revelation about Hal's abuse of their daughter seemed to fit with some things they had heard him say when he was unaware they were within earshot. On the other hand, how could this be happening to them? After all, John gave Hal a strong and beautiful blessing at their wedding ceremony and, during their seven years of marriage, he had treated him like his own son. This was a betrayal of the worst kind. How could anyone treat their daughter so ruthlessly? What had the children seen and experienced? Emma and John felt anxiety, uncertainty, and fear when wondering how they would protect their daughter and grandchildren, and what the future would look like.

A few months after learning how Hal had been treating their daughter, Emma and John were relieved to learn that after Dee called 911, law enforcement showed up and arrested Hal. After his parents bailed him out, he called Emma and John to tell them he did not hurt their daughter. Dee's parents simply listened and said, "We hear you and will not talk with you about this." A restraining order prevented him from contacting Dee, who said she would never go back to Hal. Her parents did not want to jeopardize her future court proceedings by saying anything wrong to Hal.

John and Emma felt that if you hurt one of their children, you hurt them. John viewed himself as protector of his family, even after his children were grown. If his daughter's husband would not protect his family, then John would. Saying that he wanted to write a book on "How to Get Rid of Hal" seemed cathartic for John. However, this expression of catharsis scared Emma.

After a long talk, Emma and John agreed that they both needed to think redemptively. Dee's lawyer used to say, "The greatest revenge is success." Emma and John then thought in terms of Hal watching Dee succeed. He had made her quit school and jobs, but he did not have that kind of power anymore. They made it their goal to have Dee succeed with her children, in court, in school, and in her job. Hal will watch her succeed when he has tried so hard to push her down.

In order to learn what her daughter and grandchildren were going through physically and emotionally, Emma threw herself into time-consuming research. She had always thought that knowledge was power, but, in this instance, the more she learned and the more she experienced Hal's continued abuse of their daughter and children through Social Services and the court system, the more she feared and the deeper her feelings of utter powerlessness prevailed.

During the first year of separation, the court prevented Hal from making contact with Dee, and, during this time, he had supervised visitation with his children. Dee and the children spent most of their time living with Emma and John during the first few years of court proceedings until Dee went back to college and lived in family housing with the children. Hal lied in court motions not only about Dee and the children, but he also lied about Emma and John. He lied to Social Services, saying that Dee lived in squalor and abused the children. Emma spent many hours at the computer performing paralegal work to counter the assertions Hal made in motions. She spent countless hours with Dee in interviews with Social Services to try to explain what was really happening, and that Hal was using their department to abuse Dee.

On one occasion, Hal had lied about the children's relationship with Emma and John, saying the children were terrified of them. As she drew up to the computer to begin the process of addressing each claim in the motion, as she had done countless times to date, Emma's feelings of fear and emotional exhaustion broke through. Emma, John, and Dee already had a history of many disappointments in court with a judge who never viewed the situation accurately and with the opposing lawyer literally lying about their daughter and her parents before the judge.

Emma stared hopelessly at the blank screen and cried out to the Lord in anguish, sobbing, "Lord! How much more can we take of this before someone in the court system really understands what is happening here! When will it stop! When will this awful, evil man get what he deserves? God! Please make it stop! I can't do this anymore! I'm exhausted! I'm angry!" Emma had never cried or shouted out in "prayer" this way before. In that moment, through her own frustrations, she cried out to the Lord with her deepest and too-often suppressed feelings. She put Philippians 4:13 ("I can do all things through Him who strengthens me") on a neon sticker and placed it just to the upper right of her computer so it would catch her eye periodically and remind her that she would not be given more than she could handle.

The guardian ad litem assigned to their case was enamored with Hal's parenting and connection to the children. She found herself unimpressed with Dee, who was nervous and distracted. Even though Hal ended up in a batterer's program and went to jail because he had beaten Dee, and in spite of allegations of sexual abuse, the court system treated him like a good dad. Emma and John persevered as wisely and strongly as they could, but realized that lawyers, guardians ad litem, and judges had no clue about Dee's and the children's experiences. It felt like they were losing their grandchildren to an abuser.

During this entire time, Dee's brother, Dan, felt helpless. So, when he received a job offer 3,000 miles away, he took it readily. Emma and John felt the loss of his presence. Their son saw his parents do everything humanly possible for his sister and her children. The stress and pressure on his family and Dan's desire for Hal to be gone out of their lives became increasingly more difficult to manage. When Dee's oldest child described sexual abuse by her father to her therapist, Dan's feelings of helplessness became too great. Although law enforcement and Social Services were again involved, nothing was done. Social Services said they had every reason to believe Dee's daughter, given the physical evidence, but that the father probably told the child to lie when she was interviewed.

After Dee's daughter's interview, the law enforcement official in attendance turned to Emma and said, "If you see evidence that he [meaning Hal] has broken the law, please inform the police." Emma responded, looking him squarely in the eye, "We keep doing that, but it goes nowhere, because no one is willing to hold this man accountable—not the court, not law enforcement, not his lawyer, not his own parents, not Social Services, no one. So, my daughter, and especially my grandchildren, all continue to be held at risk and Hal's abuse continues." John and Emma felt, more than ever, fear for their daughter's and grandchildren's safety.

Emma and John experienced guilt over needing emotional support while their daughter and her children were the ones who urgently needed help. Emma and John saw a therapist who diagnosed them both with situational depression and anxiety. In other words, if the situation they found themselves in did not exist, their depression and anxiety would not exist. The therapist understood their plight and tried to be encouraging and helpful, but her efforts were not successful. Even well-intentioned and caring friends and family members were unable to understand why Emma and John were seemingly always either preparing for court or in court. Dee's lawyer said that her case file was the largest one he had in his twenty-year career.

Every time the phone rang, Emma and John were convinced that it would be bad news. A few months into the separation process, the sound of a ringing phone would make Emma startle. Both her tears and adrenalin would flow even before she answered the phone. Emma recognized that an unwelcome intruder, posttraumatic stress disorder, had moved in. She kept her PTSD feelings and triggers to herself. John had enough to worry about and she did not tell the therapist because Emma did not want that truth on record.

Hal's continued abuse and efforts to control Dee led to court proceeding after court proceeding and countless social service investigations that continued for nine years. Emma and John took out substantial home equity loans three times to cover the cost of lawyers while trying to protect their daughter and grandchildren. Emma worked exhaustively on court motions and other related tasks. Emma and John went to court with Dee every time she needed to appear. John worked tirelessly on financial documents to show proof of Hal's lies and to be sure his financial paperwork for court was accurate.

During this time, Emma taught courses in their church that prepared attendees for ministerial certification. Their pastor showed his profound ignorance when he asked Emma a question: "When do you think your daughter will be able to float her own boat?" Emma responded by saying: "When her former husband stops putting holes in it." Then Emma left the church. John had already left the church a few months prior, because the pastor showed himself to be very unsupportive. This pastor never asked how they were doing or if he could pray with them.

No one from church called to check in with Emma and John to see how they were doing. Those in the church never had any encouragement for them. Their well-meaning therapist could not help or give any insight to their situation. Friends and family, except for possibly their son, could not understand what they were going through.

After several years working toward a final divorce decree, the court ultimately gave Hal liberal, unsupervised parenting time and shared legal custody. Consequently, he had access to all of them. He could and did keep on abusing Dee and the children physically and emotionally. John and Emma viewed this conclusion as the result of ignorance and complacency on the part of everyone involved. John spent sleepless nights staring out of their back door into the darkness, trying to control his anger and sense of helplessness.

Dee had her life and hands full trying to navigate safety for her children and herself. Emma and John felt his abuse as if he was abusing them directly. They also felt the ineffectiveness of Social Services and felt abused by the opposing lawyer, the guardian ad litem, and the court system overall. The lack of knowledge and understanding about domestic violence on the part of every person and every entity involved with this case created a situation where Dee and her children remained at risk. Emma and John continued to grieve as the abuse of their daughter and grandchildren continued. They shared their daughter's feelings of pain, anger, frustration, disillusionment, grief, sadness, fear, and betrayal.

## A Woman's Parents' Choices

A few decades ago, a newly married friend shared that she really needed to make the best of her marriage no matter what happened, because her mother said, "You got married, you made your bed, now you have to lie in it." After asking what she thought her mother meant, she said that even in the worst of circumstances, her parents would not help her, and that she needed to find a way to take care of all her own marital problems. Some parents of daughters caught in a domestic violence marriage espouse this philosophy. They have nothing to offer and do not provide support of any kind to their daughter and their grandchildren. However, nearly two decades of personal experience with abused women reveals that there are very few parents of victims that do not want to help their daughters. Those who do want to help their abused daughter and their grandchildren are the ones we will address in this chapter.

Domestic Violence

## The Difficulty

### Three Generations

Grandparents realize that they not only have to try to help their daughter move through her situation and emotions, but also their grandchildren's situation and emotions, and also their own. An abused woman is concerned for her children and for herself, while the woman's parents focus on three generations. Grandparents offer the last line of defense or active involvement.

The main concerns revolve around the daughter and the children, and rightfully so. Both the mom and children are in danger as long as they live with the abuser as well as during and after separation and divorce. At the same time, the grandparents need support as well. Sadly, the parents of the victim are usually left with little support, and they have little understanding of the domestic violence situation they are dealing with. The result is too little wisdom at a time when much wisdom is needed. In the case study, Emma grappled for as much information she could get quickly, which was a wise thing to do.

### Physical Health, Emotions, and Mental Health

Supportive grandparents feel the trauma of their loved ones' experiences, but they also experience their own trauma.

#### Physical.

Physical manifestations of trauma may include sleep loss (as shown in John's sleepless nights staring out the back door), heightened blood pressure, weight loss (from worry, depression, or anxiety) or weight gain (using food to comfort), irritable bowel, chronic fatigue, headaches, and more. At the same time, "just because you go through trauma doesn't mean you'll have health problems. Other factors are at play, like your life experiences, the support you have from loved ones, and your genes."[1]

1. Richmond, "Emotional Trauma and the Mind-Body Connection," para 10.

*Emotions and Mental Health.*

The emotions grandparents experience include depression, anxiety, pain, anger, frustration, disillusionment, grief, loss, sadness, fear, hopelessness, powerlessness, and betrayal. Grandparents may try hard to protect their daughter from their own emotions, so the daughter can misinterpret what they are actually feeling and wonder why her parents do not experience the same feelings that she does. Grandparents do feel what their daughter feels, but try not to show those emotions in an effort not to add to their daughter's trauma.

The daughter may wonder why she had not been able to see through the façade of who their abuser really is. Likewise, the grandparents wonder why their good social skills did not pick up on something that would indicate this man's true nature. In some instances, grandparents did warn their daughter, but she took no heed. This is not the time to say, "I told you so." Just help her. You have all been betrayed. Grandparents can experience the same mental health concerns as abused women. Emma and John both had depression and anxiety, and Emma had PTSD as well.

## LACK OF SUPPORT

*Extended Family and Greater Community.*

The parents of the victim are too often overlooked. Friends and extended family ask about their daughter and grandchildren and how they are managing, and may even tell the grandparents how sorry they are for their circumstances, but few take the time to sit and talk with the grandparents to find out how they are doing. Those who take an active, regular interest in the grandparents' wellbeing under these circumstances should be highly commended for insight, wisdom, and kindness.

The church, community, and mental health professionals have nothing specific to support grandparents during this experience. Grandparents may view their situation and resulting emotions as burdensome for others. Moreover, the violence is not aimed directly against them. Sometimes grandparents want to keep their daughter's situation private because they believe her story is not theirs to tell. Friends and family may find the subject uncomfortable and not want to approach the matter of intimate partner violence with the grandparents. Others prefer to sidestep the conversation because they do not want to create an upset.

*Each Other.*

The grandparents experience raw emotions. Their feelings, however, may remain unspoken because they both share a common experience. Even when they have a close relationship, grandparents have a hard time supporting each other because they are both struggling with little outside support. When one grandparent has to vent, the other grandparent already knows all of it, identifies with it, and has nothing to offer to help. They go down that proverbial "rabbit hole" together. No one feels better, and their angst increases. They do not have the emotional resources to nurture each other through their daughter's trauma.

When one grandparent wants to support their abused daughter but the other believes that the daughter needs to handle her own situation, the grandparent who wants to help loses affection for the other spouse. The spouse who wants to help does not even have the support of the other. As one supportive grandparent said, "At some point they will need to have 'that' dance" whereby they either do or do not come to terms with their differences.

Whether the grandparents support one another or not, they find themselves in a very lonely place.

## Grieving

The grandparents experience a grieving process very much like their daughter's, but without the help of a domestic violence counselor, who can give them understanding and wisdom. A very wise psychologist once said, "Counselors and therapists can provide the tools needed to help a person's situation, but real healing happens in community." Where can the grandparents find their community of understanding and healing?

We do not grieve only when someone dies. The feelings of loss an abused woman and her parents experience can go on for years and years because the abuse continues and healing is thwarted. This kind of grief is not generally recognized or understood, and so receives little support.

Since the daughter's parents want to present her with a positive and encouraging demeanor, they will hide their grief. The grandparents may even hide their grief from each other. This "masked grief" creates additional emotional and mental health issues. Masked grief "can cause mental illnesses and disorders as the person who is grieving does not give themselves the time or space to actually grieve."[2] If one does not express one's grief, these emotions can emerge in unhealthy ways, such as "overeating, drinking, compulsive shopping, excessive sex,"[3] or another such manifestation. Physical manifestations can also occur. "Masked grief will manifest in headaches, stomachaches, sleeplessness, heartburn, and changes in appetite. You may also suffer from frequent occurrences of illness."[4]

## Spiritual Encouragement

Many Scriptures express the need for us to encourage others, but 2 Corinthians 1:3–5 stands out:

> Blessed be the God and Father of our Lord Jesus Christ, the Father of mercies and the God of all consolation, who consoles us in all our affliction, so that we may be able to console those who are in any affliction with the consolation with which we ourselves are consoled by God. For just as the sufferings of Christ are abundant for us, so also our consolation is abundant through Christ.

God shows us compassion and provides comfort. Then we show others the same comfort we have received from God.

But how do we do this? What does showing others compassion and comfort look like? Offering reassuring words from the heart and from the Scriptures can help immensely, but let us not stop there.

Sometimes we need to think in practical terms. For example, what can I do to relieve some of this person's, couple's, or family's burden? Because of all the time Emma spent helping her daughter with court, social services, and childcare, she would have appreciated someone cleaning, or fixing a dinner, or gathering mail at the post office. John, outside of his professional work, spent untold hours working on Dee's and Hal's financial court documents, juggling his and Emma's finances, attending court, and helping with the grandchildren. He would have welcomed someone picking up the branches in the yard after spring winds, or trimming the bushes, or helping him and Emma move their daughter and the children into their apartment. Sometimes the gospel, or loving and supporting someone in pain, comes in the form of a casserole, yard work, or other practical works of service.

2. Wallace, "Types of Grief," para. 52, 55.
3. Roldan, "Masked Grief," para. 27.
4. Roldan, "Masked Grief," para. 18.

When one does this, they are coming alongside someone else in their pain, which is an irreplaceable gift.

In the process of helping someone who hurts, we show love. First John 4:7–8 tells us: "Beloved, let us love one another, because love is from God; everyone who loves is born of God and knows God. Whoever does not love does not know God, for God is love."

# Conclusion

ONE SEPTEMBER EVENING, JOE and Karen attended their children's Parent-Teacher Association open house for parents and students. One father stood out as a model parent. His engaging tone when greeting others, his winsome smile as he put his signature on a form to do volunteer tutoring, his "obvious" care for his family as he displayed loving interactions with his children, all while holding hands with his adoring wife, made an unmistakable impression. This scenario could be one of a loving, engaged husband and father or could be one describing a batterer.

What might we see if we looked inside a courtroom to view a domestic violence couple during a divorce proceeding? The abuser smiles and looks self-assured. He presents his information and answers questions with confidence, and often does so as he evades the truth or lies about his victim. For emphasis, he furrows his brow just the right amount at just the right times. On the other hand, the victim has a flushed face and eyes rimmed with tears. Her voice quivers and her confidence falters. She has a hard time remembering events and important points she wanted to make to the judge. This protective mother presents as an anxious, fearful person, who has a hard time staying focused. The judge awards custody to the father because the mother gives the appearance of being a mentally unstable parent.

This book presents information that will allow professionals and the general reader to understand intimate partner violence and to make more appropriate, less harmful decisions for those involved. The reader will be able to better understand the abuser, the victim, and the children. Also included are practical helps and encouragement for protective mothers and children caught in domestic violence families, as well as information to help the protective mother better understand herself, her situation, and her children. The material helps the victim understand that, whether she stays with the abuser or leaves, she has exhibited great courage.

Working successfully to reduce domestic violence means an increase in safe homes and fewer hospital visits for women and children, less engagement with law enforcement, better mental health and lowered mental health expenditures, fewer court cases, a decrease in incest and child abuse, less risk in school for all children as good behaviors increase and acting out decreases, less Social Service involvement, an increase in children's abilities educationally and socially, and less crime in our communities.

Violence against women is widespread globally, and is a violation of women's human rights. Nonetheless, domestic violence is not handled with the same overall attention and care as other human rights issues. Marianna Yang of Harvard Law School states:

> Since the pandemic [Covid-19], violence against women has increased to unprecedented levels. The *American Journal of Emergency Medicine* said that domestic violence cases increased by 25 to 33 percent globally. The National Commission on COVID-19 and criminal justice shows an increase in the US by a little over 8 percent, following the imposition of lockdown orders during 2020.[1]

If you know grandparents who are going through this experience, encourage them to find someone to talk with. Maybe that person is you. When they cannot or do not open up about their experience, they exist behind locked doors until someone comes along with a key that opens the door to sharing their emotions. Making the statement, "If you are able, please tell me what you are experiencing and feeling, and if not now, I will wait until you can," brings relief, because someone is showing them interest. The grandparents are being given an opportunity to experience better physical and mental health as opposed to hanging onto emotions and grief. Be available and sincere when you use that key.

The first step in helping the world to become a safer, healthier place for everyone is to become knowledgeable about domestic violence. You, the reader, have just done that. Now, you will know when to take that second step.

1. Mineo, *The Harvard Gazette*, para. 3.

# Appendix

RESOURCES ABOUND FOR THOSE who need help or information about domestic violence. Those listed here in alphabetical order provide only a few, but many sites contain additional information one may want for safety as well as information.

**Alliance for HOPE International:** 1–888-511–3522
Their goal is to meet the needs of survivors of domestic violence and sexual assault, as well as their children; elder and child abuse; human trafficking.
https://www.allianceforhope.com/

**Childhelp National Child Abuse Hotline:** 1–800-A-CHILD (2–24453)
This site has a map with phone numbers for each state.
https://childhelphotline.org/

**Compensation Compass**
Offers possible financial help for victims of domestic violence.
https://compass.freefrom.org/

**Domesticshelters.org (Canada)**
This site has resources and help for those in Canada.
https://www.domesticshelters.org/en-ca/domestic-abuse-help-in-canada

**Domesticshelters.org (USA)**
A resource for finding a shelter near you, with access to more than 1,100 helpful articles.
https://www.domesticshelters.org/

**National Domestic Violence Hotline:**
1–800-799-SAFE (7233) and TTY 1–800-787–3224
https://www.thehotline.org/

**National Organization for Victim Assistance**
Victim assistance resources and information
https://www.trynova.org/

**National Sexual Assault Hotline:** 1–800-656-HOPE (4673)
https://www.rainn.org/about-national-sexual-assault-telephone-hotline
https://hotline.rainn.org/online

**National Teen Dating Abuse Helpline:**
1–866-331–9474 and TTY 1–866-331–8453

**National Child Traumatic Stress Network**
https://www.nctsn.org/

**Rape, Abuse, and Incest National Network (RAINN):**
1–800-656-HOPE (4673)
https://www.rainn.org/

**Safe Helpline** (for members of the military): 1–877-995–5247
https://www.safehelpline.org/

**Women's Advocates:** 1–651-227–8284
Their mission is to work with victim-survivors and the community to
break domestic violence cycle.
https://www.wadvocates.org/

**WomensLaw.org**
Provides legal information for victims.
https://www.womenslaw.org/

# Bibliography

Aas, Monica, Henry Chantal, Ole A. Andreassen, Frank Bellivier, Ingrid Melle, and Bruno Erain. "The Role of Childhood Trauma in Bipolar Disorders." *International Journal of Bipolar Disorders* 4, no. 1 (2016). https://journalbipolardisorders.springeropen.com/articles/10.1186/s40345-015-0042-0.

Ackerman, Courtney E. "What is Attachment Theory? Bowlby's 4 Stages Explained." Positive Psychology.com. April 15, 2020. https://positivepsychology.com/attachment-theory/.

ActionAid UK, Gender & Development Network, Womankind International Planned Parenthood Federation, and Orchid Project. "Gender Equality: The Key to Ending Violence Against Women." Accessed 2023. https://www.ippf.org/sites/default/files/violence_against_women_and_girls_-_gender_equality.pdf.

Al-Zubi, Yasmin. "Reversing Real-Life Violence Desensitization in Children." *Journal of Neurology and Clinical Neuroscience* 5, no. 4, (2021), 1–3. https://www.pulsus.com/scholarly-articles/reversing-reallife-violence-desensitization-in-children.pdf.

American Psychiatric Association. "What are Dissociative Disorders?" August 2018. https://psychiatry.org/patients-families/dissociative-disorders/what-are-dissociative-disorders.

———. "What is Schizophrenia?" Accessed 2023. https://www.psychiatry.org/patients-families/schizophrenia/what-is-schizophrenia.

American Psychological Association. *APA Dictionary of Psychology*. Washington, DC: American Psychological Association, 2023. https://dictionary.apa.org.

———. "Sexual Assault and Harassment." Accessed 2022. https://www.apa.org/topics/sexual-assault-harassment.

Angelakis, Ioannis, Jennifer L. Austin, and Patricia Gooding. "Association of Childhood Maltreatment with Suicide Behaviors among Young People: A Systematic Review and Meta-analysis." *JAMA Network Open* 3, no. 8 (August 5, 2020). https://jamanetwork.com/journals/jamanetworkopen/fullarticle/2769030.

Aristotle. *On the Generation of Animals*. Translated by Arthur Platt. Accessed March 8, 2020. https://en.wikisource.org/wiki/On_the_Generation_of_Animals/Book_IV.

Assohoto, Barnabe, and Samuel Ngewa. "Genesis." In the *Africa Bible Commentary*, edited by Tokunboth Adeyemo. Nairobi: WordAlive/Zondervan, 2006.

Attorneys.com. "Legal Defenses for Battered Women." Legal Articles, Domestic Violence. Accessed 2022. https://www.attorneys.com/domestic-violence/legal-defenses-for-battered-women.

Bacon-Davis, Amanda. *This Thing Has a Name*. Illustrated by Jinjer Markley. Amanda Bacon-Davis, 2022.

Bahk, Yong-Chun, Seon-Kyeonj Jang, Kee-Hong Choi, and Seunj-Hwan Lee. "The Relationship between Childhood Trauma and Suicidal Ideation: Role of Maltreatment and Potential Mediators." *Psychiatry Investigation* 13, no. 1, 37–43. DOI 10.4306/pi.2017.14.1.37.

Bancroft, Lundy. "The Connection between Batterers and Child Sexual Abuse Perpetrators." Lundy Bancroft, 2007. https://lundybancroft.com/articles/the-connection-between-batterers-and-child-sexual-abuse-perpetrators/.

———. "Healing and Recovery in Children Exposed to Domestic Violence." Domesticshelters.org, Webinar, Phoenix, AZ., May 12, 2022. https://www.domestic shelters.org/.

———. *When Dad Hurts Mom: Helping Your Children Heal the Wounds of Witnessing Abuse*. New York: Penguin, 2004.

———. *Why Does He Do That? Inside the Minds of Angry and Controlling Men*. New York: Penguin, 2002.

Bancroft, Lundy, and Jay G Silverman. *The Batterer as Parent*. London: SAGE Publications, 2002.

Banks, Duncan. "What is Brain Plasticity and Why is it so Important?" The Conversation. April 4, 2016. https://theconversation.com/what-is-brain-plasticity-and-why-is-it-so-important-55967.

Bender, Eve. "PTSD, Other Disorders Evident in Kids Who Witness Domestic Violence." Psychiatric News: American Psychiatric Association. June 4, 2004. https://psychnews.psychiatryonline.org/doi/full/10.1176/pn.39.11.0390014a.

Benoit, Diane. "Infant-Parent Attachment: Definition, Types, Antecedents, Measurement and Outcome." *Paediatrics Child Health* 9, no. 8 (October 2004), 541–45. https://www.ncbi.nlm.nih.gov/pmc/articles/PMC2724160/.

Bensley, Lillian, Juliet Van Eenwyk, and Katrina Wynkoop Simmons. "Childhood Family Violence History and Women's Risk for Intimate Partner Violence and Poor Health." *American Journal of Prevevntive Medicine* 25, no. 1 (July 2003), 38–44. https://pubmed.ncbi.nlm.nih.gov/12818308/.

Bering, Jesse. "Pedophiles, Hebephiles and Ephebophiles, Oh My: Erotic Age Orientation." *Scientific American*, July 1, 2009. https://blogs.scientificamerican.com/bering-in-mind/pedophiles-hebephiles-and-ephebophiles-oh-my-erotic-age-orientation/.

Bevan, Emma, and Daryl Higgins. "Is Domestic Violence Learned? The Contribution of Five Forms of Child Maltreatment to Men's Violence and Adjustment." *Journal of Family Violence* 17 (2002) 223–45. DOI:10.1023/A:1016053228021.

Boseley, Sarah. "Domestic Abuse Victims More Likely to Suffer Mental Illness—Study." *The Guardian*, June 7, 2019. https://www.theguardian.com/society/2019/jun/07/domestic-abuse-victims-more-likely-to-suffer-mental-illness-study.

Brown, Brett V., and Sharon Bzostek. "Violence in the Lives of Children." *Cross Currents* 1 (August 2003). https://cms.childtrends.org/wp-content/uploads/2003/01/2003-15ViolenceChildren.pdf.

Calvete, Esther. Mental Health Characteristics of Men Who Abuse Their Intimate Partner. *Revista Espanola de Sanidad Penitenciaria* 10 (June 2008), 48–55. http://scielo.isciii.es/pdf/sanipe/v10n2/revision.pdf.

Camber Children's Mental Health. "What's the Connection between Child Abuse and Depression?" KVC Health Systems. April 13, 2021. https://www.cambermentalhealth. org/2021/04/13/whats-the-connection-between-child-abuse-and-depression/.

*Cambridge Dictionary*, s.v. "undermine." Cambridge: Cambridge University Press, 2021. https://dictionary.cambridge.org/us/dictionary/english/undermine.

Cameranesi, Margherita, and Caroline C. Piotrowski. "Self-Esteem in Children Exposed to Intimate Partner Violence: a Critical Review of the Role of Sibling Relationships and Agenda for Future Research." *Journal of Child and Adolescent Trauma* 11, no. 3 (September 2018), 339–51. https://www.ncbi.nlm.nih.gov/pmc/articles/PMC7163827/.

Centers for Disease Control and Prevention. *Preventing Adverse Childhood Experiences: Leveraging the Best Available Evidence*. Atlanta: National Center for Injury Prevention and Control, Centers for Disease Control and Prevention, 2019.

CHADD. "Finding Help for ADHD and Domestic Violence." Accessed 2023. https://chadd.org/adhd-weekly/finding-help-for-adhd-and-domestic-violence/.

Child Abuse Solutions, Inc. "Fact Sheet: Child Sexual Abuse in Custody Disputes." Center for Judicial Excellence, Berkeley, CA, no date. https://centerforjudicialexcellence.org/wp-content/uploads/2013/12/2008-FINAL-CSA-FACT-SHEET.pdf.

Children's Hospital of Philadelphia. "Domestic Violence and Child Abuse." Accessed 2020. https://violence.chop.edu/domestic-violence-and-child-abuse.

Children's Services. "How Trauma Affects Child Brain Development," *Practice Notes* 17, no. 2 (May 2012). North Carolina Division of Social Services and the Family and Children's Resource Program. https://practicenotes.org/v17n2/brain.htm.

Clay, Rebecca. "Suicide and Intimate Partner Violence." *Monitor on Psychology* 45, no. 10 (2014), 30. https://www.apa.org/monitor/2014/11/suicide-violence.

Clayton, Ingrid. "What is Trauma-Bonding?" *Psychology Today*. September 16, 2021. https://www.psychologytoday.com/us/blog/emotional-sobriety/202109/what-is-trauma-bonding.

Cleveland Clinic. "Reactive Attachment Disorder." Accessed 2023. https://my.clevelandclinic.org/health/diseases/17904-reactive-attachment-disorder.

Clute, Penny. "The Law and You: Strangulation Always Serious." Alliance for HOPE, International, Family Justice Center. January 15, 2019. https://www.familyjusticecenter.org/the-law-and-you-strangulation-always-serious/.

*Collins English Dictionary*, s.v. "undermine." New York: HarperCollins, 2021. https://www.collinsdictionary.com/us/dictionary/english/undermine.

Cordoza, Kavitha, and Clare Marie Schneider. "The Importance of Mourning Losses." North Carolina Public Radio. June 14, 2021. https://www.npr.org/2021/06/02/1002446604/the-importance-of-mourning-losses-even-when-they-seem-small.

Criminal Justice Research. "Female Suicide and Domestic Violence," 2022. https://criminal-justice.iresearchnet.com/types-of-crime/domestic-violence/female-suicide/.

Currie, Janet, and Erdal Tekin. "Does Child Abuse Cause Crime?" Institute for the Study of Labor: Discussion Paper Series No. 2063 (April 2006). https://docs.iza.org/dp2063.pdf.

Custody X Change. "Family Court Bias Against Mothers: Real or Not?" (No Date.) https://www.custodyxchange.com/topics/custody/family-members/bias-against-mothers.php.

Davis, Charles Patrick. "Definition of Attention Deficit Disorder (ADD)." MedicineNet. Accessed March 29, 2021. https://www.medicinenet.com/attention_deficit_disorder_add/definition.htm.

Degges-White, Suzanne. "Intimate Partner Abuse: Walk Away Before the Cycle Starts." *Psychology Today,* February 2015. https://www.psychologytoday.com/us/blog/lifetime-connections/201502/intimate-partner-abuse-walk-away-the-cycle-starts.

Dibdin, Emma. "Why Childhood Trauma Could Be Causing Your Anxiety." PsychCentral. Accessed January 31, 2022. https://psychcentral.com/anxiety/the-connection-between-childhood-trauma-and-generalized-anxiety-disorder.

Dimock, Jean A. "Influence of Plato and Aristotle's Patriarchy on Christian Hierarchy Today." In *Christian Egalitarian Leadership: Empowering the Whole Church according to the Scriptures,* edited by Aída Besançon Spencer and William David Spencer, 83–114. House of Prisca and Aquila Series. Eugene, OR: Wipf & Stock, 2020.

Dissociative Identity Disorder Research. "Types of Trauma." Accessed October 10, 2020. https://did-research.org/origin/trauma/.

DomesticShelters.org. "Barriers to Leaving, Part 1." Accessed January 1, 2016. https://www.domesticshelters.org/articles/escaping-violence/barriers-to-leaving-part-i.

———. "5 Myths about Child Custody and Domestic Violence." September 16, 2016. https://www.domesticshelters.org/articles/child-custody/5-myths-about-child-custody-and-domestic-violence.

———. "Do Survivors Lie?" April 3, 2013. https://www.domesticshelters.org/articles/escaping-violence/do-survivors-lie.

———. "Forbidden Food." November 29, 2017. https://www.domesticshelters.org/articles/true-survivor-stories/forbidden-food.

———. "Getting Kids Out of Harm's Way." July 6, 2014. https://www.domesticshelters.org/articles/escaping-violence/getting-kids-out-of-harm-s-way.

———. Strangulation Can Leave Long-Lasting Injuries." April 4, 2016. https://www.domesticshelters.org/articles/health/strangulation-can-leave-long-lasting-injuries.

———. "When Incest Accompanies Domestic Violence." July 20, 2016. https://www.domesticshelters.org/articles/identifying-abuse/when-incest-accompanies-domestic-violence.

———. "When it's Time to Go: Part I." July 11, 2014. https://www.domesticshelters.org/articles/escaping-violence/when-it-s-time-to-go-part-i.

Early Learning Childhood Education. "5 Reasons to Empower Children (and 5 Ways to Do It)." BonkersBeat.com. March 15, 2017. https://musicearlychildhoodpresenter.com/5-reasons-to-empower-children.

Edleson, Jeffrey L., Lyungai F. Mbilinyi, and Shetty, Sudha. "Parenting in the Context of Domestic Violence." Judicial Council of California Administrative Office of the Courts: Center for Families, Children & the Courts: March 2003. http://ce-classes.com/exam_format/Parenting-in-the-Context-of-Domestic-Violence.pdf.

Edwards, Blake Griffin. "Alarming Effects of Children's Exposure to Domestic Violence." *Psychology Today,* February 26, 2019. https://www.psychologytoday.com/us/blog/progress-notes/201902/alarming-effects-childrens-exposure-domestic-violence.

Ennis, Liam, Carissa Toop, Sandy Jung, and Sean Bois. "Instrumental and Reactive Intimate Partner Violence: Offender Characteristics, Reoffense Rates, and Risk Management." *Journal of Threat Assessment and Management* 4, no. 2 (2017), 61–76.. http://dx.doi.org/10.1037/tam0000080.

Evers, Kelly Ann. "Batterers: Characteristics that Help Identify a Potential Abuser." www. domestic-violence-help.org. Accessed 2023. https://www.domestic-violence-help. org/batterers.html.

Fagan, Anna. "Why Didn't She Call Police?" Genesis Women's Shelter & Support. May 11, 2020. https://www.genesisshelter.org/why-didnt-she-call-police/.

Farney, Andrea C., and Roberta L. Valente. "Creating Justice Through Balance: Integrating Domestic Violence Law into Family Court Practice." *Juvenile and Family Court Journal* 54, no. 4 (Fall 2003), 35–55. DOI:10.1111/j.1755–6988.2003.tb00085.x.

Florida Coalition against Domestic Violence. "Exploring the Intersection Between Intimate Partner Violence and Substance Use/Abuse." (No Date.) http:// centerforchildwelfare.fmhi.usf.edu/Training/2018cpssummit/Domestic_Violence_ and_Substance_Abuse.original.1534343264.pdf.

Fontes, Lisa Aronson. "8 Common Post-Separation Domestic Abuse Tactics." Domesticshelters.org. April 27, 2022. https://www.domesticshelters.org/articles/ legal/8-common-post-separation-domestic-abuse-tactics.

———. "From Romance to Isolation: Understanding Grooming." Domesticshelters.org. February 11, 2019. https://www.domesticshelters.org/articles/identifying-abuse/ from-romance-to-isolation-understanding-grooming.

———. "How Domestic Abusers Groom and Isolate their Victims." *Psychology Today*, February 19, 2019. https://www.psychologytoday.com/us/blog/invisible-chains/201902/how-domestic-abusers-groom-and-isolate-their-victims.

———. "4 Phases Before an Abuser Kills." Domesticshelters.org. May 18, 2022. https://www. domesticshelters.org/articles/identifying-abuse/4-phases-before-an-abuser-kills.

———. "10 Risks of Domestic Abusers as Parents." Domesticshelters.org. September 5, 2022. https://www.domesticshelters.org/articles/children-and-domestic-violence/ unsupervised-visitation-for-abuser-s-kids-is-risky.

———. "Yes, Abusive Partners Brainwash their Victims." Domesticshelters.org. April 7, 2021. https://www.domesticshelters.org/articles/identifying-abuse/yes-abusive-partners -brainwash-their-victims.

Ford, Kathryn. "Children's Exposure to Intimate Partner Sexual Assault." *Family & Intimate Partner Violence Quarterly.* 1, no. 2 (Fall 2008), 141–49. https://www. innovatingjustice.org/sites/default/files/child_exposure.pdf.

Foy, Chris. "What is the Relationship between Domestic Violence and Bipolar Disorder?" FHE Health. January 27, 2023. https://fherehab.com/learning/link-domestic-violence-bipolar.

Fraley, R. Chris. "Adult Attachment Theory and Research: A Brief Overview." University of Illinois at Urbana-Champaign, Department of Psychology, 2018. http://labs. psychology.illinois.edu/~rcfraley/attachment.htm.

Fuller, J. Ryan. "Intimate Partner Violence: Characteristics of Abusers and Victims." New York Behavioral Health. Accessed 2023. https://newyorkbehavioralhealth.com/ domestic-violence-characteristics-of-abusers-and-victims-part-i-of-ii.

Fuller-Thomson, Esme, and Stephen R. Hooper. "The Association between Childhood Physical Abuse and Dyslexia: Findings from a Population-Based Study." *Journal of Interpersonal Violence* 30, no. 9 (May 2015), 1583–92. DOI: 10.1177/0886260514540808.

Goldstein, Barry. "California Courts Harm Kids by Ignoring the Science." Domesticshelters. org. March 28, 2022. https://www.domesticshelters.org/articles/domestic-violence-op-ed-column/courts-refuse-to-listen-to-scientists-despite-kids-in-harm.

———. "How Can Protective Mothers Find a Good Attorney?" Domesticshelters.org. April 11, 2022. https://www.domesticshelters.org/articles/domestic-violence-op-ed-column/how-can-protective-mothers-find-a-good-attorney.

Grana, Jose Luis, Natalia Redondo, Marina J. Munoz-Rivas, and Arthur L. Cantos. "Subtypes of Batterers in Treatment: Empirical Support for a Distinction between Type I, Type II, and Type III." *PLOS ONE*, 9, no. 10 (October 16, 2014). https://doi.org/10.1371/journal.pone.0110651.

Guy-Evans, Olivia. "Frontal Lobe Function, Location in Brain and Function." Simply Psychology. May 8, 2021. https://www.simplypsychology.org/frontal-lobe.html.

Hadianfard, Habib. "Child Abuse in Group of Children with Attention Deficit-Hyperactivity Disorder in Comparison with Normal Children." *International Journal of Community Based Nursing and Midwifery* 2, no. 2 (April 2014) 77–84. https://www.ncbi.nlm.nih.gov/pmc/articles/PMC4201192/.

Healthdirect. "Mental Illness Stigma." September, 2021. https://www.healthdirect.gov.au/mental-illness-stigma.

Herman, Judith. *Trauma and Recovery: The Aftermath of Violence—From Domestic Abuse to Political Terror*. New York: Basic, 1997.

Herrenkohl, Todd I., Hyunzee Jung, Jungeun Olivia Lee, and MooHyun Kim. "Effects of Child Maltreatment, Cumulative Victimization Experiences, and Proximal Life Stress on Adult Crime and Antisocial Behavior." US Department of Justice: National Criminal Justice Reference Service, January 2017. https://www.ojp.gov/pdffiles1/nij/grants/250506.pdf.

Higuera, Valencia. "What is Uninvolved Parenting?" Healthline. September 20, 2019. https://www.healthline.com/health/parenting/uninvolved-parenting.

Hodel, Amanda S. "Rapid Infant Prefrontal Cortex Development and Sensitivity to Early Environmental Experience." *Developmental Review* 48 (2018), 113–44. DOI 10.1016/j.dr.2018.02.003.

Holland, Kimberly. "PTSD and Depression: How are they Related?" Healthline. March 22, 2019. https://www.healthline.com/health/ptsd-and-depression.

Holt, Stephanie, Helen Buckley, and Sadhbh Whelan. "The Impact of Exposure to Domestic Violence and Young People: A Review of the Literature." *Child Abuse & Neglect* 32 (2008), 797–810. https://citeseerx.ist.psu.edu/document?repid=rep1&type=pdf&doi=554513b61a88a64354ebb0075c0bc76c00102c52.

Huecker, Martin R., Kevin C. King, Gary A. Jordan, and William Smock. "Domestic Violence." National Institute of Health. March 7, 2022. https://www.ncbi.nlm.nih.gov/books/NBK499891/.

Hunter, Cathryn. "Effects of Child Abuse and Neglect for Adult Survivors." Australian Institute of Family Studies. January 2014. https://aifs.gov.au/cfca/publications/effects-child-abuse-and-neglect-adult-survivors.

Karin, Omer, Moriya Raz, Avichai Tendler, Alon Bar, Yael Korem Kohanim, Tomer Milo, and Uri Alon. "A New Model for the HPA Axis Explains Dysregulation of Stress Hormones on the Timescale of Weeks." *Molecular Systems Biology* 16 (2020). https://www.embopress.org/doi/full/10.15252/msb.20209510.

Katz, Emma. "Coercive Control, Domestic Violence, and a Five-Factor Framework: Five Factors That Influence Closeness, Distance, and Strain in Mother–Child Relationships." *Violence Against Women* 25, no. 15 (2019), 1829–53.

Kesner, John E., and Patrick C. McKenry. "The Role of Childhood Attachment Factors in Predicting Male Violence Toward Female Intimates." *Journal of*

*Family Violence* 13, no. 4 (1998), 417–32. https://www.researchgate.net/profile/John_Kesner/publication/251112620_The_Role_of_Childhood_Attachment_Factors_in_Predicting_Male_Violence_Toward_Female_Intimates/links/545cb2ffocf2c1a63bf8dob1.pdf.

Kippert, Amanda. "The Warning Signs an Abusive Partner May Try to Kill You." *A&E True Crime.* September 20, 2021. https://www.aetv.com/real-crime/signs-an-abusive-partner-may-kill-you.

———. "What is Emotional Abuse?" Domesticshelters.org. May 12, 2021. https://www.domesticshelters.org/articles/identifying-abuse/what-is-emotional-abuse.

Kochanowska, Maja. "The Biology of Stress." Reliably about Biology and Neurobiology. March 29, 2020. https://neuroskoki.pl/en/biology-of-stress/.

Kookogey, Kevin S. *An Apologetic for Liberty.* Franklin, TN: Stoddard, 2022.

Layton, Julia, and Alia Hoyt. "How Brainwashing Works." Howstuffworks.com. October 4, 2021. https://science.howstuffworks.com/life/inside-the-mind/human-brain/brainwashing.htm.

Legal Momentum. "History of the Violence against Women Act." The Women's Legal Defense and Education Fund. Accessed 2023. https://www.legalmomentum.org/history-vawa.

Lewis, T., D. C. Schwebel, M. N. Elliott, S. N. Visser, S. L. Toomey, K. A. McLaughlin, P. Cuccaro, S. Tortolero Emery, S. W. Banspach, and M. A. Schuster. "The Association between Youth Violence Exposure and Attention-Deficit/Hyperactivity Disorder (ADHD) Symptoms in a Sample of Fifth-Graders." *American Journal of Orthopsychiatry* 85, no. 5 (2015), 504–13. https://www.ncbi.nlm.nih.gov/pmc/articles/PMC4636211/.

Li, Pamela. "4 Types of Parenting Styles and Their Effects on the Child." Parenting for Brain. July 25, 2022. https://www.parentingforbrain.com/4-baumrind-parenting-styles/.

———. "Uninvolved Parenting—Why It's the Worst Parenting Style." Parenting for Brain. 2022. https://www.parentingforbrain.com/uninvolved-parenting/.

MacLaren, Alexander. "Psalm 27." *MacLaren Expositions of Holy Scripture.* Bible Hub, 2004–2023. https://biblehub.com/commentaries/maclaren/psalms/27.htm.

Mair, Christina, Carol B. Cunradi, and Michael Todd. "Adverse childhood experiences and intimate partner violence: testing psychosocial mediational pathways among couples." *Annals of Epidemiology* 22, no. 12 (December 2022), 832–39. DOI 10.1016/j.annepidem.2012.09.008.

Martin, Sharon. "What Kind of Boundaries Do You Need to Set?" Betterboundariesworkbook.com. 2023. https://betterboundariesworkbook.com/types-of-boundaries/.

Massachusetts Citizens for Children (MassKids). "Behavior and Physical Signs that Might Indicate Sexual Abuse." Enough Abuse Campaign. 2022. https://www.enoughabuse.org/gtf/possible-signs-in-children.html.

———. "Behavior Signs of Abusers: Grooming Tactics Used by Sexual Abusers." Enough Abuse Campaign. 2022. https://www.enoughabuse.org/gtf/who-are-the-abusers-2.html.

———. "Who are the Abusers?" Enough Abuse Campaign. 2022. https://www.enoughabuse.org/gtf/who-are-the-abusers.html.

Mayo Clinic. "Dissociative Disorders." Mayo Foundation for Medical Education and Research. 2022. https://www.mayoclinic.org/diseases-conditions/dissociative-disorders/symptoms-causes/syc-20355215.

McBride, Karyl. "Shaming Children is Emotionally Abusive." *Psychology Today*, September 10, 2012. https://www.psychologytoday.com/us/blog/the-legacy-distort ed-love/201209/shaming-children-is-emotionally-abusive.

McDonald, Renee, Ernest N. Jouriles, Suhasini Ramisetty-Mikler, Raul Caetano, and Charles E. Green. "Estimating the Number of American Children Living in Partner-Violent Families." US Department of Health and Human Services, Office on Women's Health. February 15, 2021. https://www.womenshealth.gov/relationships-and-safety/domestic-violence/effects-domestic-violence-children.

MedicineNet. "Medical Definition of Perinatal." March 29, 2021. https://www.medicinenet.com/perinatal/definition.htm.

Miller, Alison. "Intimate Family Violence: A Dissociative Family Dance." International Society for the Study of Trauma and Dissociation. October 26, 2016. https://news.isst-d.org/%EF%BB%BF%EF%BB%BFintimate-partner-violence-a-dissociative-family-dance/.

Mineo, Liz. "'Shadow Pandemic' of Domestic Violence." *Harvard Gazette*, June 29, 2022. https://news.harvard.edu/gazette/story/2022/06/shadow-pandemic-of-domestic-violence.

Moynihan, Jennifer, and Matthew Copeland. "911's Deadly Flaw: Why Dialing 911 from a Cell Phone Can Cost You Precious Time." CBS: WTLV. February 5, 2020. https://www.cbs19.tv/article/news/local/9-1-1s-deadly-flaw-why-dialing-9-1-1-from-a-cell-phone-can-cost-you-precious-time/501-2f89f766-726e-4ef4-b434-14b2b57b1ffo.

Mueller, Isabelle, and Ed Tronick. "Early Life Exposure to Violence: Developmental Consequences on Brain and Behavior." *Frontiers in Behavioral Neuroscience* 13 (2019). https://www.frontiersin.org/articles/10.3389/fnbeh.2019.00156/full.

National Center on Domestic Violence, Trauma, and Mental Health. "Preparing for Court Proceedings with Survivors of Domestic Violence." March 2013. http://www.nationalcenterdvtraumamh.org/wp-content/uploads/2013/03/NCDVTMH-2013-Preparing-for-Court-Proceedings.pdf.

National Child Traumatic Stress Network. "Effects." Accessed 2023. https://www.nctsn.org/what-is-child-trauma/trauma-types/complex-trauma/effects.

———. "Helping Your Teen Cope with Traumatic Stress and Substance Abuse: A Guide for Parents." October 2008. https://www.nctsn.org/sites/default/files/resources//helping_your_teen_cope_traumatic_stress_substance_abuse_parents.pdf.

———. "Making the Connection: Trauma and Substance Abuse." June 2008. https://www.nctsn.org/resources/making-connection-trauma-and-substance-abuse.

National Domestic and Family Violence Bench Book. "Cultural and Spiritual Abuse." June 2021. https://dfvbenchbook.aija.org.au/understanding-domestic-and-family-violence/cultural-and-spiritual-abuse/.

National Domestic Violence Hotline. "Is Change Possible in an Abuser?" Accessed 2023. https://www.thehotline.org/resources/is-change-possible-in-an-abuser/.

———. "What is Gaslighting?" Accessed 2023. https://www.thehotline.org/resources/what-is-gaslighting/.

National Health Service (United Kingdom). "Causes—Bipolar Disorder." January 3, 2023. https://www.nhs.uk/mental-health/conditions/bipolar-disorder/causes/.

National Institute of Justice, U.S. Department of Justice. "Batterer Intervention Programs Have Mixed Results." October 9, 2019. https://nij.ojp.gov/topics/articles/batterer-intervention-programs-have-mixed-results.

———. "Children Exposed to Violence." September 21, 2016. https://nij.ojp.gov/topics/articles/children-exposed-violence.

———. "Mandatory Divorce Custody Mediation and Intimate Partner Violence." April 17, 2018. https://nij.ojp.gov/topics/articles/mandatory-divorce-custody-mediation-and-intimate-partner-violence.

———. "Pathways between Child Maltreatment and Adult Criminal Involvement." October 11, 2017. https://nij.ojp.gov/topics/articles/pathways-between-child-maltreatment-and-adult-criminal-involvement.

National Institute of Mental Health. "Attention-Deficit/Hyperactivity Disorder." September, 2021. https://www.nimh.nih.gov/health/topics/attention-deficit-hyperactivity-disorder-adhd.

———. "Bipolar Disorder." October 2018. https://www.nimh.nih.gov/sites/default/files/documents/health/publications/bipolar-disorder/19-mh-8088.pdf.

Neuro Health. "Types of Dyslexia." Laurie H. C. Philips & Associates. 2022. https://neurohealthah.com/blog/types-of-dyslexia.

Neuroscientifically Challenged. "Know Your Brain: Amygdala." 2022. https://neuroscientificallychallenged.com/posts/know-your-brain-amygdala.

New Jersey Division of Criminal Justice. "Handling a Domestic Violence Call: In-Service Training for Police Dispatchers." May, 2003 and December 2001. https://www.nj.gov/oag/dcj/njpdresources/dom-violence/dv-dispatcher-stud.pdf.

Northwest Justice Project. "Getting Ready for a Court Trial or Hearing." Washington LawHelp. November 2021. https://www.washingtonlawhelp.org/files/C9D2EA3F-0350-D9AF-ACAE-BF37E9BC9FFA/attachments/392541D4-E185-CAA9-028E-45925FFDD37B/3210en_gettingreadyforahearingortrial_final_20211203.pdf.

Nova Southeastern University. Lenore Walker Faculty Profile. 2020. https://psychology.nova.edu/faculty/profile/walker.html.

Olivares, Vianey. "The Most Misogynistic Movies and Film Franchises of All Time." Cultura Colectiva. June 29, 2019. https://culturacolectiva.com/movies/most-misogynistic-films-of-all-time.

Orenstein, Beth W. "Understanding Battered Woman Syndrome." Everyday Health. November 25, 2014. https://www.everydayhealth.com/news/understanding-battered-womens-syndrome/.

Ortlund, Dane. ESV Devotional Psalter. Wheaton: Crossway, 2016.

Paradigm Treatment. "What are the Effects of Domestic Violence on Teens?" August 23, 2017. https://paradigmtreatment.com/effects-of-domestic-violence-teens/.

Paybarah, Azi. "Mother of Children Killed by Their Father Said She Lived in Fear." New York Times, March 2, 2022. https://www.nytimes.com/2022/03/02/us/sacramento-church-shooting.html.

Pence, Ellen, Gabrielle Davis, Cheryl Beardslee, and Denise Gamache. "Mind the Gap: Accounting for Domestic Abuse in Child Custody Evaluations." U.S. Department of Justice, Office of Violence Against Women, Battered Women's Justice Project. June 2012.

Perrin, Ruth Leah. "Overcoming Biased Views of Gender and Victimhood in Custody Evaluations When Domestic Violence Is Alleged," American University Journal of Gender, Social Policy & the Law 25 no. 2 (2017), 155–77. https://digitalcommons.wcl.american.edu/cgi/viewcontent.cgi?article=1694&context=jgspl.

Plato. Laws. Internet Classics Archive. Translated by Benjamin Jowett. 1994–2009. http://classics.mit.edu/Plato/laws.11.xi.html.

Popovic, David, Andrea Schmitt, Lalit Kaurani, Fanny Senner, Sergi Papiol, Berend Malchow, Andre Fischer, Thomas G. Schulze, Nikolaos Koutsouleris, and Peter Falkai. "Childhood Trauma in Schizophrenia: Current Findings and Research Perspectives." *Frontiers in Neuroscience* 13 (2019), 274. https://www.ncbi.nlm.nih.gov/pmc/articles/PMC6448042.

Promises Behavioral Health. "Domestic Violence and Depression—Breaking the Cycle." June 20, 2013. https://www.promises.com/addiction-blog/domestic-violence-and-depression-breaking-the-cycle/.

Psychology Today. "Hebephilia." Accessed 2022. https://www.psychologytoday.com/us/basics/hebephilia.

———. "Pedophilia." Accessed 2022. https://www.psychologytoday.com/us/conditions/pedophilia.

Queensland Health. "Brain Map Frontal Lobes." Queensland Government. July 12, 2022. https://www.health.qld.gov.au/abios/asp/bfrontal.

Raypole, Crystal. "5 Mental Health Issues that Could Trigger Dissociation." GoodTherapy. December 24, 2018. https://www.goodtherapy.org/blog/5-mental-health-issues-that-could-trigger-dissociation-1224187.

Raypole, Crystal, and Tom Rush. "How to Recognize and Break Traumatic Bonds." Healthline. November 24, 2020. https://www.healthline.com/health/mental-health/trauma-bonding.

Recovery Village. "Dissociative Disorders Statistics." August 23, 2022. https://www.therecoveryvillage.com/mental-health/dissociative-disorders/dissociative-disorders-statistics.

Resto, Luis Edgardo, and Marshall B. Mathers III. *So Much Better*. Universal Music Publishing Group. 2013.

Richmond, Christine. "Emotional Trauma and the Mind-Body Connection." WebMD. November 29, 2018. https://www.webmd.com/mental-health/features/emotional-trauma-mind-body-connection.

Rivera, Echo A., Heather Phillips, Carole Warshaw, Eleanor Lyon, Patricia J. Bland, and Orapan Kaewken. "The Relationship between Intimate Partner Violence and Substance Use." Chicago, IL: National Center on Domestic Violence, Trauma, and Mental Health. 2015. http://www.nationalcenterdvtraumamh.org/wp-content/uploads/2014/09/IPV-SAB-Final202.29.1620NO20LOGO-1.pdf.

RN.com. "Kentucky Domestic Violence." AMN Healthcare. 2017. https://lms.rn.com/getpdf.php/2066.pdf.

Robinson, Kara Mayer. "Sociopath vs. Psychopath: What's the Difference?" WebMD. 2014. https://www.webmd.com/mental-health/features/sociopath-psychopath-difference#2.

Roldan, Karen. "Masked Grief: 10 Things to Know About Stuffing Your Grief." USUrnsOnline. 2022. https://www.usurnsonline.com/grief-loss/masked-grief/.

Rollè, Luca, Giulia Giardina, Angela M. Caldarera, Eva Gerino, and Piera Brustia. "When Intimate Partner Violence Meets Same Sex Couples: A Review of Same Sex Intimate Partner Violence." *Frontiers in Psychology* 9 (2018). https://doi.org/10.3389/fpsyg.2018.01506.

Safe Steps Family Violence Response Centre. "Submission to the Senate Finance and Public Administration Inquiry into Domestic Violence and Gender Inequality." Melbourne. April 5, 2016. https://www.safesteps.org.au/wp-content/uploads/2017/10/safe-steps

-submission-Senate-Inquiry-into-Domestic-Violence-and-Gender-Inequality-FINAL.pdf.

Samsel, Michael. "Grooming." Abuse and Relationships. 2008–2018. https://www.abuseandrelationships.org/Content/Behaviors/grooming.html.

Saunders, Daniel G., Kathleen C. Faller, and Richard M. Tolman. "Child Custody Evaluators' Beliefs about Domestic Abuse Allegations: Their Relationship to Evaluator Demographics, Background, Domestic Violence Knowledge and Custody-Visitation Recommendations." Document No.: 238891. U.S. Department of Justice. Award Number: 2007-WG-BX-0013. June 2012. https://www.ojp.gov/pdffiles1/nij/grants/238891.pdf.

Science Daily. "People with Bipolar Disorder More than Twice as Likely to Have Suffered Childhood Adversity." October 12, 2016. https://www.sciencedaily.com/releases/2016/10/161012095744.htm.

Scott, Shelby B., Galena K. Rhodes, Scott M. Stanley, Elizabeth S. Allen, and Howard J. Markman. "Reasons for Divorce and Recollections of Premarital Intervention: Implications for Improving Relationship Education." National Library of Medicine, National Center for Biotechnology Information. June 1, 2014. https://www.ncbi.nlm.nih.gov/pmc/articles/PMC4012696/.

Selby, Jenn. "Why Didn't She Fight Back? The Myth That's Used to Justify Sexual Violence." *Refinery 29*, March 18, 2020. https://www.refinery29.com/en-gb/2020/03/9547973/freezing-up-response-rape.

Sharecare.com. "How is Brainwashing Achieved?" Accessed 2022. https://www.sharecare.com/health/personality/how-is-brainwashing-achieved.

Silvers, Ann. "Brainwashing in Abusive Relationships." PsychCentral. September 14, 2015. https://psychcentral.com/blog/brainwashing-in-abusive-relationships#1.

Sissons, Beth. "What is the Link between Trauma and Schizophrenia?" Medical News Today. July 7, 2022. https://www.medicalnewstoday.com/articles/trauma-and-schizophrenia.

Smith, Rita, "911: The Gateway to the Criminal Justice System." Domesticshelters.org webinar, Arizona, March 17, 2022. https://www.domesticshelters.org/videos/911-the-gateway-to-the-criminal-justice-system.

Smith, Tracy. "Dissociative Disorder Facts and Statistics." The Recovery Village. May 26, 2022. https://www.therecoveryvillage.com/mental-health/dissociative-identity-disorder/dissociative-identity-disorder-statistics.

Snyder, Briana L. "Women with Dissociative Identity Disorder Who Experience Intimate Partner Violence." *Journal of Psychosocial Nursing and Mental Health Services* 56, no. 5 (May 2018), 26–32. https://pubmed.ncbi.nlm.nih.gov/29447414/.

Soper, Richard G. "Intimate Partner Violence and Co-Occurring Substance Abuse/Addiction." *American Society of Addiction Medicine Magazine*, October 6, 2014, 1–9.

Spencer, William David. "Equal Leadership: God's Intention at Creation." In *Christian Egalitarian Leadership: Empowering the Whole Church according to the Scriptures*, edited by Aída Besançon Spencer and William David Spencer, 60–82. House of Prisca and Aquila Series. Eugene, OR: Wipf & Stock, 2020.

StoneRidge Centers. "Can Traumatic Stress Change Our Brains?" 2021. https://pronghornpsych.com/how-emotional-trauma-changes-the-brain.

Strucke, Michelle, and Kate Hajjar. "Battered Woman Syndrome." Cornell University Law School. 2010. https://courses2.cit.cornell.edu/sociallaw/student_projects/BatteredWomanSyndrome.htm.

Thicke, Robin, with Clifford Joseph Harris, Jr., and Pharrell Williams. "Blurred Lines." Star Trak Records, 2013.

Thurrott, Stephanie. "Is Mutual Abuse Real?" Domesticshelters.org. April 25, 2022. https://www.domesticshelters.org/articles/identifying-abuse/is-mutual-abuse-real.

Tomison, Adam M. "Exploring Family Violence: Links between Child Maltreatment and Family Violence." *Issues in Child Abuse Prevention.* Australian Institute of Family Studies. Winter 2000. https://aifs.gov.au/sites/default/files/publication-documents/issues13_0.pdf.

Trauma and Learning Policy Initiative. "Helping Traumatized Children Learn: Frequently Asked Questions about Trauma-Sensitive Schools." Accessed 2023. https://traumasensitiveschools.org/frequently-asked-questions.

Tsavoussis, Areti, Sstanislaw P. A. Stawicki, Nicoleta Stoicea, and Thomas J. Papadimos. "Child-Witnessed Domestic Violence and its Adverse Effects on Brain Development: A Call for Societal Self-Examination and Awareness." *Frontiers in Public Health* 2 (October 10, 2014). https://www.frontiersin.org/articles/10.3389/fpubh.2014.00178/full.

Tschampa, Jean. "Can Childhood Trauma Cause Anxiety? Yes, and Here's Why." Life Care Wellness. October 26, 2019. https://life-care-wellness.com/can-childhood-trauma-cause-anxiety/.

Tull, Matthew. "The Relationship Between PTSD and Depression." Verywellmind. March 26, 2020. https://www.verywellmind.com/ptsd-and-depression-2797533.

———. "Understanding PTSD and Dissociation: Links Between Trauma, PTSD, and Dissociative Disorder." Verywellmind. June 3, 2020. https://www.verywellmind.com/how-trauma-can-lead-to-dissociative-disorders-2797534.

Tunkle, Caroline R. "Parentification in the Context of Diverse Domestic Violence Exposure Experiences." Master's Thesis, Auburn University: Auburn, Alabama. August 5, 2017.

United Nations Office on Drugs and Crime. "Killings of Women and Girls by Their Intimate Partner or Other Family Members: Global Estimates 2020." UNODC, November 2021. https://www.unodc.org/documents/data-and-analysis/statistics/crime/UN_BriefFem_251121.pdf.

United States Department of Justice: Office of Justice Programs. "Children Exposed to Violence." January 8, 2020. https://www.ojp.gov/program/programs/cev.

United States Department of Veterans Affairs. "Spirituality and Trauma: Professionals Working Together." National Center for PTSD. October 6, 2022. https://www.ptsd.va.gov/professional/treat/care/spirituality_trauma.asp.

US Legal. "Friendly-Parent Principle Law and Legal Definition." USLegal.com. 2022. https://definitions.uslegal.com/f/friendly-parent-principle.

Vehling, Sara. "Taking Your Breath Away—Why Strangulation in Domestic Violence is a Huge Red Flag." Mobile ODT. October 16, 2019. https://www.mobileodt.com/blog/taking-your-breath-away-why-strangulation-in-domestic-violence-is-a-huge-red-flag.

Walker, Brandi. "How Domestic Violence Impacts Women's Mental Health." Step Up for Mental Health. November 5, 2020. https://www.stepupformentalhealth.org/how-domestic-violence-impacts-womens-mental-health/.

Walker, Lenore. "Battered Woman Syndrome." *Psychiatric Times* 26, no. 7 (July 8, 2009). https://www.psychiatrictimes.com/view/battered-woman-syndrome.

———. Battered Woman's Syndrome and Self-Defense. *Notre Dame Journal of Law, Ethics, and Public Policy* 6, no. 2 (January 1, 2012), 321–34. https://scholarship.law.nd.edu/cgi/viewcontent.cgi?referer=&httpsredir=1&article=1476&context=ndjlepp.

Wallace, Tracy. "Types of Grief: Grief Reactions, Grief Symptoms, and FAQ's for Your Own Grief Expression." Austin: Eterneva. Accessed 2023. https://www.eterneva.com/resources/types-of-grief.

Wang, Phillip. "What are Dissociative Disorders?" American Psychiatric Association. August 2018. https://psychiatry.org/patients-families/dissociative-disorders/what-are-dissociative-disorders.

Weaver, Terri L., Louisa Gilbert, Nabila El-Bassel, Heidi S. Resnick, and Samia Noursi. "Identifying and intervening with substance-using women exposed to intimate partner violence: phenomenology, comorbidities, and integrated approaches within primary care and other agency settings." *Journal of Women's Health* 24, no. 1 (2015), 51–56. DOI 10.1089/jwh.2014.4866.

Webermann, Aliya R., Bethany L. Brand, and Gregory S. Chasson. "Childhood Maltreatment and Intimate Partner Violence in Dissociative Disorder Patients." *European Journal of Psychotraumatology* 5 (September 12, 2014). https://www.ncbi.nlm.nih.gov/pmc/articles/PMC4163757/.

WebMD. "What is Dyslexia?" March 22, 2021. https://www.webmd.com/children/understanding-dyslexia-basics.

WebMD Editorial Contributors, edited by Dan Brennan. "What to Know About Disenfranchised Grief." WebMD. October 25, 2021. https://www.webmd.com/mental-health/what-to-know-about-disenfranchised-grief.

Westerfield, Caitlin M., and Benjamin R. Doolittle. "Spirituality of the Traumatized Child: A Call for Increased Faith Community Participation in the Trauma-Healing Process for Children." *Journal of Religion and Health* 61 (2022), 203–13. DOI https://doi.org/10.1007/s10943-021-01416-1.

Wheeler, Brenisen. "Loss of Agency: How Domestic Violence Impacts Mental Health." Women's Advocates. May 26, 2020. https://www.wadvocates.org/2020/05/26/loss-of-agency-how-domestic-violence-impacts-mental-health/.

Wilcox, W. Bradford, Laurie DeRose, and Jason S. Carroll. "The Ties that Bind: Is Faith A Global Force for Good or Ill in the Family?" Institute for Family Studies, 2019. https://ifstudies.org/ifs-admin/resources/reports/worldfamilymap-2019-051819.pdf.

World Health Organization. "Intimate Partner Violence during Pregnancy." 2011. https://apps.who.int/iris/bitstream/handle/10665/70764/?sequence=1.

Wright, Anthony. "Limbic System: Amygdala." McGovern Medical School, University of Texas. October 10, 2020. https://nba.uth.tmc.edu/neuroscience/m/s4/chapter06.html.

Xiang, Yanhui, Weixin Wang, and Fang Guan. "The Relationship between Child Maltreatment and Dispositional Envy and the Mediating Effect of Self-Esteem and Social Support in Young Adults." *Frontiers in Psychology* 9 (2018). https://www.frontiersin.org/articles/10.3389/fpsyg.2018.01054/full.

Yasharoff, Hannah. "Pharrell Williams on Realizing 'Blurred Lines' was Problematic: 'That Blew My Mind.'" *USA Today*, October 15, 2019. https://www.usatoday.com/story/entertainment/music/2019/10/15/pharrell-how-robin-thicke-blurred-lines-backlash-opened-his-eyes/3983316002/.

# Index

abuse, definition and characterization of, 15, 44. *See also* intimate partner violence (IPV)

actively motivated abusers, defined, 21. *See also* batterer

Adam, 93

Adams, David, 72

addiction, 21–22. *See also* substance abuse

adrenalin, 136–37

adverse childhood experiences (ACEs), 65, 122

African Americans, parenting by, 100

aggressiveness, 138–39

Ahasuerus (king), 37–38

Ainsworth, Mary, 17

alcohol abuse, 7–8, 21–22, 83–84, 147

Alliance for HOPE International, 177

amygdala, 66

anger, 23

antisocial personality disorders, 22–23

anxiety, 75–78, 143–45

anxious-resistant attachment, 17

Aristotle, 91–92

armor of God, 129–30

Artaxerxes (king), 37

Asian Americans, parenting by, 100

attachment, 16–19

attachment theory, 17

attention deficit disorder (ADD), 74–75

attention deficit/hyperactivity disorder (ADHD), 74–75, 142

Augustine, 92

authoritarian parenting, 98, 119. *See also* parenting

authoritative parenting, 97–98. *See also* parenting

avoidant attachment, 17

Bancroft, Lundy, 42–43

battered women syndrome (BWS), 79–80

batterer
    ability to change, 28–29
    abuse as influence to, 15–16
    abusive past partners myths regarding, 24
    anger myths regarding, 23
    characteristics of, 8
    childhood abuse myths regarding, 23–24
    children's literature influence to, 13–14
    class myths regarding, 26
    court advantage of, 120–21
    culture myths regarding, 26
    cycle of abuse and, 10–11
    deception by, 53–54, 57, 164
    defined, 4, 6–11
    entertainment as influence to, 12–13
    entitlement mentality of, 7
    environmental influences to, 11–14
    exerting control by, 8–10
    explosion and battering phase of, 10
    foundation of control of, 6–8
    gender inequality influence to, 19–20
    honeymoon phase of, 10–11

191

tension-building phase of abuse, 10
therapy, 24–26, 28–29, 105, 132–33
Thicke, Robin, 12–13
Thomas of Aquinas, 92
threats, 27, 44
touching, boundaries of, 157
trauma
    brain development and, 66–67,
        135–39
    physical health and, 68, 168
    spiritual welfare and, 150–51
    substance abuse and, 147
    suicide and, 149
    triggers of, 125
    See also mental health
trauma bonding, 82–83, 146–47
trauma-induced dyslexia, 150
trivializing, 36
Trouble with Homework (Berenstain
    Bears series), 14
Tunkle, Caroline, 101

undermining, 31–39, 104
uninvolved parenting, 99. See also
    parenting

Vashti (queen), 37–38
verbal abuse, 27
victim, defined, 4
violence, types of, 8
Violence Against Women Act (VAWA), 19
visitation, 3

Walker, Leonore, 10, 79
weapons, 71
websites
    Alliance for HOPE International, 177
    Childhelp National Child Abuse
        Hotline, 177
    Compensation Compass, 177
    DomesticShelters.org, 90, 177
    National Child Traumatic Stress
        Network, 178
    National Domestic Violence Hotline,
        178
    National Organization for Victim
        Assistance, 178

National Sexual Assault Hotline, 178
Rape, Abuse, and Incest National
    Network (RAINN), 178
Safe Helpline, 178
Women's Advocates, 178
WomensLaw.org, 90, 178
Williams, Pharrell, 12–13
withholding, 36
women
    with adverse childhood experiences
        (ACEs), 65
    anxiety in, 75–78
    attention deficit disorder (ADD) in,
        74–75
    attention deficit/hyperactivity
        disorder (ADHD) in, 74–75
    background of, 64–66
    battered women syndrome (BWS)
        in, 79–80
    bias against, in court system, 115–16
    bipolar disorder in, 78–79
    brain effects of domestic violence to,
        66–67
    in the church, 95
    in couples counseling, 25
    custody advantages of, 120–21
    death of, 71–72
    decisions of, 86–91
    depersonalization in, 81–82
    depression in, 75–78
    derealization in, 82
    disenfranchised grief in, 84–85
    dissociation disorder in, 80–82
    dissociative amnesia in, 81
    dissociative disorder in, 80–82
    dissociative identity disorder in, 81
    gender inequality and, 19–20
    God's intention for, 92–95
    growing up years of, 64–65
    historical treatment of, 11–12,
        91–92, 116–17
    low self-esteem in, 75
    mental health of, 72–85, 103, 116,
        119–20
    mutual abuse and, 88
    parents of, 162–72
    physical injury to, 68–69

www.ingramcontent.com/pod-product-compliance
Lightning Source LLC
Chambersburg PA
CBHW061732270326
41928CB00011B/2209